The Political Economy of HIV in Africa

Biomedical revolutions seem to have radically altered the environment for HIV transmission: anti-retrovirals (ARVs) and drugs to reduce mother-to-child transmission promise to cut HIV transmission rates, as does male medical circumcision. However, the hopeful messages of UNAIDS are tempered with warnings about expenditure shortfalls and calls for funding. Contributions to this book remind us that, along with the external financial constraints, there have been new fractures in state power and in the organisation of health systems. More than this, the book fundamentally calls into question whether biomedical interventions can change the social roots of this disease. As well as considering new policy approaches, the book reasserts a long-standing political economy approach to HIV and to adapt it to reflect new competing theoretical approaches. The chapters attempt to connect the debates about HIV/AIDS to larger discussions about globalisation, class differentiation, inequity and uneven development in African countries.

This book was originally published as a special issue of the *Review of African Political Economy*.

Deborah Johnston is a Reader in Development Economics at SOAS University of London, UK. She is a development economist whose research looks at the application of economics, political economy and feminist economics to issues of poverty, ill-health and wellbeing.

Kevin Deane is a Senior Lecturer in International Development at the University of Northampton, UK. His educational background is in development economics, but his research draws on a range of disciplines including political economy, development studies, economics, public health and epidemiology, with an application to the economic and social drivers of the HIV/AIDS epidemic.

Matteo Rizzo is a Senior Lecturer in Development Research Methods at the Department of Development Studies, Senior Lecturer in the Economics of Africa at the Department of Economics and a Member of the Centre of African Studies, all at SOAS University of London, UK. He is an editorial board member of the *Review of African Political Economy*.

The Political Economy of HIV in Africa

Edited by
Deborah Johnston, Kevin Deane and
Matteo Rizzo

LONDON AND NEW YORK

First published 2018 by Routledge

2 Park Square, Milton Park, Abingdon, Oxfordshire OX14 4RN
52 Vanderbilt Avenue, New York, NY 10017

Routledge is an imprint of the Taylor & Francis Group, an informa business

First issued in paperback 2019

British Library Cataloguing in Publication Data
A catalogue record for this book is available from the British Library

ISBN 13: 978-1-138-74163-8 (hbk)
ISBN 13: 978-0-367-23482-9 (pbk)

Typeset in Times New Roman
by RefineCatch Limited, Bungay, Suffolk

Publisher's Note
The publisher accepts responsibility for any inconsistencies that may have
arisen during the conversion of this book from journal articles to book chapters,
namely the possible inclusion of journal terminology.

Disclaimer
Every effort has been made to contact copyright holders for their permission to
reprint material in this book. The publishers would be grateful to hear from any
copyright holder who is not here acknowledged and will undertake to rectify
any errors or omissions in future editions of this book.

Contents

Citation Information   vii

Notes on Contributors   ix

Introduction: The political economy of HIV   1
Deborah Johnston, Kevin Deane and Matteo Rizzo

1. Trapped in the prison of the proximate: structural HIV/AIDS prevention
   in southern Africa   8
   Bridget O'Laughlin

2. The political economy of concurrent partners: toward a history of
   sex–love–gift connections in the time of AIDS   28
   Mark Hunter

3. Wealthy and healthy? New evidence on the relationship between wealth
   and HIV vulnerability in Tanzania   42
   Danya Long and Kevin Deane

4. Paying the price of HIV in Africa: cash transfers and the depoliticisation
   of HIV risk   60
   Deborah Johnston

5. Exploring the complexity of microfinance and HIV in fishing communities
   on the shores of Lake Malawi   80
   Eleanor MacPherson, John Sadalaki, Victoria Nyongopa, Lawrence Nkhwazi,
   Mackwellings Phiri, Alinafe Chimphonda, Nicola Desmond, Victor Mwapasa,
   David G. Lalloo, Janet Seeley and Sally Theobald

6. Revisiting the economics of transactional sex: evidence from Tanzania   103
   Kevin Deane and Joyce Wamoyi

Debates

7. The key questions in the AIDS epidemic in 2015   121
   Alan Whiteside OBE

8. 15 years of 'War on AIDS': what impact has the global HIV/AIDS response
   had on the political economy of Africa?   133
   Sophie Harman

CONTENTS

9. Breaking out of silos – the need for critical paradigm reflection in HIV prevention 143
   Justin O. Parkhurst and Moritz Hunsmann

10. Microfinance and HIV prevention 154
    Janet Seeley

    Index 163

Citation Information

The chapters in this book were originally published in the *Review of African Political Economy*, volume 42, issue 145 (September 2015). When citing this material, please use the original page numbering for each article, as follows:

Editorial

The political economy of HIV
Deborah Johnston, Kevin Deane and Matteo Rizzo
Review of African Political Economy, volume 42, issue 145 (September 2015), pp. 335–341

Chapter 1

Trapped in the prison of the proximate: structural HIV/AIDS prevention in southern Africa
Bridget O'Laughlin
Review of African Political Economy, volume 42, issue 145 (September 2015), pp. 342–361

Chapter 2

The political economy of concurrent partners: toward a history of sex–love–gift connections in the time of AIDS
Mark Hunter
Review of African Political Economy, volume 42, issue 145 (September 2015), pp. 362–375

Chapter 3

Wealthy and healthy? New evidence on the relationship between wealth and HIV vulnerability in Tanzania
Danya Long and Kevin Deane
Review of African Political Economy, volume 42, issue 145 (September 2015), pp. 376–393

Chapter 4

Paying the price of HIV in Africa: cash transfers and the depoliticisation of HIV risk
Deborah Johnston
Review of African Political Economy, volume 42, issue 145 (September 2015), pp. 394–413

Chapter 5

Exploring the complexity of microfinance and HIV in fishing communities on the shores of Lake Malawi
Eleanor MacPherson, John Sadalaki, Victoria Nyongopa, Lawrence Nkhwazi, Mackwellings Phiri, Alinafe Chimphonda, Nicola Desmond, Victor Mwapasa, David G. Lalloo, Janet Seeley and Sally Theobald
Review of African Political Economy, volume 42, issue 145 (September 2015), pp. 414–436

Chapter 6

Revisiting the economics of transactional sex: evidence from Tanzania
Kevin Deane and Joyce Wamoyi
Review of African Political Economy, volume 42, issue 145 (September 2015), pp. 437–454

Debates

Chapter 7

The key questions in the AIDS epidemic in 2015
Alan Whiteside OBE
Review of African Political Economy, volume 42, issue 145 (September 2015), pp. 455–466

Chapter 8

15 years of 'War on AIDS': what impact has the global HIV/AIDS response had on the political economy of Africa?
Sophie Harman
Review of African Political Economy, volume 42, issue 145 (September 2015), pp. 467–476

Chapter 9

Breaking out of silos – the need for critical paradigm reflection in HIV prevention
Justin O. Parkhurst and Moritz Hunsmann
Review of African Political Economy, volume 42, issue 145 (September 2015), pp. 477–487

Chapter 10

Microfinance and HIV prevention
Janet Seeley
Review of African Political Economy, volume 42, issue 145 (September 2015), pp. 488–496

For any permission-related enquiries please visit:
http://www.tandfonline.com/page/help/permissions

Notes on Contributors

Alinafe Chimphonda was a Research Assistant with the Malawi Liverpool Wellcome Trust in Malawi.

Kevin Deane is a development economist based at the University of Northampton, UK. He has a PhD in Economics from SOAS, University of London, UK. His research draws on economics, development studies, public health and epidemiology with application to the HIV/AIDS epidemic in sub-Saharan Africa.

Nicola Desmond is Wellcome Trust Research Fellow and Head of Social Science at the Malawi-Liverpool-Wellcome Trust Clinical Research Programme (MLW) based in Blantyre, Malawi.

Sophie Harman is a Reader in International Politics at Queen Mary University of London, UK, where she teaches and conducts research in global health politics and, Africa and International Relations.

Moritz Hunsmann is a political sociologist and Researcher at the French National Centre for Scientific Research (CNRS/IRIS). He conducted his PhD research on the political economy of AIDS control in Tanzania, and his current work further explores the politics of public health in sub-Saharan Africa, with primary interests in HIV/AIDS, maternal and newborn health and, more recently, industrial pollution.

Mark Hunter is an Associate Professor in the Department of Human Geography, University of Toronto Scarborough, Canada, and Honorary Research Fellow in the School of Built Environment and Development Studies, University of KwaZula-Natal, South Africa.

Deborah Johnston is a Reader in Development Economics at SOAS University of London, UK. She is a development economist whose research looks at the application of economics, political economy and feminist economics to issues of poverty, ill-health and wellbeing.

David G. Lalloo is a Professor of Tropical Medicine and Dean of Clinical Sciences and International Public Health at the Liverpool School of Tropical Medicine, UK.

Danya Long has an MSc in Economics with reference to Africa from SOAS, University of London, UK. Her dissertation looked at the relationships between wealth, gender and HIV/AIDS in Tanzania.

Eleanor MacPherson is a Post-Doctorate Researcher at the Liverpool School of Tropical Medicine, UK.

Victor Mwapasa is an Associate Professor at University of Malawi College of Medicine.

Lawrence Nkhwazi was a Research Assistant with the Malawi Liverpool Wellcome Trust in Malawi.

Victoria Nyongopa was a Research Assistant with the Malawi Liverpool Wellcome Trust in Malawi.

Bridget O'Laughlin is a Research Associate of the Institute of Economic and Social Studies in Maputo, Mozambique. Her current research is on rural labour and rural health in Mozambique.

Justin O. Parkhurst is a social and political scientist and Associate Professor of Global Health Policy in the Department of Social Policy, London School of Economics, UK. He has conducted research on HIV/ AIDS policy and prevention in Africa, maternal health care in low-income settings, and on the political and institutional factors influencing the use of evidence in health and social policy making.

Mackwellings Phiri is a Research Assistant with the Malawi Liverpool Wellcome Trust in Malawi.

Matteo Rizzo is a Senior Lecturer in Development Research Methods at the Department of Development Studies, Senior Lecturer in the Economics of Africa at the Department of Economics and a Member of the Centre of African Studies, all based at SOAS University of London, UK. He is an editorial board member of the *Review of African Political Economy*.

John Sadalaki is a Research Manager at the College of Medicine at the University of Malawi.

Janet Seeley is a Professor of Anthropology and Health at London School of Hygiene and Tropical Medicine, UK.

Sally Theobald is a Professor of Social Science and International Health at Liverpool School of Tropical Medicine, UK.

Joyce Wamoyi is a Social and Behavioural Research scientist at the National Institute for Medical Research, Mwanza, Tanzania. She has an MSc in Public Health and a PhD in Social and Behavioural Sciences and has worked on various health research topic areas for over 16 years.

Alan Whiteside ran the Health Economics and HIV and AIDs Research Division in Durban, South Africa, until 2013 when he joined the Balsiliie School of International Affairs in Waterloo, Canada. He was awarded an OBE in the New Year's Honour's List in 2014.

INTRODUCTION

The political economy of HIV

Given all the positivity and self-congratulation over HIV in the international policy world, it might be hard to remember how many lives have been destroyed and continue to be devastated by this illness. Looking to UNAIDS headlines, we hear of plans for an 'AIDS-free generation in Africa', 'ending the epidemic by 2030' and 'eliminating stigma and discrimination'. In this case, the boldness of the goals is partly driven by what Michel Sidibé, Executive Director of UNAIDS, called 'game-changers' in his World AIDS Day message in 2011. Biomedical revolutions seem to have radically altered the environment for HIV transmission: antiretrovirals (ARVs) and drugs to reduce mother-to-child transmission promise to cut HIV transmission rates, as does male medical circumcision.

Of course, the hopeful messages of UNAIDS are tempered with warnings about expenditure shortfalls and calls for funding. With austerity as the watchword in the world's wealthy countries, the problem of gaining sufficient pledges, and then turning those pledges into money, is harder than ever. In this special issue, the debate piece by Alan Whiteside throws the question of funding into sharp relief. To what extent is the end to HIV in sight, when the costs of providing ARVs under the present approach are potentially 'crippling' for high-prevalence countries? Whiteside questions the HIV-free narrative, highlighting the 'treatment tension' that exists as the absolute number of those living with HIV rises and ARVs continue to be costly.

Two of the debate pieces in this issue, by Whiteside and by Sophie Harman, remind us that, along with the external money that has been central to the HIV response, there have been new fractures in state power and in the organisation of health systems. Harman argues that the positive progress narrative on HIV overlooks several limitations to the global response. Funding is a major issue given the cost of treatment, HIV continues to be transmitted, and stigma persists. At the same time, the governance of HIV/AIDS has seen competition among international institutions, an expansion of the market into health care and the co-option of many civil society organisations. More specifically, Harman argues that health systems have been fragmented, distorted and an extra layer of bureaucracy added.

More than this, the contributions to this special issue fundamentally call into question the biomedical approach. The problem is even more serious than one of a crisis of funding and a fracture of the state and the health service. While biomedical interventions promise to change HIV transmission, there are doubts about whether they will be able to affect 'the social roots of this disease' (Hunter 2010, 225). A clear reading of international public health history, from malaria to measles, shows us that technical fixes to health problems tend to leave the social and economic determinants of health, and the relationships that underpin them, untouched. For this reason, technical fixes can be far less successful than public health policy makers predict – even disastrous for the population they intend to help.

Alternative approaches

From the very beginning, social scientists fought to get attention for an alternative to the narrow narrative of HIV transmission arising from the public health literature. One reason for this is that the biomedical response to HIV has at times been inaccurate, divisive and stigmatising. So, for example, the initial view that HIV in African countries was driven by an aberrant sexual behaviour has disappeared. How could it survive when sexual behaviour surveys, anthropological accounts and activists have challenged it so comprehensively? Amid this maelstrom, brave and committed academics, such as Stillwaggon (Stillwaggon 2002, 2006), named the origin of such views as a combination of racism and the dregs of a colonial view of African 'otherness'. Public health officials consequently can no longer argue that the origins of HIV lie in a substantially different pattern of sexual partnership – even though they may argue that its transmission is heightened by sexual behaviour inappropriate to high-prevalence environments. As Whiteside argues, the origins of HIV in Africa remain an unanswered public health question, even though critical social scientists have raised a range of issues pertinent to the creation of a high-risk environment.

However, whilst early responses were overwhelmingly framed within a biomedical/behavioural paradigm (Campbell and Williams 1999), Justin Parkhurst and Moritz Hunsmann in this issue discuss the (re-)emergence of the focus on structural drivers and the acknowledgement of their importance by key global institutions, and remind us of the context and long history of the social science battle against over-medicalisation of HIV analysis. Whilst this is encouraging and has opened up new spaces for the social sciences (and humanities), this also raises a further set of questions and challenges that will influence the degree to which social scientists are able to impact the response in a meaningful way. Parkhurst and Hunsmann locate these challenges in the potential misalignment of the needs and priorities of donors and non-governmental organisations and what they term HIV-prevention realities, such as the need for structural interventions (which are, by their nature, aimed at addressing complex social issues) to demonstrate quantifiable short-term impacts on transmission rates or related behaviours to justify initial funding, which in turn influences the nature of interventions implemented in the first place. Further, they emphasise the silo-based response to the epidemic, in which disciplinary boundaries limit the potential for the design of responses that are truly holistic, although it is emphasised that these boundaries work both ways, and that social scientists are also required to engage constructively with their biomedical colleagues.

The success of the social/structural drivers literature in forcing this issue onto the global agenda (Sumartojo et al. 2000; Gupta et al. 2008; Auerbach et al. 2011) has created both opportunities for radical rethinking of the responses to the epidemic, as well as a space in which biomedical and behavioural methods and ways of thinking attempt to reassert themselves. This is seen particularly in relation to methodology, with randomised control trials increasingly being used to address 'social' issues, and there is hence a danger that the structural drivers agenda is subjected, through the application of inappropriate technical frameworks, to a reductionism and individualisation that is paradoxically at the heart of the critical rejection of biomedical and behavioural approaches. This is best illustrated by the uncritical borrowing of currently fashionable strategies, such as microfinance and cash transfers, from the international development sphere (where these strategies are themselves hotly contested), as they provide interventions that can be viewed as addressing 'structural issues', but are also easily assimilated into standard biomedical and behavioural methodological frameworks.

This reductionism of the structural emphasises the need for alternative approaches that go beyond these narrow conceptualisations, a challenge that political economy approaches are well placed to take up. What have the alternative views been? All the authors in this issue show that the pattern of HIV prevalence in African countries reflects complex social and economic inequalities, enabling a reflection on both how structural drivers can be better conceptualised, and also the limitations of microfinance and cash transfers as 'structural' interventions.

Bridget O'Laughlin discusses the way in which structural drivers have been conceptualised by those emanating from the public health silo, and presents an alternative political economy perspective in which, rather than a focus on how structures and contexts influence individual disease outcomes and behaviours, structural drivers are viewed as the factors that determine how infection and risk are distributed across the population. This provides a more nuanced notion of the term 'structural', directing attention to broader socio-economic processes, structures, and social relations, and the need for a radical political economy approach that is able to address them.

However, political economy has to compete in its explanations for HIV with mainstream economics. Mainstream economics presents a picture of rational individuals who 'optimise' their risk of acquiring HIV. Increasingly, this framework is used to justify microfinance and cash transfer strategies as it directs attention to the incentives that individuals face, and the trade-offs that they have to make when weighing up whether to engage in risky (and potentially harmful) sexual behaviour. As the articles in this issue by Deborah Johnston and by Kevin Deane and Joyce Wamoyi show, mainstream economics offers an inaccurate, over-stylised view of individual behaviour. In relation to transactional sex, Deane and Wamoyi note that mainstream economics fails to address the central concerns related to transactional sexual practices, such as gendered power, that are reflected in the progressive public health literature, which consistently emphasises the role of unequal gender relations. In the Tanzanian context, and it is likely elsewhere in sub-Saharan Africa, the focus on individual incentives is limited due to the lack of engagement with local sexual norms around sex and exchange, to the historical socio economic roots of this practice, and to how the ongoing dynamics of this practice are influenced by developmental processes and the penetration of capitalist relations.

Mark Hunter's article in this issue also addresses the role of economic and social relations in creating sexual norms around concurrency that are related to the growing materiality of sex and to how concurrency is shaped by the giving of gifts in this context. UNAIDS (2009, 6) formally defines concurrency as 'overlapping sexual partnerships where sexual intercourse with one partner occurs between two acts of intercourse with another partner'. Relatively high rates of concurrency have been seen by some working in this field as the strongest explanation for Africa's high HIV prevalence rates. Always under debate, however, concurrency as a driver of HIV has undergone some critical inspection as more recent empirical research has found rather limited support. Further, Hunter reflects, in a more nuanced way, on differences in the forms of concurrency between rich and poor countries. These differences, and the recognition of transactional sex in Northern countries, are important to tease out in a sensitive manner to enhance our understandings of these practices, but also to ensure that this analysis is divorced from the derogatory and racist framing noted above. As with other papers here, the role of a range of structural factors, such as high unemployment in the context of expanding informal settlements and reduced marriage rates, shape concurrent relationships, offering alternative sites for intervention.

Danya Long and Kevin Deane show how simple stories about poverty and HIV are confounded by the data on the relationship between HIV prevalence and HIV infection, which for Tanzania shows that the poorest do not have the highest rates of prevalence. Whilst there is a range of biases within the data, such as the longer life expectancies and better access by the wealthy to ARVs, the data present a challenge to the notion that the poorest are most impacted, and suggest that more comprehensive understandings of the dynamics of the epidemic must account for the role of both poverty and wealth. This also enables a reflection on responses – such as microfinance targeted at poor women, who typically do not have the highest prevalence rates – that are presented as 'structural', but that do not engage with broader socio-economic structures that shape economic dependence and unequal access to economic opportunities that are experienced by women of all income groups.

HIV transmission policies: fashions and fads

The response to biomedical policies has been complex. Behaviour change policies have widely been seen as failing to change behaviour (see, for example, Whiteside, and Parkhurst and Hunsmann, both in this issue). This failure has not only been recognised in the social sciences, but is also widely acknowledged within biomedical circles. Whilst the reasons for this failure depend on perspective, social scientists, and political economists, are well placed to comment. Rather than simple technical solutions or simplistic approaches to behaviour change, a political economy approach has instead focused on the complexity of the analysis, not least because the patterns of capitalist development and labour flows in Africa are complex and not reducible to easy simplification (O'Laughlin 2013). The outcomes for HIV risk will be differentiated, with different patterns of nutrition, different sexual norms and different kinds of access to health facilities. This will mean that it will not be possible to chart unambiguous HIV risks, and so not possible to assert that there is an HIV 'magic bullet'. However, as O'Laughlin, in this issue, argues, while it is difficult to describe the linkages between wider social processes and health, it is vitally important to do so if we want to explain the general population-wide incidence of disease.

Certainly, policy has to have a wider focus than individual decision-making. Indeed, Stillwaggon (2006) argues that broader structural change may be easier to accomplish than approaches that require all individuals to change their sexual behaviour. More than this, rather than solely local solutions, radical political economy approaches argue that HIV risk reduction needs global change in several respects (Johnston 2013). First, in order to counter uneven development, the policy space for active industrial and trade policy needs to be expanded. Second, migrant health rights need to be improved and protected if we are to end the health externalities of migrant labour systems that endanger workers and abandon them when they are ill. Third, the fiscal space for health expenditure must be expanded if we are to heal fractured and inadequate public health systems. Fourth, long-term, low-cost access to the latest generation of ARVs must be negotiated.

Johnston discusses the fashion for HIV-related cash transfers, which aim to reduce HIV risk by changing behaviour. Cash transfers have offered a new and attractive policy option to international agencies trying to reduce HIV prevalence. Measurable and time-bound, they promise quick but long-lasting results. The analytical starting point for these policies is varied, but all start out with a simplified set of assumptions about the way that cash payments can change sexual behaviour. In a rereading of the empirical record, Johnston argues that these policies and projects have been far less successful than the sound bites of international organisations would suggest. The evidence on reductions in HIV is extremely limited, while in at least one case, HIV risk was *increased* by a cash-transfer project. More than that, it is not clear how ethical or sustainable these interventions are. They are unlikely to have any effect on the underlying causes of the HIV epidemics in African countries: uneven development, inequality and inadequate health service access.

In her debate piece in this issue, Janet Seeley discusses the fashion for microfinance initiatives and questions whether providing short-term loans to poor women, an intervention arising from a drastically oversimplified structural approach, could ever have the potential to reduce HIV transmission by transforming power structures within society. Seeley also discusses the broader debate on the role of microfinance in relation to other developmental issues such as poverty and gender-based violence, and emphasises the mixed and inconclusive nature of the evidence on microfinance, suggesting that the case for microfinance as a one-size-fits-all solution rests on analytical and empirical grounds that are both shaky.

The limitations of microfinance as a core component of women's economic empowerment and HIV prevention are laid bare in the case study of female fish traders on the shores of Lake Malawi in this issue. Eleanor MacPherson and her co-authors provide evidence from a recent research project to show that provision of loans to female fish traders in a vulnerable socio-economic context led to situations in which they were unable to meet repayment schedules, in part due to the way that loans were disbursed, and ended up engaging in transactional sexual interactions so that they could pay the loans back. Paradoxically then, some fish traders were compelled to engage in the sorts of sexual interactions that the microfinance intervention was supposed to prevent. The unintended (and perhaps unanticipated) consequences of the programme were thus greatly at odds with the initial project aims, and this is a prime example of the potentially disastrous impact of poorly framed HIV policy.

Conclusion

This special issue acts to reassert a long-standing political economy approach to HIV, and to adapt it to reflect new competing theoretical approaches and new policy initiatives. However, there are many challenges to anyone constructing an alternative analytical approach to HIV. Knowledge about HIV/AIDS is not complete or uncontested. The debate over some of the key 'game-changers', treatment-as-prevention and male medical circumcision, illustrates this well. While UNAIDS believe that the epidemiological evidence for reductions in HIV transmissions is clear-cut, others argue about the quality of the epidemiological data, the consistency of results in different settings or the potential to scale up these interventions (Wamai et al. 2011; Wilson et al. 2014)

On one level, of course, this special issue is a snapshot of what is known in time (about biomedical responses to HIV transmission, about the impact of microfinance or cash transfers). If this was all it was, then the special issue would quickly become a reservoir of dated evidence. However, at the same time, this special issue aims for something of longer-lasting value – to connect the current debates about HIV/AIDS to larger discussions about globalisation, class differentiation, inequity and uneven development in African countries. In doing so, this special issue hopes to carry on the work of *ROAPE*, and connect to earlier publications. A Special Issue on AIDS was compiled in 2000 (Baylies and Bujra 2000), in addition to other articles on AIDS and social science research, livelihoods, social reproduction, class and injustice by authors such as Carolyn Baylies, Roy Love, and Janet Bujra in issues of the journal dating back to 1997 (see Baylies and Bujra 1997; Baylies 1999; Love 2004; Bujra 2006). This reflects a long history of challenging narrow, inaccurate and potentially dangerous interpretations of HIV in African countries

Acknowledgements

This special issue was developed on the basis of a workshop hosted at SOAS in May 2012 on "Conceptualising the political economy of HIV risk in Africa", which was generously funded by the *Review of African Political Economy* and the Centre for African Studies, University of London. We thank all the participants of this workshop for the discussion and debate. Clare Smedley has provided a huge amount of editorial guidance throughout the process. We are grateful to all anonymous reviewers who were involved in reviewing the special issue papers, and also the editorial board of the *Review of African Political Economy* for the opportunity to produce this special issue with them. Finally, we appreciate the efforts of all the contributing authors.

Deborah Johnston

Kevin Deane

Matteo Rizzo

References

Auerbach, J., J. Parkhurst, C. Cacáres and K. Keller. 2011. "Addressing Social Drivers of HIV/AIDS: Some Conceptual, Methodological, and Evidentiary Considerations." *Global Public Health* 6 (Suppl. 3): S293–S309.

Baylies, C. 1999. "International Partnership in the Fight against AIDS: Addressing Need and Redressing Injustice?" *Review of African Political Economy* 26 (81): 387–414.

Baylies, C. and J. Bujra. 1997. "Social Science Research on AIDS in Africa: Questions of Content, Methodology and Ethics (Recherches dans les Sciences Humaines sur le SIDA en Afrique: Problèmes de contenu, de méthodologie et de déontologie)." *Review of African Political Economy* 24 (73): 380–388.

Baylies, C. and J. Bujra. 2000. "Editorial: Special Issue on AIDS." *Review of African Political Economy* 27 (86): 483–486.

Bujra, J. 2006. "Class Relations: AIDS & Socioeconomic Privilege in Africa." *Review of African Political Economy* 33 (107): 113–129.

Campbell, C. and B. Williams. 1999. "Beyond the Biomedical and Behavioural: Towards an Integrated Approach to HIV Prevention in the Southern African Mining Industry." *Social Science & Medicine* 48 (11): 1625–1639.

Gupta, G. R., J. O. Parkhurst, J. A. Ogden, P. Aggleton and A. Mahal. 2008. "Structural Approaches to HIV Prevention." *The Lancet* 372 (9640): 764–775.

Hunter, M. 2010. *Love in the Time of AIDS: Inequality, Gender, and Rights in South Africa.* Bloomington, IN: Indiana University Press.

Love, R. 2004. "HIV/AIDS in Africa: Links, Livelihoods and Legacies." *Review of African Political Economy* 31 (102): 639–648.

Johnston, D. 2013. *Economics & HIV: The Sickness of Economics.* London: Routledge.

O'Laughlin, B. 2013. "Land, Labour and the Production of Affliction in Rural Southern Africa.". *Journal of Agrarian Change* 13 (1): 175–196. doi: 10.1111/j.1471-0366.2012.00381.x.

Stillwaggon, E. 2002. "HIV/AIDS in Africa: Fertile Terrain." *Journal of Development Studies* 38 (6): 1.

Stillwaggon, E. 2006. "Reducing Environmental Risk to Prevent HIV Transmission in Sub-Saharan Africa." *Africa Policy Journal* 1 (Spring): 37–57.

Sumartojo, E., L. Doll, D. Holtgrave, H. Gayle and M. Merson. 2000. "Enriching the Mix: Incorporating Structural Factors into HIV Prevention." *AIDS* 14 (Suppl. 1): S1–2.

UNAIDS [Joint United Nations Programme on HIV/AIDS]. 2009. "Consultation on Concurrent Sexual Partnerships: Recommendations from a Meeting of UNAIDS Reference Group on Estimates, Modelling and Projections held in Nairobi, Kenya, April 20–21st 2009." [Online] Available from https://www.k4health.org/sites/default/files/Concurrency%20meeting% 20recommendations_eng.pdf [Accessed June 15, 2015].

Wamai, R. G., B. J. Morris, S. A. Bailis, D. Sokal, J. D. Klausner, R. Appleton, N. Sewankambo, D. A. Cooper, J. Bongaarts, G. de Bruyn, A. D. Wodak, and J. Banerjee. 2011. "Male Circumcision for HIV Prevention: Current Evidence and Implementation in Sub-Saharan Africa." *Journal of the International AIDS Society* 14: 49. doi: 10.1186/1758-2652-14-49.

Wilson, D., J. Taaffe, N. Fraser-Hurt, and M. Gorgens. 2014. "The Economics, Financing and Implementation of HIV Treatment as Prevention: What Will it Take to Get There?" *African Journal of AIDS Research* 13 (2): 109–119.

Trapped in the prison of the proximate: structural HIV/AIDS prevention in southern Africa

Bridget O'Laughlin

There is now agreement in HIV/AIDS prevention that biomedical and behavioural interventions do not sufficiently address the structural causes of the epidemic, but structural prevention is understood in different ways. The social drivers approach models pathways that link structural constraints to individuals at risk and then devises intervention to affect these pathways. An alternative political economy approach that begins with the bio-social whole provides a better basis for understanding the structural causes of HIV/AIDS. It demands that HIV/AIDS prevention in southern Africa should not be a set of discrete technical interventions but a sustained political as well as scientific project.

[Piégé dans la prison de l'approximatif : la prévention structurelle du VIH/SIDA en Afrique australe.] Il existe maintenant un consensus en matière de prévention du VIH : les interventions biomédicales et comportementales ne traitent pas assez les causes structurelles de l'épidémie, mais la prévention structurelle peut être comprise de différentes manières. L'approche des facteurs sociaux modélise des relations qui lient des contraintes structurelles aux individus à risque et conçoit des interventions qui influent sur ces relations. Une approche alternative de l'économie politique qui prend en compte l'ensemble biologique et social fournit une meilleure base pour la compréhension des causes structurelles du VIH/SIDA. Elle nécessite une prévention du VIH/SIDA en Afrique australe qui ne soit pas un ensemble d'interventions techniques discrètes mais un projet politique et scientifique durable.

Introduction

The HIV/AIDS pandemic has ravaged southern Africa for almost three decades. Given the relative wealth of many countries of the region, some were surprised by the rapidity of its spread and the resilience of the epidemic. Yet one can also ask, as Shula Marks (2002) did in relation to South Africa, if HIV/AIDS was not an epidemic waiting to happen in southern Africa, given its history of impoverishment, inequality, disenfranchisement, rapid urbanisation, labour migration, war and social disruption.

Initially, prevention followed established global approaches focused on the transformation of individual sexual behaviour: targeting high-risk groups, using social marketing techniques to provide information and to persuade people to use condoms, avoid concurrent sexual relations and, when testing became available, to know their status. Yet from the outset there were also critics who argued that prevention programmes focusing on changing individual sexual behaviour were failing to confront the structural causes of the epidemic. Some in South Africa particularly (but not only) even argued that the structural causes were the disease, thus compromising both the public health response and the legitimacy of their critique of prevention approaches focused exclusively on sexual behaviour (Fassin 2007).

South Africa's treatment action campaign (TAC) around access to antiretroviral therapy (ART) drugs for all successfully challenged both government health policy and multinational pharmaceutical companies (Robins and Von Lieres 2004). Its success largely resolved the clinical debate on provisioning of ARTs across the region and underlined the importance and political possibility of addressing structural causes of the disease. Recognition of structural causes of HIV/AIDS has also acquired new legitimacy in global health policy. The Working Group on Social Drivers is one of nine set up by the AIDS2031 Consortium 'to question conventional wisdom, stimulate new research, spark public debate and examine social and political trends regards AIDS' (AIDS2031 Consortium 2011, xi). PEPFAR, the Global Fund and the World Bank now promote combined HIV-prevention packages that include structural, biomedical and behavioural interventions.

Reading through the literature on these new structural interventions, one encounters a bewildering array of different meanings and measures. Some are very specific, such as income-generating activities for adolescent girls or laws enforcing 100% condom use in brothels. Others are very general, such as improving public health and education systems. Some pursue the 'gold standard' of the randomised control trial (RCT) in pursuit of measures that have 'demonstrated or promising efficacy' (Kurth et al. 2011). Others emphasise that the social embedding, contextual specificity, political contingency and multiple outcomes of structural intervention make it difficult to sort out cause and effect statistically or to standardise interventions (Hankins and De Zalduondo 2010).

These differences in interpretation and practical approaches to structural intervention reflect the theoretical ambiguity of the field. This ambiguity goes beyond the inevitable conceptual blurring that emerges out of the negotiation process in the writing of institutional policy documents and funding proposals to fundamentally divergent ways of thinking about structural approaches to HIV/AIDS prevention. The same language is being used for different things. This essay argues that it is clarifying to distinguish two very different ways of conceptualising the structural causes of HIV/AIDS, each with different implications for strategies of prevention: the social drivers approach and an alternative biosocial political economy approach.

Social drivers: conceptualising the structural causes of HIV/AIDS

Global HIV/AIDS prevention has focused on controlling the sexual transmission of the disease. Yet many scholars of HIV/AIDS have long been convinced that its dynamics, like those of other epidemics before it, are grounded in structures of poverty and inequality (inter alia Farmer 1999; Barnett and Whiteside 2002). In their contribution to going 'beyond condoms', Klein, Easton, and Parker (2002) argued that HIV/AIDS prevention had to address the reasons for selective social vulnerability to infection. They identified different kinds of causes, all of which have relevance in southern Africa: poverty resulting from long-term patterns of economic development, gender inequality, migration and population displacement related to political instability. Stillwaggon (2009) has given particular attention to triggering co-factors and hence to the failures of public health systems in the wake of structural adjustment.

It has proven difficult, however, to confirm statistically a relation of causality between poverty and the incidence of HIV/AIDS. In a careful sifting through of available data, Johnston (2013, ch. 4) shows that there are no clear correlations between the various dimensions of poverty and being vulnerable to HIV/AIDS at either national or individual level. The relations are complex and variable over place and time. How then can the importance of social vulnerability for disease be captured empirically? Or must prevention retreat to what it has been able to measure – changes (or not) in sexual behaviour?

A thoughtful, detailed and accessible answer on how to integrate structure in HIV/AIDS prevention has been laid out by Justin Parkhurst (Parkhurst 2010, 2012, 2013, 2014), building on his earlier work with Rao Gupta (Gupta et al. 2008) and Auerbach, Parkhurst, and Cáceres (2011) on social drivers. Their approach now dominates the prevention policy literature; it uses social driver as a synonym for structural driver.

The social drivers approach models the processes that link social variables to sexual behaviour and hence to individual biological outcomes, in this case becoming HIV positive. Health outcomes are shaped directly by the immediate determinants of individual risk (the proximate determinants). In the case of HIV/AIDS these are exposure to, transmission of and infection by the HIV virus. But the proximate determinants are themselves structured by a multiplicity of social, cultural and environmental determinants (distal determinants) that make a particular group of people vulnerable to situations of immediate risk. 'Pathways' tie distal to proximate determinants and should thus be the focus of structural interventions. For example, poverty is a structural factor that gives rise to financial inability to meet daily food needs, which may lead to a parent engaging in transactional sex (Parkhurst 2014, 4). Identifying such links allows prevention to target the processes that aggregate individual risk into social vulnerability. Such causal pathways are contextually specific and often interdependent, i.e. health outcomes have multiple determinants and structural factors such as poverty have multiple, even countervailing, health outcomes (Parkhurst 2012, 4).

This approach thus begins with the decision-making, risk-calculating, health-seeking individual whose choices reflect social and cultural constraints as well as biological processes. Its methodological strategy is to begin with individuals whose choices have failed them; it identifies high-risk groups on the basis of HIV prevalence, and looks outwards for possible causes of vulnerability. Changes in individual behaviour or preferences are measures of successful intervention.

Analytical rigour is maintained in the identification of pathways by the insistence that the link to individual biological risk be statistically measurable. In looking, for example, at the ways in which migration might affect vulnerability to HIV/AIDS, Deane, Parkhurst, and Johnston (2010, 1459) emphasise:

> Finally, and critically, to influence HIV risk, any distal factor must do so by changing one or more direct proximal factors – migration must affect a factor that is related to the number of potential exposures (number of partners, number of sex acts, partners from a higher prevalence community, etc.) or affect factors that mediate risk for any given sex act (condom use, presence of other infections, etc.) – all of which may change over the course of an HIV epidemic.

Parkhurst (2014, 3) argues that broad definitions of structure that include things such as human behaviour, health systems functioning or biomedical research are not operationally useful. He prefers to focus either on social factors that fundamentally shape or influence patterns of individual risk behaviour or on those that mediate how people can avoid HIV within a given context.

The proximate/distal approach is a familiar one to demographers and epidemiologists. Its language has long been used by the large international population non-governmental organisations (NGOs), such as Pathfinder, that initially dominated HIV/AIDS prevention in southern Africa. They used social marketing to promote change in sexual behaviour and emphasised gender relations in households as an important variable limiting women's ability to choose for HIV testing or condom use. The analytical framework employed in the social drivers approach is also similar to that of contemporary micro-economics, the dominant framework in health economics, which assumes the utility-maximising individual operating within a universe of resources and constraints and thus construes population health as an aggregate of individual choices (Johnston 2013, ch. 3).

This paradigmatic congruence of theoretical approaches focused on individual choice orients the kinds of structural interventions deemed suitable in 'combination approaches' to prevention, the strategy favoured by UNAIDS, the AIDS2031 Consortium and many of the most prominent epidemiological experts on HIV/AIDS (e.g. Padian et al. 2011; Verboom, Melendez-Torres, and Bonell 2014). Structural interventions are designed to be part of prevention 'packages' that include existing biomedical and behavioural interventions. The new 'structural interventions' in HIV/AIDS prevention maintain a focus on changing the behaviour of individuals at risk but they add a social component intended to address the economic, social and cultural drivers that prevent individuals from exercising healthy choices.

To prove their efficacy rigorously, the social drivers approach prefers that interventions be tested by public health experts before being 'scaled up' to reach greater numbers of people at risk. Though Parkhurst (2014, 6) envisions the inclusion of qualitative evidence in designing and assessing interventions, others give almost exclusive priority to quantitative evidence, even demanding that packages be tested on the basis of the 'gold standard' of evidence-based medicine, RCTs (Kurth et al. 2011). Parkhurst emphasises the importance of contextually related variation in the drivers of HIV/AIDS and the limitations of a top-down approach, but translates this as searching for 'generalisable strategies to provide what target groups need in "tailored" ways that respond to the specific set of multiple structural factors influencing the group's risk and vulnerability' (Parkhurst 2013, 2).

McMichael famously characterised modern epidemiology as a 'prisoner of the proximate', adept at determining which individuals are at increased risk, but not at understanding disease distribution within and between populations (McMichael 1999, 888–889). Certainly Auerbach, Parkhurst and the Social Drivers Working Group, all of whom recognise social inequality as a determinant of inequalities of health, have been concerned with finding ways to avoid the prison of the proximate. Yet existing examples of the combination approach in southern Africa suggest that their attempts fall short of an escape.

Experimental 'structural interventions' in southern Africa

As Hargreaves (2013, 3) has noted, the evidence base is thus far rather weak, but in an extended literature search I found a small number of well-documented studies on combined approaches to structural intervention in HIV/AIDS prevention in southern Africa. All are experimental in design, use RCTs and include various components. Interestingly, all focus on gender inequality as a pathway and identify women as subjects of intervention. I have chosen three that have been described in the literature as promising examples. They differ by location, by group of women targeted and by forms of intervention. They illustrate the kinds of theoretical and methodological conundrums that the social drivers approach confronts when it defines structure in terms of the determinants of individual choice.

Microfinance with gender training

The IMAGE project (Intervention with Microfinance for Aids and Gender Equity) is often cited as a successful or promising structural intervention in the policy, popular and scholarly literature (Epstein 2007; Gupta et al. 2008; Gibbs et al. 2012; AIDSTAR-ONE 2013). IMAGE was carried out in rural Limpopo Province in South Africa (Pronyk et al. 2005, 2006; Kim et al. 2008) as a joint project of prestigious institutions – the School of Public Health of Witwatersrand University and the London School of Hygiene and Tropical Medicine. It was intended to test whether a micro-credit programme could reduce intimate-partner violence, unprotected sexual intercourse and HIV incidence among poor rural women.

The study paired communities chosen for intervention with similar control communities elsewhere. The intervention included a group-lending scheme and gender training, both implemented by South African NGOs. The gender training featured HIV/AIDS education and political mobilisation, culminating in a political demonstration against violence against women. Women mainly used the loans as working capital for tailoring or for selling clothes, fruit and vegetables. Follow-up interviews with participants and their paired counterparts from similar communities were done about two years later.

The organisers of the study were initially quite modest about the significance of their findings (cf. Pronyk et al. 2006). Women in the intervention group were more likely than the control group to be economically better off, had more household assets, were more often members of rotating savings societies and spent more on food, but they did not achieve higher food security nor did their children improve their school attendance. Interview data suggested that those in the intervention group had a stronger sense of community, reported more participation in collective action, expressed different attitudes towards gender roles and talked more about sex to the members of their households than did women in the control communities, but this is, after all, how they had learned to speak in the gender-training module. They registered fewer incidents of domestic violence than the women of the control group, but there was no change in frequency of unprotected sex. The incidence of new HIV infections did not decline in the aftermath of the project in the communities of intervention.

Conditional cash transfers to keep girls in school

A rising star in the list of structural interventions for HIV/AIDS prevention in southern Africa is conditional cash transfers (see *inter alia* Gibbs et al. 2012; Pettifor et al. 2012; Strathdee et al. 2013; Fieno and Leclerc-Madlala 2014). Attention has thus far been focused on a World Bank-funded experiment in southern Malawi (Zomba) in 2008–2009 (Baird et al. 2010, 2012; Baird, McIntosh, and Ozler 2011). The study sought to affect the length of time that adolescent women between the ages of 15 and 24 remain in school, a possible determinant of sexual activity and hence of exposure to HIV. They wanted to explore the notion that schooling is a kind of 'social vaccine' against risky sexual behaviour (Baird et al. 2012). The researchers also sought to intervene in the social policy debate in southern Africa around the efficacy of conditional versus non-conditional transfers. They tried to see what size transfer was required to be effective and to find out whether giving money to girls themselves would have better or worse outcomes than giving it to their parents.

There were three sampling zones in the study area: the city of Zomba, surrounding peri-urban areas and a rural area. The researchers did not try to target poor households though they excluded areas regarded as too affluent from the study. They included girls who had dropped out of school (who were asked to re-enrol) as well those still studying. The girls were randomly assigned to three different groups: the control group that received no cash payments, one group that received an unconditional cash payment and one that received a payment subject to monthly controls on their school attendance. School fees were paid directly by the project. Both girls and their parents received separate payments of varying amounts, again randomly determined.

After a year, researchers interviewed all the girls and found that, as expected, those who had received the conditional cash transfer had better school attendance than the other two groups. They also had a lower incidence for some outcomes regarded as evidence of risky sexual behaviour: first-time sex, having sexual intercourse at least once a week and having a partner over 25. Yet the differences between the girls who got *conditional* transfers and those receiving an *unconditional* payment were minimal. The researchers conclude that cash transfers in general could promote school attendance and improve sexual behaviour. They speculate that the monthly transfers may have allowed girls to spend less time in transactional sex with 'sugar daddies' (Baird, McIntosh, and Ozler 2011, 1736). Even these results were somewhat contradictory, however; the control group who got no payment was less likely, for example, to have unprotected intercourse than those who got transfers (Baird et al. 2012).

Their strongest finding is thus not surprising: if girls' school fees are paid and they and their parents receive a cash payment for going to school, then they do. What has made this project famous, however, is that 18 months after it began, when cash payments were still being disbursed, participants were tested for HIV1 and HIV2 (Herpes). The conditional transfer group had a lower HIV prevalence of infection (3/235, 1%) than both the control group (17/799, 3%) and the unconditional transfer group (4/255, 2%) (Baird et al. 2012, Table 4, 1327). These are small numbers and there could be no control of changes in the respective rates of incidence since there was no baseline testing done. The conclusion is nonetheless drawn that secondary schooling can be a kind of social vaccine for girls, facilitated by conditional cash transfers.

Raising sex-workers' gender consciousness

A recent review in the *Annual Review of Public Health* focused on combination approaches to HIV among women at high risk of infection in low- and middle-income countries (Strathdee et al. 2013). One of the model projects discussed was the Women's Health CoOp intervention, aimed at substance-using women, sex-workers and other vulnerable women in Pretoria, South Africa. Contrary to expectations raised by its name, no local women's health cooperative was involved. This was a community-based RCT, funded by the US National Institute on Drug Abuse and based on a United States 'best-evidence' intervention developed for crack cocaine-using, inner city African-American women (Wechsberg et al. 2011). It rests its claim to being a structural intervention on having addressed substance use and gender-based violence as pathways towards risky sexual behaviour.

It was difficult to find sufficient self-identified, drug-using, professional sex-workers for the study, so eligibility was broadly defined. Participants had to be women, 18 years or older, South African citizens living in Gauteng, have consumed alcohol on at least 13 of the past 90 days, and be an active sex worker or had unprotected sex in the past 90 days. Eighty-three per cent of the group reported they were unemployed and 63% identified themselves as sex-workers (obviously not exclusive categories). Most had a regular sexual partner other than clients. Participants accepted for the programme were tested for HIV

They received small payments for their time in cash and supermarket gift vouchers as well as toiletries and risk-reduction items such as condoms 'to facilitate continued behaviour change'. Participants were randomly assigned to two groups: one had a brief counselling session on risky sexual behaviour and substance use. The other received women-centred information and counselling on women's particular risk for HIV and other sexually trans-mitted infections, substance use and intimate-partner violence, role-playing practice on negotiation and preparation of a personal action plan.

Self-reported baseline information on sexual behaviour and clinical data on substance use from an initial baseline interview were compared with the results at the end of the pro-gramme. Women who had followed the intensive women's intervention programme were much more likely than the control group to report that they had used condoms the last time they had intercourse with their partners (not clients) and, if they were sex-workers, to have experienced a reduction in sexual and physical abuse. Yet, contrary to the expec-tations of the researchers, women who were not sex-workers in the control group reported much greater reduction in drug use and physical abuse than those who participated in the specially designed women's intervention. Nonetheless, the intervention has been assessed as successful and is being 'packaged' for 'scaling up' in local community health centres and NGOs (*Ibid.*).

The claims of this experiment strain credibility. No matter how clever the role-playing and creative the life-planning, it is hard not to think that in a group with an 80% unemploy-ment rate the cash and small gifts were more important in shaping reported answers than was the consciousness-raising power of two 50-minute educational sessions and two subsequent interviews. This programme has been adapted from one developed for African-American women in inner cities in the United States. The project has imported the definition of a high-risk group, urban women substance-users, from a very different profile of risk and then blurred the definition of vulnerability when those who volunteered to participate did not fit the model of the drug-using commercial sex-worker.

The limits of the social drivers approach to structural intervention

These three 'structural interventions' more or less fulfilled the comparative requirements of experimental design and all addressed gender as a structural driver, but they otherwise vary in quality and results. The Women's CoOp project arguably violates Parkhurst's emphasis on contextualisation and shows how flexibly 'tailoring' to context can be interpreted. The Domba project was originally an intervention on girls' school attendance; measuring HIV prevalence was a tag-on. The IMAGE intervention did not lead to a statistically significant impact on HIV incidence and the CoOp project did not attempt to measure it. Yet all have been promoted as promising new forms of HIV/AIDS prevention by influential institutions of global public health. A closer look raises some questions about the limitations of the social drivers approach to structural intervention.

The first problem is that the approach is atheoretical in its questions, choice of subjects of intervention and identification of pathways. When theoretical premises are not specified they remain implicit assumptions, reflecting our common sense or the dominant theoretical paradigms of the world in which we live. This is particularly dangerous if we are taking an unknown 'other' as the subject of intervention.

The current list of structural interventions for southern Africa focuses narrowly on various categories of high-risk women: in these cases poor rural women in Limpopo, non-wealthy adolescent rural women in Malawi, women commercial sex-workers in Gauteng. The studies refer to gender relations as a pathway but they are remarkably uninformed by gender theory, either by the concept of intersectionality linking gender and class or by inquiry into how and why gender relations change.

The questions asked are entirely about what would give poor women more choices in their sexual behaviour. The importance (not exclusivity) of sexual intercourse in HIV transmission makes gender relations an appropriate pathway to look at in prevention but gendered vulnerability to HIV/AIDS is not an exclusive or fixed condition. To say that 59% of those living with AIDS in sub-Saharan Africa are women (Strathdee et al. 2013, 302) does not mean that the remaining 41% are unimportant or that these proportions are fixed.

The first prevention programmes in the 1990s in southern Africa targeted migrant men, commercial sex-workers and people living in cities. High-risk groups were targeted on the basis of current national prevalence and assumptions based on experiences elsewhere. Loewenson and Whiteside (1997), reviewing HIV prevalence rates in the region in the early 1990s, found that prevalence was up to 2.5 times higher in urban than in rural areas, very different to the situation today. Rural women were not initially flagged as a vulnerable group in prevention programmes despite the well-known gendered patterns of circulating migration in the region. Epidemics have dynamic histories so prevention has to be prepared to meet a moving target. Recent studies have shown that in discordant couples it can now be the woman rather than the man who is HIV positive (Eyawo et al. 2010). With prevalence as high as it is in southern Africa, arguably everyone is potentially at risk.

These interventions focus narrowly on increasing women's resources and awareness with little attention to the lives and consciousness of men. The African heterosexual male appears in these studies to be a shadowy, homogeneous, somewhat pathological presence. The Domba study refers to 'sugar daddies'. In the CoOp study, all men of African descent appear by tradition to be omnipotent, predatory and sources of infection:

> South African women more often lack control over their sexuality and often face victimization. African men are usually expected to be in control in the home and are often abusive and have concurrent partners. Interrelated HIV risk factors that are particularly prevalent among South African women are intimate partner violence (IPV), exposure to alcohol and other drug use, and unprotected sex with male partners with high HIV prevalence. (Strathdee et al. 2013, 304)

Men would seem to be steadfastly unconcerned either about their own health or that of their partners. Challenging gender relations seems to lie entirely within the powers and responsibilities of women and gender struggles to be limited to the domains of culture, sex and domestic violence. The rich southern African literature on the changing shape of sexualities, including masculinities (Niehaus 2002; Hunter 2004), does not figure here, nor does the differentiation of experience resulting from intersecting relations of class and political struggle. The labelling of women as victims and men as aggressors reinforces the moral culture of blame that Fassin's (2007, 2013) work has shown to be so destructive to HIV/AIDS prevention efforts in South Africa. It is not at all safe to presume that HIV transmission in southern Africa today takes place only in transactional sex or in sex under duress, when men are perpetrators of contagion and women are victims.

The second problem is that these interventions subordinate external validity to internal validity (Cartwright 2010; Woolcock 2013); the requirements of experimental design take priority over evidence that may give us qualifying or even different answers to our research questions. Both Adams (2013) and Hunsmann (2012) document how the rigid methodological requirements of experimental 'evidence based medicine' (EBM) preclude the ethnographic and historical information needed to understand the experience of the subjects of intervention. Parkhurst (2013, 7) includes focus groups, individual interviews, observation and historical data in his list of evidence to be used in a structural approach, but the bibliographies of these three studies include few references to the historical and ethnographic literature on health in South Africa and Malawi. This is understandable since, as Adams (2013, 55–56) points out, the 'gold standard' of EBM, the top level on a scale of five, is the properly designed random controlled trial, the RCT. Eyewitness non-expert testimony lies outside the scale, classified as 'anecdotal'.

Ironically, we learn more about the causes of vulnerability to HIV/AIDS and the limitations of micro-credit interventions from the admirably frank discussion by Dunbar et al. (2010) of SHAZ!, an experimental structural intervention that has not made it onto the list of 'successes' because the study was not concluded. A microfinance project for a group of young women in Zimbabwe, it was implemented in the period of rampant inflation before the currency devaluation. Most used the money to set up trading businesses. Only the few from better-off families were successful and repaid their loans. Moreover, those who tried to do long-distance trade and needed lodging for the night became victims of sexual violence, including rape. The dropout rate was so high that a second round of HIV testing was never carried out, so it fails the standards of EBM.

A third set of problems results from the assumption that the dynamics of the whole can be reduced to the aggregate of individual choices. Both microfinance and conditional cash transfers linked to mandatory school attendance are currently widely promoted by the major AIDS organisations and the World Bank as ways of increasing the capacity of women to refuse risky sex. In line with many World Bank projects, they locate the causes of deprivation in the poor themselves: their lack of capital blocks women's entrepreneurial spirit or the lack of willingness of parents to send their daughters to school exposes them to risk. It is presumed that if we make all poor rural women small-scale entrepreneurs or pay all poor adolescent girls in rural Malawi to go to school, we can reduce both rural poverty and strengthen women's capacity to refuse to be infected by HIV.

But it is not so easy to scale up what might work for one to all. The markets for handmade clothes and small-scale vendors in Limpopo are already saturated. To extend the conditional transfer to all adolescent girls in Malawi would require substantial investment in the scale and quality of secondary education, particularly in rural areas. Why not avoid administrative costs by skipping the conditional transfer altogether and investing directly in secondary education and extending universal free schooling to secondary level? The World Bank preference for micro-credit and conditional cash transfers over generalised social assistance is explicitly ideological, as discussed elsewhere in this special issue.[1] That HIV/AIDS intervention should follow in its wake reflects the politics of funding in prevention research, precisely one of the structural drivers Parkhurst considers too broad to be operational.

Its methodological emphasis on structure as an aggregate of individual choice also makes it difficult for the social drivers approach to recognise the importance of collective agency (Kippax et al. 2013). The organisers of the IMAGE intervention were aware of this issue and tried to recognise the importance of community by carrying out a range of activities at the local level, including working with a South African NGO that gave political mobilisation training, talking to local chiefs and police and bringing the subjects of the intervention to a political demonstration against violence against women (Pronyk et al. 2008). They then interpreted community as an aggregate of individual social capital and measured it by giving scores for social networks, for perceptions of reciprocity, community support and solidarity, and for participation in collective action. They set aside as 'secular changes' the major shifts in attitudes towards HIV/AIDS that were going on in South Africa at that time as the TAC created ' . . . new political spaces for engagement at local, national and global levels' (Robins and Von Lieres 2004, 84).

The question of political spaces raises another lacuna in the social drivers framework: silence around where researchers themselves fit politically in strategies of prevention. Universities with major public health programmes have been, like the World Bank or UNAIDS, the Gates Foundation, the pharmaceutical companies and the population and health international NGOs, major actors in global health politics, particularly around HIV/AIDS. The proximal/distal distinction puts them far off-stage, but their impact has been very direct, giving, for example, these sorts of experimental RCT studies the legitimacy of 'structural intervention'.

The packaging approach followed in these three experimental structural interventions does not alter very much the behavioural and biomedical components found wanting in critical analyses of the failures of earlier prevention programmes; they simply add in a new social component. One could argue that proximate/distal framing that currently dominates the social drivers approach to intervention could be salvaged by loosening the methodological demands of the RCT in evidence-based medicine and by following Parkhurst's directive on the importance of contextualisation. But it is not so easy to cast off the experimental methodology of RCTs; the proximate/distal framework provides its theoretical model for linking social variables to biological outcomes. A more radical alternative is to heed Kippax and Stephenson's (2012) call to go beyond the distinction between biomedical and social dimensions of HIV/AIDS prevention. This means, I would argue, scrapping the proximal/distal distinction and reclaiming the concept of structure to better reflect the kinds of concerns raised by critics of behavioural interventions in HIV/AIDS prevention.

A bio-social political economy of HIV/AIDS prevention in southern Africa

The proximate/distal approach to conceptualising the relation between social and biological processes builds on what Clifford Geertz (1973) called a stratigraphic conception of human life: a biological core surrounded by psychological, social and cultural layers. Geertz suggested that human life was more like an onion; when you strip off all its layers, there is no core. An alternative way to think about the problem is that the social and biological are inextricably linked in a single material totality that we dissect theoretically through the questions we ask. As Kippax and Stephenson (2012, 792) have argued: 'Although analytically distinct, effective prevention requires that biomedical technologies, behavioral strategies, and social structures are not treated as separate entities.' In short, the best way to escape from the prison of the proximate is to break down the walls of the prison, effacing the distinction between proximate and distal, explicitly theorising questions to determine the relevance of evidence, and thus navigate our way through a broad space that is both biological and social.

The concept of structure is relational. This means by definition, for example, that if we observe an enormous gap in rates of HIV incidence of black and white people in South Africa, our initial questions do not attempt to isolate the distinctive behavioural characteristics of black people but to understand the reasons for inequality between black and white. The concept of structure is not a synonym for the social but a way of thinking about causality. Understanding the causes of events demands going beyond the immediate sequence of events to look for social forces that exert their pressure over long periods of time, are not easy to change and are often unperceived by those who live them and make them (Pierson 2003). Such an approach applied in epidemiology means that there are rarely quick fixes for epidemics like HIV/AIDS and that solutions can be impermanent.

There are different theoretical traditions in this alternative structural epidemiology – eco-social, political economy or social medicine, for example (Krieger 2014). Many of those who have written on the political economy of HIV/AIDS take a broadly Marxist approach, emphasising the importance of capitalism as a global system in the structuring of the bio-social and thus underlining the ways that contradictions of class intersect with contradictions of gender and race in shaping the space of intervention. From this perspective, the politics of opposition, including the instruments of ideological critique, are a necessary part of prevention.

A bio-social political economy takes history not as upstream context but as the expression of structure, a beginning point for understanding the causes of inequality in health. Southern Africa shares with the rest of the world insertion in the structures of global capitalism, but it also has some distinctive structural patterns. Historically, global capitalism was intersected by a common history of settler colonialism and regional divisions between rural labour reserves and centres of accumulation. The resulting patterns of residence, work, living conditions and conjugality have shaped distinctive patterns of health and disease (O'Laughlin 2013). The long-term structural pattern of women and children residing and farming in the countryside while men migrated to work on mines and in cities as wage-workers has been eroded (Crush et al. 2005; Hunter 2010), but the region is still marked by great mobility, permeable national boundaries and the dominance of South African capital. In rural areas particularly, non-commodified production, mainly done by women and children, covers a good part of nutritional needs and care. The wage-labour force is sharply segmented, with a large proportion of jobs being casual, manual and seasonal or precarious. Women-headed households have long been common in southern Africa (O'Laughlin 1998), but today many conjugal couples never establish a common residential unit with their children.

In this region, the defence of racialised settler capitalism was violent and protracted with the apartheid regime in South Africa entangled in other wars in the region. In such a historical context the politicisation of race remains very alive. Though legal definition of racialised zones of residence and conditions of employment has been abolished, living conditions and the provisioning of formal health care are still spatially and socially discriminated. Campbell's study of an HIV/AIDS prevention project in 'Summertown', a mining community in South Africa, showed how continuing social divisions were reflected in miners' resistance to HIV/AIDS prevention messages (Campbell 2003). A racialised understanding of suffering continues to shape public AIDS discourse, particularly in South Africa (Fassin 2007).

These specificities of the region intersect in the case of HIV/AIDS with a conjunctural moment, the near hegemony of United States public health discourse – its premises, its policies, its institutions – in global HIV/AIDS policy. The shifting debates within institutions such as UNAIDS, the World Bank, WHO or the Gates Foundation normatively shape how HIV/AIDS is to be known, how its causes will be understood, who will be treated and which treatments they will receive. The dependence of many regional health budgets on donor funding, the scale of earmarked funding for HIV/AIDS and the dependence of HIV/AIDS organisations on external funding mean that a neoliberal normative vision of health care suffuses HIV/AIDS prevention and treatment (cf. Ingram 2013).

One can understand Parkhurst's (2014, 3) hesitation to employ such a broad definition of structure, his fear that it may not be epidemiologically operational. There is, however, an established methodological tradition in epidemiology that traces precisely the path that Parkhurst is reluctant to tread: Geoffrey Rose's work on prevention (Rose 2001, 2008), which distinguishes between what makes an individual sick and what makes a population sick. Rose's approach to prevention puts together two related epidemiological insights (which he does not claim as his own). First, health and disease, the normal and the pathological, are not sharply opposed conditions but part of a dynamic continuum. Those who are recognised as very sick or at high risk of becoming so lie at one end of the distribution but there are many degrees in between. Second, the distribution of risk of exposure to a particular illness within a population is often such that more cases come from the large group falling around the middle of the distribution who are individually at low risk than from the outlying high-risk but much smaller group (Rose 2008, 131). Prevention must therefore address two distinct issues: the determinants of individual cases and the determinants of the rate of incidence within a population (Rose 2001). A high-risk strategy of disease prevention conflates the two: 'it concentrates attention on the conspicuous segment of disease and risk, seeking to understand and control it as though it were the whole of the population in general' (Rose 2008, 49). This is what has happened in mainstream HIV/AIDS prevention.

Rose's strategy of prevention seeks to shift downwards the profile of risk for the entire population, considering the whole continuum from the normal to the pathological. This can have a greater impact on the total number of cases than does a restrictive focus on individuals at high risk of exposure. In the case of the incidence of HIV, for example, long-distance truck-drivers can be particularly vulnerable to HIV infection yet still account for a very small proportion of those who become HIV positive. Typically, the underlying determinants of the continuum of disease are mainly economic and social and thus their remedies must also be economic and social. This is why Rose concludes that: 'Medicine and politics cannot and should not be kept apart' (*Ibid.*, 161).

There are important methodological and practical differences between the social drivers approach to structural prevention of HIV/AIDS and Rose's strategy. The social drivers approach begins with individuals considered to be at risk, looks outward to find the social and economic forces that constrain their capacity to make healthy choices and identifies programmes that will directly affect the pathway between the individual and the structural constraint. Rose's strategy begins with the dynamic distribution of disease within the population as whole and looks for the principal social and economic processes that shape it, some of which may lay outside the direct experience of the individual at risk. Prevention must thus bring epidemiological knowledge to bear on political processes that are collective and involve challenges to economic and social institutions that will certainly meet political opposition.

Rose's approach applied to HIV/AIDS prevention in southern Africa thus obliges us to look at the dynamics of its broader political economy. He provides a way of thinking about the interdependence of the biological and the social that brings HIV/AIDS prevention back towards the classic concerns of public health with conditions of living. His caution against focusing only on the characteristics of those who are ill rather than on the distribution of risk within the population as a whole obliges us to think about those social relations that determine why particular groups are vulnerable to infection and others are less so and how the boundaries between them change over time. His emphasis on politics allows us to recognise that health too is an area of power, contradiction and struggle.

Structural HIV/AIDS prevention as a bio-political process

The social drivers approach to structural HIV/AIDS prevention strives to find a set of globally applicable discrete social interventions that can be tailored to particular contexts and plugged into intervention packages designed by epidemiological experts. The alternative intervention strategy is to identify the structural relations that affect the incidence of the disease, to look for possible points of intervention and to ally with and learn from those who can be involved in the long term in struggles to challenge the structural causes of the disease. Such efforts cannot be tailored into packaged interventions and are unlikely to be supported by PEPFAR or the Global Fund. There is much to be learned from looking at other experiences of intervention, but it would be unwise to try to implement them purely on the basis of statistical success.

This strategy implies a long-term commitment to political struggles in particular places around particular issues. To show what it would mean to operationalise this approach, I use two cases drawn from Mozambique, where the nature of intervention is likely to affect the patterns of incidence of the disease. The first discusses an area where intervention has focused on the sexual behaviour of migrant male cane-cutters but not on their conditions of recruitment, residence and work. The second has to do with attempts to address the structural determinants of adherence to antiretroviral therapy.

Capital, labour and public health in sugar production[2]

The Xinavane Sugar Estate in southern Mozambique is mainly owned by the large multinational sugar corporation Tongaat-Hulett. It took over a derelict sugar estate and has expanded up-river in the Incomati valley. It now employs around 4800 workers on permanent contracts and up to 3700 casual workers. Cane-cutters are mainly migrants from other areas of Mozambique, recruited on six-month contracts and housed in walled guarded hostels located close to the fields and away from the towns. Most return home to their families when cane-cutting is finished.

At the end of the day, particularly on Sundays and after wages are paid at the end of the month, migrant workers socialise with local men and local women at nearby beer-stands. In these districts, rural families are heavily dependent on remittances from labour migration to South Africa. There is no need to appeal to tradition to understand the presence of concurrent sexual relationships here. A study done in an area neighbouring the Xinavane estate found overall HIV prevalence to be 39.9% (González et al. 2012, 584), higher among women than among men. It is inevitable that without condom use some migrants will contract HIV and that they will transmit it to their wives in areas that currently have lower prevalence.

As Campbell (2003) found in 'Summertown', large corporations employing migrants can be interested in HIV/AIDS prevention, if only on grounds of worker productivity, though they may be reluctant to yield authority over workplace activities. The Xinavane estate is a leading member of ECOSIDA, a HIV/AIDS business council set up in 2005 to provide information to businesses, unions and labour inspectors on workplace prevention programmes that raise HIV awareness and promote implementation of existing laws against stigma and discrimination in the workplace. The Xinavane employee responsible for workplace AIDS awareness training told me of the reprimand he received from workers on one of the new outlying plantations of the estate after delivering his talk on condom use. Exasperated, they told him that they wanted to use condoms but there were none available anywhere near the hostel. Neither the small number of local shops nor the itinerant vendors who came on payday carried them. He went off to the capital city and brought back a three-month supply.

Xinavane Estate could probably be convinced to distribute free condoms, but just as important is the eradication of the ideological premises that informed the behavioural prevention interventions promoted by international AIDS organisations. They took responsibility for developing HIV/AIDS education away from national public health systems to vest it in advertising agencies that organised glossy social-marketing campaigns and claimed that the success of health promotion was only demonstrated if people paid for the condoms they needed and used. This intervention was structural – it has had lasting consequences – but so could be the reorientation of condom distribution and health promotion training, an effort to which academic institutions could contribute without much need for funding.

The company has not addressed a longer-term structural question, how migrant workers are recruited as cane-cutters. It tried outsourcing management of recruitment and the hostels, but was obliged to take them over again after a cholera outbreak in one of the hostels. Migration per se is not a structural cause of AIDS. There is no generic migrant behaviour. How people live and work within changing patterns of migration in southern Africa varies by work group, by gender, by employer, by the militancy of trade unions, by the rigour of health inspections. Those pushing employers for better living and conditions or lobbying for tighter enforcement of workplace standards could benefit from expert epidemiological advice but that would require an oppositional rhetoric and a constancy of political struggle that does not fit well with the terms of project funding from PEPFAR, the World Bank or the United Kingdom Department for International Development.

Local public health care and adherence to ART

The political struggle coordinated by TAC (the Treatment Action Campaign) obliged the South African government to introduce free antiretroviral therapy in the public health system and forced the big pharmaceutical companies to lower prices and allow for the production or import of cheap generics. This was a process, not a single event, and involved a broad range of allies: people living with AIDS, community health activists, churches, health workers, epidemiologists, lawyers and COSATU (the Congress of South African Trade Unions) (Robins and von Lieres 2004). Their tactics ranged from educational presentations of relevant epidemiological research, through mass demonstrations, to pleading legal cases to the constitutional court. Their campaign had political resonance throughout southern Africa.

Antiretroviral treatment has now entered the list of measures promoted in mainline prevention, based on the possibility that reduction of viral load and hence contagion will allow the epidemic to die out gradually (Padian et al. 2012). Clinical challenges are recognised: acute early infection may go disregarded, or drug-resistant variants of HIV arise or chronic opportunistic infections could overwhelm the public health system (*Ibid.*). Further, for ART to function as prevention, adherence to treatment must be sufficient to keep viral load down and to avoid the development of resistant strains. Although adherence is sometimes understood as a matter of individual choice, here too structural issues intrude.

One aspect of adherence to treatment is nutrition, an issue insightfully discussed for Mozambique by Kalofonos (2010). To stay healthy on antiretrovirals, one should eat a varied and plentiful diet. For those with well-paid permanent jobs this is possible, but assuring an adequate diet is problematic for poor HIV-positive small-scale farmers, many of whom are women. Rain-fed agriculture is risky and demands intensive labour for weeding precisely when last year's stocks have already run low. Casual work is seasonal and poorly paid and remittances from migrants are irregular.

The international NGOs that introduced ART in Mozambique were aware of the nutritional issue. They distributed a monthly basic food ration, eventually provided by the World Food Programme (WFP). The family shared the ration; it is not morally or practically possible to reserve food for the person with HIV/AIDS (Kalofonos 2010; Braga 2012). But as the ART programme has expanded, it has become increasingly difficult to assure provisioning of the household ration (Pfeiffer 2013). Moreover, WFP food imports in food-producing areas presented the classic dilemma discussed by Amartya Sen (1981): there is food available in the market; those who are poor and living with AIDS simply do not have the money to buy it. Importing food potentially undercuts the working of local food markets and thus local commercial farming, reinforcing the downward spiral of poverty and illness. Yet if a cash subsidy is given instead, there is no assurance that the money will be spent on the varied and high-quality diet needed by those who are on ART. Though high rates of malnutrition do not mirror the distribution of HIV prevalence or AIDS cases in Mozambique, from a structural perspective nutritional conditions will affect the overall prevalence of full-blown AIDS among those who are HIV positive.

Adherence is also compromised by the availability and quality of care for the rapidly expanding number of those receiving ART. Initially, PEPFAR funding for HIV/AIDS was channelled through NGOs operating parallel to the ministry and the public health system (Pfeiffer 2013). When international NGOs began to offer ART they did so in clinical coordination with the public health system (Høg 2014), but usually through a separate and better facility, located within or close to a public hospital or health centre. The public health system, which was already facing a high disease burden, had both to respond to the burden of curative care and to develop the capacity to implement ART on an expanding scale in rural areas (*Ibid.*).

In 2008, the Ministry of Health ordered the NGO day-hospital programmes to integrate into regular public health facilities. This decision was not popular with HIV/AIDS patients, who typically had to wait longer both to be attended and to obtain their medicine in much less pleasant environments, or with staff, who were generally paid less and worked under more stressful conditions (Olsen 2011; Braga 2012).

Assessments of the impact of the integration of day hospitals in public health centres on ART adherence and thus ultimately on the success of a prevention strategy based on ART show mixed results. Sherr et al. (2010) reported that the quality of ART care in the health posts that functioned under trained non-physician clinicians was as good as that provided by doctors. Lambdin et al. (2013) found, however, that the kind of intensive follow-up and counselling that was done by the separate vertical ART programmes had resulted in higher levels of adherence than the public health centres achieved. Yet they opted for a long-term structural solution: to work on improving the functioning of the public health system. There is no certainty that the public health system can respond. Braga's (2012) empathetic account of the indignities confronted by AIDS patients in their transfer from a specialised day-hospital to neighbourhood public health clinics in central Mozambique showed that what patients lost was not simply privileged access to medicine but care based on the respect of specially trained staff and on the accompaniment, compassion and persistence of volunteers organised and paid a small subsidy by NGOs.

Thus the problem of adherence to treatment is certainly a clinical issue informed by clinical studies, but it raises the kinds of structural tensions – ethical and political – flagged by Rose (2001) when balancing the treatment of individuals against the causes of incidence of the disease. Focusing on the latter requires long-term involvement in political struggles of both alliance and opposition. Public health researchers cannot precisely predict the outcomes of the structural interventions they advocate but the positions they take, in efforts unlikely to be funded by PEPFAR, the World Bank or the Global Fund, will affect what happens.

What constitutes structural intervention in HIV/AIDS prevention?

The London cholera epidemic of 1854 ended after Dr Snow took the handle off a pump that spewed infected water, and epidemiologists have been arguing ever since over the significance of what he proved: that bacteria are the cause of cholera or that investing in public systems of clean water provisioning could end centuries of periodic cholera epidemics (Kunitz 2007). HIV/AIDS prevention belongs in this core debate in public health. Early HIV/AIDS prevention in southern Africa focused on the causes of contagion, particularly the sexual transmission of the HIV virus, but there was from the outset a concurrent stream that argued for the importance of understanding the structural causes of the disease. How to do this is, however, also a subject of debate, the terms of which this article has sought to clarify.

There are two different ways of thinking about confronting structural causes in prevention of HIV/AIDS. The social drivers approach begins with the proximate biomedical causes of the disease and works outwards to find the pathways that link structural constraints such as gender inequality to individual behaviour. It proposes to identify programmes such as micro-credit that can disrupt these pathways, test them through rigorously controlled experiments and then plug them into packages of interventions that can be scaled up and implemented in tailored ways in different places.

I have argued that the social drivers approach remains trapped in McMichael's prison of the proximate. It is conceptually and methodologically very difficult to identify and give importance to the structural causes of HIV/AIDS if individual agency is both the beginning and the end of the analysis and if the dynamics of the whole are understood as no more than the sum of individual choices. Metaphorically speaking, it is better to destroy the prison by breaking down the wall between proximate and distal to work analytically with a bio-social totality. To do so demands that questions are posed within an explicit theorisation that takes account of the particular historical patterns that give rise to structures that are both dynamic and resistant to change. The southern African region is such a totality, made distinctive by the ways a racialised settler capitalism has become intertwined with shifting patterns of global capital accumulation. The structural consequences for health, including both vulnerability to HIV/AIDS and the nature of the responses to it, are political, economic, social and cultural.

It is understandable that Parkhurst would feel unsure about such a broad perspective, why he would argue that things such as the functioning of the health system or the funding of HIV/AIDS research cannot be operationalised epidemiologically. Rose's distinction between why individual people get sick and why populations get sick provides, however, a way of thinking about what kinds of intervention make sense and measuring their impact. The aim of HIV/AIDS prevention should be reducing the incidence of the disease across the population as a whole. This usually means confronting processes that are structural – contradictory, long-term, politically contested and often difficult to perceive in everyday individual decisions about health.

Operationally, a structural approach to HIV/AIDS prevention in southern Africa should not be expected to find or adapt 'proven' social components for clearly delimited technical 'packages' of prevention interventions marketed across the world. It could mean HIV/AIDS experts reflexively locating themselves and their institutions structurally before proposing any kind of intervention: e.g. reading critically the literature on micro-credit before launching a scheme or considering the external validity of the assumptions underlying condom social marketing. If the intention is more fundamentally to weaken the structural causes of HIV/AIDS, then it means understanding the patterns of incidence of the disease in particular places at particular times and putting that knowledge to work in collective action, as was done in the TAC campaign. That would mean participating in political processes that aim, without any certainty of success, to alter the conditions under which a not very robust virus has spawned a very stubborn epidemic. Good politics are informed by evidence, but the uncertainty of outcomes will not be resolved by controlled experimental testing.

Disclosure statement

No potential conflict of interest was reported by the author.

Notes

1. On the relation of the choice of interventions to neoliberalism, see Johnston on conditional cash transfers and MacPherson, Sadalaki, Nyongopa, et al. on microfinance, both in this issue.
2. This section relies on research in Xinavane carried out in 2012 by the Institute of Economic and Social Studies (Maputo). See O'Laughlin and Ibraimo 2013.

References

Adams, V. 2013. "Evidence-based Global Public Health." In *When People Come First: Critical Studies in Global Health*, edited by J. Biehl, and A. Petryna, 54–90. Princeton: Princeton University Press.

AIDSTAR-ONE. 2013. "Structural Interventions: An Overview of Structural Approaches to HIV Prevention." Accessed August 31, 2012. http://www.aidstar-one.com/focus_areas/prevention/pkb/structural_interventions/overview_structural_approaches_hiv_prevention.

AIDS2031 Consortium. 2011. *AIDS: Taking a Long-term View.* Upper Saddle River, NJ: Pearson Education/FT Press Science.

Auerbach, J. D., J. O. Parkhurst, and C. F. Cáceres. 2011. "Addressing Social Drivers of HIV/AIDS for the Long-term Response: Conceptual and Methodological Considerations." *Global Public Health* 6 (Suppl. 3): S293–S309.

Baird, S., E. Chirwa, C. McIntosh, and B. Ozler. 2010. "The Short-term Impacts of a Schooling Conditional Cash Transfer Program on the Sexual Behavior of Young Women." *Health Economics* 19 (S1): 55–68.

Baird, S. J., R. S. Garfein, C. T. McIntosh, and B. Ozler. 2012. "Effect of a Cash Transfer Programme for Schooling on Prevalence of HIV and Herpes Simplex Type 2 in Malawi: A Cluster Randomised Trial." *The Lancet* 379 (9823): 1320–1329.

Baird, S., C. McIntosh, and B. Ozler. 2011. "Cash or Condition? Evidence from a Cash Transfer Experiment." *The Quarterly Journal of Economics* 126 (4): 1709–1753.

Barnett, T. and A. Whiteside. 2002. *AIDS in the Twenty-first Century: Disease and Globalisation.* Basingstoke: Palgrave Macmillan.

Braga, C. M. T. 2012. "'Death is Destiny': Sovereign Decisions and the Lived Experience of HIV/AIDS and Biomedical Treatment in Central Mozambique." PhD, State University of New York at Buffalo.

Campbell, C. 2003. *'Letting Them Die': Why HIV/AIDS Prevention Programmes Fail.* Oxford and Indianapolis: James Currey and Indiana University Press.

Cartwright, N. 2010. "What are Randomised Controlled Trials Good For?" *Philosophical Studies* 147 (1): 59–70.

Crush, J., B. Williams, E. Gouws, and M. Lurie. 2005. "Spaces of Vulnerability: Migration and HIV/AIDS in South Africa." *Development Southern Africa* 22 (3): 293–318.

Deane, K. D., J. O. Parkhurst, and D. Johnston. 2010. "Linking Migration, Mobility and HIV." *Tropical Medicine & International Health* 15 (12): 1458–1463.

Dunbar, M. S., M. C. Maternowska, M. S. J. Kang, S. M. Laver, I. Mudekunye-Mahaka, and N. S. Padian. 2010. "Findings from SHAZ!: A Feasibility Study of a Microcredit and Life-skills HIV Prevention Intervention to Reduce Risk among Adolescent Female Orphans in Zimbabwe." *Journal of Prevention & Intervention in the Community* 38 (2): 147–161.

Epstein, H. 2007. *The Invisible Cure: Africa, the West, and the Fight against AIDS*. New York: Farrar, Straus & Giroux.

Eyawo, O., D. de Walque, N. Ford, G. Gakii, R. T. Lester, and E. J. Mills. 2010. "HIV Status in Discordant Couples in Sub-Saharan Africa: A Systematic Review and Meta-analysis." *The Lancet Infectious Diseases* 10 (11): 770–777.

Farmer, P. 1999. *Infections and Inequalities: The Modern Plagues*. Berkeley: University of California Press.

Fassin, D. 2007. *When Bodies Remember, Experiences and Politics of AIDS in South Africa*. Berkeley: University of California Press.

Fassin, D. 2013. "Children as Victims." In *When People Come First: Critical Studies in Global Health*, edited by J. Biel, and A. Petryna, 109–129. Princeton: Princeton University Press.

Fieno, J. and S. Leclerc-Madlala. 2014. "The Promise and Limitations of Cash Transfer Programs for HIV Prevention." *African Journal of AIDS Research* 13 (2): 153–160.

Geertz, C. 1973. *The Interpretation of Cultures*. New York: Basic Books.

Gibbs, A., S. Willan, A. Misselhorn, and J. Mangoma. 2012. "Combined Structural Interventions for Gender Equality and Livelihood Security: A Critical Review of the Evidence from Southern and Eastern Africa and the Implications for Young People." *Journal of the International AIDS Society* 15 (3 (Suppl. 1): 1–10.

González, R., K. Munguambe, J. Aponte, C. Bavo, D. Nhalungo, E. Macete, P. Alonso, C. Menéndez, and D. Naniche. 2012. "High HIV Prevalence in a Southern Semi-rural Area of Mozambique: A Community-based Survey." *HIV Medicine* 13 (10): 581–588.

Gupta, G. R., J. O. Parkhurst, J. A. Ogden, P. Aggleton, and A. Mahal. 2008. "Structural Approaches to HIV Prevention." *The Lancet* 372 (9640): 764–775.

Hankins, C. A. and B. O. De Zalduondo. 2010. "Combination Prevention: A Deeper Understanding of Effective HIV Prevention." *Aids* 24: S70–S80.

Hargreaves, J. R. 2013. *Incorporating a Structural Approach within Combination HIV Prevention*. Arlington, VA and London: AIDSTAR-ONE and STRIVE.

Høg, E. 2014. "HIV Scale-up in Mozambique: Exceptionalism, Normalisation and Global Health." *Global Public Health* 9 (1–2): 210–223.

Hunsmann, M. 2012. "Limits to Evidence-based Health Policymaking: Policy Hurdles to Structural HIV Prevention in Tanzania." *Social Science & Medicine* 74 (10): 1477–1485.

Hunter, M. 2004. "Masculinities, Multiple-sexual-partners, and AIDS: The Making and Unmaking of Isoka in KwaZulu-Natal." *Transformation: Critical Perspectives on Southern Africa* 54: 123–153.

Hunter, M. 2010. "Beyond the Male-migrant: South Africa's Long History of Health Geography and the Contemporary AIDS Pandemic." *Health & Place* 16 (1): 25–33.

Ingram, A. 2013. "After the Exception: HIV/AIDS beyond Salvation and Scarcity." *Antipode* 45 (2): 436–454.

Johnston, D. 2013. *Economics and HIV: The Sickness of Economics*. Milton Park: Routledge.

Kalofonos, I. A. 2010. "'All I Eat is ARVs'." *Medical Anthropology Quarterly* 24 (3): 363–380.

Kim, J., P. Pronyk, T. Barnett, and C. Watts. 2008. "Exploring the Role of Economic Empowerment in HIV Prevention." *AIDS* 22: S57–S71.

Kippax, S. and N. Stephenson. 2012. "Beyond the Distinction between Biomedical and Social Dimensions of HIV Prevention through the Lens of a Social Public Health." *American Journal of Public Health* 102 (5): 789–799.

Kippax, S., N. Stephenson, R. G. Parker, and P. Aggleton. 2013. "Between Individual Agency and Structure in HIV Prevention: Understanding the Middle Ground of Social Practice." *American Journal of Public Health* 103 (8): 1367–1375.

Klein, C., D. Easton, and R. Parker. 2002. "Structural Barriers and Facilitators in HIV Prevention: A Review of International Research." In *Beyond Condoms, Alternative Approaches to HIV Prevention*, edited by A. O'Leary, 17–46. New York: Kluwer Academic/Plenum.

Krieger, N. 2014. "Got Theory? On the 21st c. CE Rise of Explicit Use of Epidemiologic Theories of Disease Distribution: A Review and Ecosocial Analysis." *Current Epidemiology Reports* (1): 45–56.

Kunitz, S. J. 2007. *The Health of Populations: General Theories and Particular Realities.* New York: Oxford University Press.

Kurth, A. E., C. Celum, J. M. Baeten, S. H. Vermund, and J. N. Wasserheit. 2011. "Combination HIV Prevention: Significance, Challenges, and Opportunities." *Current HIV/AIDS Reports* 8 (1): 62–72.

Lambdin, B. H., M. A. Micek, K. Sherr, S. Gimbel, M. Karagianis, J. Lara, S. S. Gloyd, and J. Pfeiffer. 2013. "Integration of HIV Care and Treatment in Primary Health Care Centers and Patient Retention in Central Mozambique: A Retrospective Cohort Study." *JAIDS Journal of Acquired Immune Deficiency Syndromes* 62 (5): e146–e152.

Loewenson, R. and A. Whiteside. 1997. *Social and Economic Issues of HIV/AIDS in Southern Africa.* Consultancy Report ed. Harare: SAfAIDS.

Marks, S. 2002. "An Epidemic Waiting to Happen? The Spread of HIV/AIDS in South Africa in Social and Historical Perspective." *African Studies* 61 (1): 13–26.

McMichael, A. 1999. "Prisoners of the Proximate: Loosening the Constraints on Epidemiology in an Age of Change." *American Journal of Epidemiology* 149 (10): 887–897.

Niehaus, I. 2002. "Renegotiating Masculinity in the South African Lowveld: Narratives of Male-male Sex in Labour Compounds and in Prisons." *African Studies* 61 (1): 77–97.

O'Laughlin, B. 1998. "Missing Men? The Debate Over Rural Poverty and Women-headed Households in Southern Africa." *Journal of Peasant Studies* 25 (2): 1–48.

O'Laughlin, B. 2013. "Land, Labour and the Production of Affliction in Rural Southern Africa." *Journal of Agrarian Change* 13 (1): 175–196.

O'Laughlin, B., and Y. Ibraimo. 2013. *The Expansion of Sugar Production and the Well-being of Agricultural Workers and Rural Communities in Xinavane and Magude.* Maputo: Cadernos, IESE (Institute for Social and Economic Studies).

Olsen, B. S. 2011. "Decentralised AIDS Care in Mozambique: Dream or Delusion?" Paper presented at the 1 ECAS 4 panel 15 paper. Accessed July 29, 2013. www.nai.uu.se/ecas-4/panels/1–20/panel-15/bent-olsen-full-paper.pdf.

Padian, N. S., M. T. Isbell, E. S. Russell, and M. Essex. 2012. "The Future of HIV Prevention." *JAIDS Journal of Acquired Immune Deficiency Syndromes* 60 (Suppl. 2): S22–S26.

Padian, N. S., S. I. McCoy, S. S. A. Karim, N. Hasen, J. Kim, M. Bartos, E. Katabira, S. M. Bertozzi, B. Schwartlander, and M. S. Cohen. 2011. "HIV Prevention Transformed: The New Prevention Research Agenda." *The Lancet* 378 (9787): 269–278.

Parkhurst, J. O. 2010. "Understanding the Correlations between Wealth, Poverty and Human Immunodeficiency Virus Infection in African Countries." *Bulletin of the World Health Organization* 88 (7): 519–526.

Parkhurst, J. O. 2012. "HIV Prevention, Structural Change and Social Values: The Need for an Explicit Normative Approach." *Journal of the International AIDS Society* 15 (3 (Suppl. 1):17367): 1–10.

Parkhurst, J. O. 2013. "Structural Drivers, Interventions and Approaches for Prevention of Sexually Transmitted HIV in General Populations: Definitions and an Operational Approach." Structural Approaches to HIV Prevention Position Paper Series. Arlington, VA and London: USAID's AIDS Support and Technical Assistance Resources, AIDSTAR-One, Task Order 1 and UKaid's STRIVE Research Consortium.

Parkhurst, J. O. 2014. "Structural Approaches for Prevention of Sexually Transmitted HIV in General Populations: Definitions and an Operational Approach." *Journal of the International AIDS Society* 17 (1): 1–10.

Pettifor, A., C. MacPhail, N. Nguyen, and M. Rosenberg. 2012. "Can Money Prevent the Spread of HIV? A Review of Cash Payments for HIV Prevention." *AIDS and Behavior* 16 (7): 1729–1738.

Pfeiffer, J. 2013. "The Struggle for a Public Sector." In *When People Come First: Critical Studies in Global Health*, edited by J. Biehl, and A. Petryna, 166–181. Princeton: Princeton University Press.

Pierson, P. 2003. "Big, Slow-moving, and … Invisible: Macro-social Processes in the Study of Comparative Politics." In *Comparative Historical Analysis in the Social Sciences*, edited by J. Mahoney, and D. Rueschemeyer, 177–207. Cambridge: Cambridge University Press.

Pronyk, P. M., J. R. Hargreaves, J. C. Kim, L. A. Morison, G. Phetla, C. Watts, J. Busza, and J. D. H. Porter. 2006. "Effect of a Structural Intervention for the Prevention of Intimate-partner Violence and HIV in Rural South Africa: A Cluster Randomised Trial." *The Lancet* 368 (9551): 1973–1983.

Pronyk, P. M., T. Harpham, J. Busza, G. Phetla, L. A. Morison, J. R. Hargreaves, J. C. Kim, C. H. Watts, and J. D. Porter. 2008. "Can Social Capital be Intentionally Generated? A Randomized Trial from Rural South Africa." *Social Science & Medicine* 67 (10): 1559–1570.

Pronyk, P. M., J. C. Kim, J. R. Hargreaves, M. B. Makhubele, L. A. Morison, C. Watts, and J. D. H. Porter. 2005. "Microfinance and HIV Prevention – Emerging Lessons from Rural South Africa." *Small Enterprise Development* 16 (3): 26–38.

Robins, S. and B. Von Lieres. 2004. "AIDS Activism and Globalisation from Below: Occupying New Spaces of Citizenship in Post-apartheid South Africa." *IDS Bulletin* 35 (2): 84–90.

Rose, G. 2001. "Sick Individuals and Sick Populations." *International Journal of Epidemiology* 30 (3): 427–432.

Rose, G. 2008. *Rose's Strategy of Preventive Medicine*, with commentary by K-T. Khaw and M. Marmot. Oxford: Oxford University Press.

Sen, A. 1981. *Poverty and Famines: An Essay on Entitlements and Deprivation.* Oxford: Clarendon Press.

Sherr, K. H., M. A. Micek, S. O. Gimbel, S. S. Gloyd, J. P. Hughes, G. C. John-Stewart, R. M. Manjate, J. Pfeiffer, and N. S. Weiss. 2010. "Quality of HIV Care Provided by Non-physician Clinicians and Physicians in Mozambique: A Retrospective Cohort Study." *AIDS (London, England)* 24 (Suppl. 1): S59–S66.

Stillwaggon, E. 2009. "Complexity, Cofactors, and the Failure of AIDS Policy in Africa." *Journal of the International AIDS Society* 12 (1): 12–21.

Strathdee, S. A., W. M. Wechsberg, D. L. Kerrigan, and T. L. Patterson. 2013. "HIV Prevention Among Women in Low- and Middle-income Countries: Intervening Upon Contexts of Heightened HIV Risk." *Annual Review of Public Health* 34: 301–316.

Verboom, B., G. Melendez-Torres, and C. P. Bonell. 2014. *Combination Methods for HIV Prevention in Men who have Sex with Men (MSM)*. The Cochrane Library. www.thecochranelibrary.com. Accessed February 4, 2015. doi: 10.1002/14651858.CD010939.

Wechsberg, W. M., W. A. Zule, W. K. Luseno, T. L. Kline, F. A. Browne, S. P. Novak, and R. M. Ellerson. 2011. "Effectiveness of an Adapted Evidence-based Woman-focused Intervention for Sex Workers and Non-sex Workers: The Women's Health CoOp in South Africa." *Journal of Drug Issues* 41 (2): 233–252.

Woolcock, M. 2013. "Using Case Studies to Explore the External Validity of 'Complex' Development Interventions." *Evaluation* 19 (3): 229–248.

The political economy of concurrent partners: toward a history of sex–love–gift connections in the time of AIDS

Mark Hunter

Over the last decade, one of the most influential explanations for high HIV prevalence in sub-Saharan Africa is the existence of sexual networks characterised by concurrent partners. Recently, however, a growing number of scholars have challenged the evidential basis for the concurrency argument. While this dispute has led to a call for more sophisticated quantitative methods to measure concurrency, this article widens the discussion to emphasise the political economic roots and qualitative dimension of concurrent partnered relations. Specifically, the paper argues for the importance of situating concurrency within key historical processes and, to that end, gives special consideration to the growth of 'transactional sex' – non-prostitute but material relations between men and women. Critics of the concurrency–HIV thesis have sometimes dismissed as anecdotal accounts of sex–gift exchanges in Africa. Yet by exploring through an ethnographic/historical lens the changing configuration of sex, love and gifts in South Africa, this article illuminates different manifestations of concurrency, including connections between concurrency and condom use.

[L'économie politique des partenaires multiples et simultanés : vers une histoire des connexions sexe-amour-don aux temps du SIDA.] Durant la dernière décennie, une des explications les plus influentes de la prévalence élevée du VIH en Afrique subsaharienne est l'existence de réseaux sexuels caractérisés par des partenaires multiples et simultanés. Récemment, un certain nombre d'académiques ont cependant contesté le fondement de l'argument de la multiplicité des partenaires. Alors, qu'en raison de ce différent, des méthodes quantitatives plus sophistiquées pour mesurer la multiplicité et la simultanéité des partenaires sont demandées, cet article élargit la discussion en mettant l'accent sur les racines politico-économiques et la dimension qualitative du phénomène des relations avec des partenaires multiples. En particulier, l'article plaide en faveur de l'importance de situer la multiplicité des partenaires dans les processus historiques clés et, à cette fin, prête une attention particulière à la croissance du « sexe transactionnel » - c'est-à-dire des relations matérielles entre hommes et femmes, mais qui ne sont pas de la prostitution. Les critiques de la thèse du VIH lié à la multiplicité des partenaires ont parfois considéré les explications basées sur les échanges sexe-don en Afrique comme anecdotiques. Pourtant, en explorant avec une vision historique/ethnographique la configuration changeante du sexe, de l'amour et des dons en Afrique du Sud, cet article montre différentes manifestations de la multiplicité des partenaires, notamment les connexions entre cette dernière et l'utilisation du préservatif.

The concurrency debate

One of the most influential recent explanations for high HIV prevalence in sub-Saharan Africa is the existence of sexual networks characterised by concurrent partners. The strength of the main argument has been well rehearsed: the number of overall sexual partners is not the key driving force of HIV, instead *concurrent relationships* rather than *serial monogamy* provide for the virus's rapid spread. One important reason for this is that those who are newly infected with HIV are more infectious themselves and thus able to pass on the virus to a concurrent sexual partner (for instance Epstein and Morris 2011; Halperin and Epstein 2004; Kenyon and Zondo 2011; Kretzschmar and Caraël 2012; Morris et al. 2013; Morris and Kretzschmar 1997; Thornton 2008).

Recently, however, a growing number of scholars have challenged the evidential basis for the concurrent partners thesis (Lurie and Rosenthal 2010; Sawers and Stillwaggon 2010; Tanser et al. 2011). The principal arguments in favour of the concurrency thesis, this critique goes, are based on mathematical models and not the actual demonstration of high rates of concurrency in sub-Saharan Africa or the relationships between concurrency and HIV prevalence. In response, proponents have argued that traditional epidemiological studies do not capture the empirical signature of concurrency which is revealed at the societal and not the individual level (Morris 2010, 31; see also Epstein 2010; Epstein and Morris 2011; Mah and Halperin 2010). Questions of method have therefore become pivotal to this debate: indeed, UNAIDS (2010) is now actively promoting methodological consistency through a series of 'consensus indicators' on concurrent partners (see also Boily, Alary, and Baggaley 2011).

Without doubt, collecting more accurate quantitative data on concurrency will provide a better evidential basis for investigating the importance of sexual networking to HIV/AIDS. Qualitative work that develops typologies of concurrency is also useful in highlighting different forms of concurrency, for instance polygamy or relationships outside of marriage. At the same time, we need to interpret this data, and its limitations, in contextualised ways. We need to understand the social processes that might lead to, or not lead to, concurrency, as well as those that affect the duration and nature of overlapping relations. In pursuing this task, this paper argues for the importance of historical and ethnographic methods, anchored in political economy, in showing the different social contexts – class and gender relations, labour market and migration dynamics, marital patterns etc. – through which concurrency is shaped and operates.

Studying the political economy of sexuality: from variables to processes

This article's working assumption about sexuality is as follows: sexuality is not simply a set of biological acts centred on male/female genitals – acts that can be turned into variables – but a complex social phenomenon embedded in dynamic and not always easily measurable historical *processes*, from the very construction of a discrete domain of 'sex' (Foucault 1978), to the way that sex is inflected by gender, the labour market, migration and much more (e.g. Parker and Aggleton 1999). This starting point yields the view that sexual attitudes and practices are always in flux, and must always be studied as they interact with other social structures and practices.

The ethnographic and historical approach rooted in political economy and outlined here is reasonably well represented in sociology, geography and anthropology (for instance Burawoy 2000; Farmer 1999; Hart 2002 – see Farmer especially on health issues). But, as Schoepf (2004, 17) notes, there is a hierarchy within AIDS research that tends to advantage epidemiological methods:

[to be recognised as real,] facts must be put about by those who are socially authorized to do so. In the domain of epidemic disease, these persons are epidemiologists and specialists in public health, not social scientists, and above all, not ethnographers who use qualitative methods to examine culture: social relations, meanings, and their contexts.

The article forefronts a single process that provides insights – though, like all social research, *partial* insights – into concurrent partnerships: this is the materiality of non-marital sex. 'Transactional sex' is a term widely used today, especially in sub-Saharan Africa, to refer to non-prostitute relations where gifts and sex are closely connected (on Botswana, see Iversen 2005; on Democratic Republic of Congo, see Maclin and Kelly 2014; on Kenya, see Muchomba 2014; on Madagascar, see Cole 2004; on Malawi, see Swidler and Watkins 2007; on Mali, see Castle and Konate 1999; on Mozambique, see Groes-Green 2014; on South Africa, see Dunkle et al. 2004; Hunter 2002; LeClerc-Madlala 2003; Selikow, Zulu, and Cedras 2002; Zembe et al. 2013; on Tanzania, see Maganja et al. 2007; Wamoyi et al. 2011; on Zimbabwe, see Masvawure 2010). These 'transactional sex' relationships, though differing greatly, have some common character-istics: they involve an expectation of male–female gifts, although participants are not posi-tioned as 'prostitutes' and 'clients' but 'boyfriends' and 'girlfriends'. Men often give girlfriends money, but gifts can also take the form of food, school fees, clothes, cell phones and accommodation. A point that the rather instrumental term 'transactional sex' downplays – and I try and capture by also referring to *sex–love–gifts* connections – is that participants generally see these relationships, in part, as being about love (see Cole and Thomas 2008; Hunter 2010; Wamoyi et al. 2011). That sex creates a debt that men must pay can therefore be seen as a moral arrangement; indeed one that echoes marital love relationships whereby a man supports a wife to whom he has sexual access. What the transactional sex literature brings attention to, therefore, is not that money and sex and love interact, for this happens in most sexual relations, but that many non-marital sexual relations have a *particular* materiality in that they are unlikely to happen in the absence of significant gifts from boyfriends to girlfriends.

Although links between 'transactional sex' and concurrent partners have long been recognised, this association has faced increased questioning in recent years. Lurie and Rosenthal (2010, 21), for instance, note in their critical appraisal of the concurrency thesis that 'what tends to get reported in qualitative studies [on transactional sex] are the "interesting cases" which are often not representative and say little about the distribution of local social norms.' Others have taken this point further by suggesting that the emphasis on sex–gift links in Africa is unwarranted since courting gifts are also common in the West. In their trenchant rebuttal of the concurrency thesis, Sawers and Stillwaggon (2010, 17) ridicule the literature on transactional sex in Africa:

> All over the world, people who have sex with each other also have other dimensions to their partnership, and some of those dimensions involve exchanges of services, goods and love, not just sex ... Picture the reaction if *The Lancet* were to publish an article that said, 'About 80% of US women reported receiving flowers, poetry, candy or jewellery for Valentine's Day, and such transactions in sexual relationships are the norm in the population ....'

Though Sawers and Stillwaggon cite an imagined *Lancet* article to mock the transactional sex literature, it is true that the actual *Lancet* article that angered them (Shelton 2009) does generalise somewhat about transactional sex and concurrency in Africa. The notion of a dis-tinct and dangerous African sexuality, as Sawers and Stillwaggon point out, is rooted in centuries of racialised stereotypes about the continent. Indeed, challenges to this view congealed two decades ago in reaction to Caldwell, Caldwell, and Quiggin's (1989) influential argument that an 'African sexuality' exists and drives AIDS (e.g. Ahlberg 1994).

But even if Sawers and Stillwaggon's comments correctly point to the need for caution in approaching the concurrency thesis, it is unhelpful to write off 'transactional sex' in parts of Africa by suggesting, even in jest, that it is analogous to everyday relationships in the US. The approach outlined here, which stresses political economy analysis at the national and subnational scales, forefronts the different context in which the materiality of sex and concurrency might occur. Following this line of thinking, I argue that research on concurrency must not start from a large unit of analysis – the 'why is HIV/AIDS so prevalent in Africa?' question – and then work down in scale, but begin from detailed research in different areas. Doing so leaves an openness not only for considering the multiple (and multiply spatialised) causal processes that affect sexuality but the uneven geography of HIV cofactors from male circumcision, to nutrition rates, to the prevalence of existing sexually transmitted diseases. This is global health, but from the bottom up and not the top down.

What follows therefore is not an attempt to prove one way or another whether concurrency is the central cause of high HIV prevalence in South Africa. Though the attention to 'transactional sex' does yield the view that concurrency is one of a number of important factors driving HIV infection, it shows that concurrency cannot be seen as a single practice that a technical agenda can simply intervene to change. The rush to acronymise health issues (e.g. CP for concurrent partners or TS for transactional sex) serves to *simplify* by *bounding* complex, interconnected, processes. Yet the different ways in which sexuality intersects with other aspects of life, from gender, to the labour market, to condom use, are absolutely vital to its constitution.

To underline the importance of historicising sexuality, and develop a critical comparative lens, this paper begins with a brief overview of changing relationship patterns in the United States. There is a relatively large amount of published work on sexuality in the US that justifies and assists this task. Using this approach, I hope to give a sense of the importance of historical change to sexuality and, at the same time, rebut the suggestion by Sawers and Stillwaggon (2010) that Valentine's gifts in the West are somehow akin to 'transactional sex' in parts of Africa.

Empirically, the shorter section on the US derives from secondary data and the South Africa data derives mostly from a long-term historical-ethnographic study that explores transformations in intimacy over the last century to better understand the contemporary AIDS pandemic (this is outlined in detail in Hunter 2010). The central question that frames South African research is how HIV prevalence can remain so high – at around 30% for most of the 2000s – despite a large amount of awareness about HIV transmission among the general population. The bulk of the South African research was conducted between 2000 and 2006 and involved the author living extensively in a predominantly isiZulu-speaking area in the province of KwaZulu-Natal. More than 95% of the residents of this area would have been classified as 'African' in the apartheid era (at the end of the apartheid era there were four widely used 'racial' categories: African, White, Indian and Coloured). This article draws very selectively on this and other research to make some general points; it cannot do justice to the diversity of views and the politics of a white man undertaking this research (though see Hunter 2010).

Valentine's gifts as transactional sex? Sex, love and gifts in the US

Frederick Engels' (1971 [1884]) *Origin of the Family, Private Property and the State* first inspired debates about the relationship between capitalism, gender inequality, sex and love (see Sayers, Evans, and Redclift 1987). In recent years, attention has turned from the materiality of marriage to courting. In her influential account, Beth Bailey identifies a significant rise in the materiality of sex in the early twentieth century, as, she writes, 'dating moved courtship into the world of the economy. Money – men's money – was at the centre of the dating system . . . men became the hosts and assumed the control that came with that position' (Bailey 1988, 21). This account hinges on a change from when men 'called' on women at their homes to when they took women out on 'dates' at movies, restaurants and dances. This led to an expectation that, in return, men would have sexual access to women, even if relations often stopped short of penetrative sex. Supporting her argument, Bailey notes that in its early days the term 'date' had a close association with prostitution (22).

Drawing attention to a slightly earlier period, the turn of the twentieth century, Elizabeth Clement (2006) discusses the phenomenon of 'charity girls', who were quite explicitly 'treated' by men in order to access new consumer worlds. This form of 'sexual barter', Clement argues, was an 'ingenious compromise' between poor women's need for respectability and their wish to access the new benefits of consumption (3, 48). Clement is particularly attentive to the dynamics of race and class, arguing that it was working-class practices of treating that led to the materiality of dating noted by Bailey: 'Treating provided the model for the economic and sexual exchange that became a hallmark of dating for young people of both classes' (227). Hence, despite differences, both Clement and Bailey illustrate a growing materiality to everyday relationships: indeed, according to these accounts, 'going Dutch' (splitting the bill) was considered as an embarrassment by most men and women in the first half of the twentieth century.

The post-war era, notes Bailey, witnessed the rise of more long-term 'going steady' relations. However, a series of forces rooted in the 1960s and 70s transformed courting in ways that still reverberate today. First was the 'sexual revolution' itself, partly fuelled by the invention of the contraceptive pill, a technology which facilitated the separation of sex from childbirth. Second was the rise of the feminist movement that promoted greater equality between men and women. These changes are sometimes seen to have led to a scenario whereby '[s]ex was uncoupled from romance and love' (Seidman 1991, 121). Indeed, discussing Western society, Anthony Giddens (1992) suggests that the skewed notion of romantic love – which led to women's domestic subjection – gave way to a more equal 'confluent love' based on a 'rolling contract' centred on mutual benefits, including sexual satisfaction. In turn, popular media programmes like *Sex and the City* reflect (and help to produce) a greater acceptance that women are entitled to sexual pleasure outside of marriage (see Akass and McCabe 2004).

One can see in all the trends noted from the 1960s the *potential* for sex to be separated from romantic love and, to take this further, become more instrumentally exchanged for gifts. Yet, on the whole, most US women do not today enter into relations premised on sex–gift exchanges. In *Sex and the City*, the four female stars all wish for their men to spoil them, but it is women's independence that shines through the series – their ability to say no to men and attain sex on their own terms. A somewhat similar theme emerges from accounts of relationships among college-goers. In her book *Hooking Up*, Kathleen Bogle (2008) shows that women often initiate casual sex on college campuses, though compared to men they are more likely to prefer longer-term 'relationships'. Bogle also shows that participants in a 'hooking up' encounter can retain contact and at a later time entertain a 'booty call' (a late-night call for sex). Depending on how concurrency is defined (i.e. whether such an encounter would count as an enduring relationship that overlaps with others), this example could provide evidence that concurrency relationships are indeed quite common among certain groups of Americans.

At the same time, Bogle argues that hook-ups often do not involve penetrative sex but kissing and oral sex – the latter being a practice that young Americans today typically do not see as 'sex'. Moreover, it is striking how gifts are barely mentioned by Bogle's informants, and this suggests that male–female gifts play only a small role in encouraging lovers to hook up: college women, after all, are embarking on careers that will lead them to experience financial independence. This sense of greater equality in male–female relations, including economic equality, is clearly also important if we consider possible discussions/negotiations over condom use, though this is also not a topic addressed in any detail in the book.

College students are, of course, a relatively privileged segment of US society, and Bogle also spoke mainly with white students. A contrasting literature suggests that everyday sex–gift connections are quite common among poorer Americans. One of the most graphic studies is Phillipe Bourgois' (2009) ethnography of drug addiction in San Francisco. Here he shows how poor (largely black) men and women, marginalised from the labour market, can form affective bonds in relations that entangle love, gifts and addiction. Other studies – some themselves influenced by the 'transactional sex' literature in Africa – have found links in the US context between race (and, by association, class) and the materiality of sex (Dunkle et al. 2010).

What this admittedly very brief reading of the US literature seems to suggest, therefore, is that rather than taking concurrent partners as a single category of analysis, it needs to be handled with care. Valentine's gifts between university students, even in a 'hooking up' culture, are quite different from gifts between men and women when large discrepancies in wealth are apparent. Moreover, at least for middle-class women – and women in the US are, of course, on average considerably richer than those in Africa – sex has become arguably *less* material outside of marriage. While, at the beginning of the twentieth century, the new dating culture was formed very strongly in relation to men's role of providing for women, hooking up, in contrast, is partly an expression of women's relative economic equality with men.

Sex, love and gifts in South Africa[1]

South Africa has a very different history of sex–love–gift connections to the US. In the early part of the twentieth century, economic hardship meant that a significant number of poor black and white women were pushed into prostitution (Freed 1949). However, the state's preferential policies for whites in respect of the labour market, housing and social services, helped pull many white women out of this sexual economy. In contrast, racialised state policies discriminated violently against black South African women, especially after apartheid's introduction in 1948. For this group, prostitution – or more informal relationships that might today be called 'transactional sex' – continued to be a means of survival in urban areas (Bonner 1990; Jochelson 2001).

However, while 'transactional sex' has a long history, in the first half of the twentieth century the numbers of men in cities greatly outweighed the numbers of women and marriage rates remained high; moreover, the building of urban townships was a deliberate attempt to limit the number of single women in cities by allowing them to stay in urban areas only as wives. For courting couples separated by men's temporary migrancy from rural areas, *ilobolo* (bridewealth) constituted the most important means through which men expressed love. *Ilobolo* – usually of 11 cattle in the KwaZulu-Natal region – signified commitment in part because it took several years for a man to pay in full. Men, therefore, did not typically buy their favourite girlfriends dinner to express love but gave *ilobolo* to their fathers.

How did *ilobolo* and love become so intertwined? In the nineteenth century, cattle from a father's rural homestead allowed a man to secure *ilobolo* to marry his girlfriend. By roughly the 1930s and 40s, however, state taxes and associated rural failure had left unmarried rural men with effectively no choice but to work in order to *lobola* (pay bridewealth for) their girlfriends. As millions of men became migrant labourers, money became intertwined with love and marriage but in a very different way to the US. Notwithstanding tensions wrought by men's long absences, their roles as providers engendered something of a 'patriarchal bargain' between men and women (Kandiyoti 1988). A young man was expected to find work, *lobola* a woman and financially support a home. In turn, women raised children, performed domestic work and engaged in homestead agriculture – the latter which declined in importance as rural areas became more overcrowded and depleted. What this arrangement meant is that, by and large, monetary transactions were not channelled through men's gifts to women in pre-marital relations but through the more meaningful payments of *ilobolo* to a woman's family, usually over several years, and remittances sent to a wife residing in a distant homestead.

Certainly, evidence in the 1960s suggests that gifts from boyfriends to girlfriends did not play an important role in driving rural courting relations. In one part of KwaZulu-Natal, the anthropologist Vilakazi (1962, 49) reported great shock when asking about courting gifts because 'the boy would be accused of trying to *gwaza* (bribe) the girl to love him.' The use of the word *gwaza* suggests that courting was a domain where gifts (to influence the outcome) would be seen as improper, even immoral, interventions. In rural areas a principal aim of a young wage-earner was to channel his earnings into *ilobolo* payments for a future wife.

Even in urban areas where liaisons could be easier, marriage was still the expected path and, related, sex–gift exchanges did not appear to be prevalent. For instance Levin (1947, 22), discussing Langa township in Cape Town, reported mainly reciprocal gifts between young men and women: 'During courtship men try to win the favour of girls by giving them presents such as slabs of chocolate, jewellery, and scarves. Women, in turn, are said to give their boyfriends presents, such as ties and socks.' In sum, throughout much of the twentieth century marriage rates remained high and a large amount of unmarried men's wages were channelled into *ilobolo*.

It is possible to argue, however, that since roughly the 1970s a set of historical processes can help to explain the coming together of love, sex and gifts in a new configuration in South Africa. Rather than assuming similarity across Africa, detailed historical analysis is necessary because social processes interact in different ways and with a complexity that regression analysis or other quantitative tools cannot easily measure. Consequently, some of the themes relevant to the case of South Africa are applicable to other parts of the continent while others are not. For instance, unemployment and de-industrialisation are common across the continent after World Bank/International Monetary Fund 'structural adjustment' programmes in the 1980s; some scholars have shown links between these changes and social inequalities that result in sex–gift links (e.g Schoepf et al. 2000 in then Zaire). In Nigeria and Uganda, scholars argue that love leads to condomless sex *within* marriage, which is still the norm for young people (Parikh 2007; Smith 2006). However, marriage rates are particularly low in southern Africa (Bongaarts 2007). Social inequalities are also higher in southern Africa because the large mining and manufacturing industries were powerful forces generating wealth and poverty in the region.

Specific to South Africa, what follows are some important historical trends relevant to understanding contemporary sex–love–gift links and concurrency. These changes have left a large number of increasingly mobile, and rarely married, women dependent on men – though typically not in prostitute but girlfriend/boyfriend relations that can endure for some time.

First, the rise of chronic unemployment

Absolutely central to the materiality of sex is the tremendous rise of unemployment from the late 1970s, a trend accentuated because of trade liberalisation that followed democratic elections in 1994. Today, only 6.6 million people are in full-time work, around 3.1 million are in outsourced work, 2.2 million are in informal work and 8.4 million are unemployed (Von Holdt and Webster 2005, 28). For young people especially, unemployment has reached terrifying levels.

Second, an increase in social inequalities that is highly gendered

Linked to rising unemployment is a widening gap between the rich and the poor. Since class-based differences work through and exacerbate gender inequalities, many single women today are dependent on men. Though a gendered wage gap has long existed, what accentuated this situation is the continued movement of largely unmarried women into the labour force, especially through their migration from languishing rural areas (Posel 2006). There is therefore a vast chasm between those working (disproportionately men) and those not working (men and women).

Third, stark reductions in marriage rates

Marriage rates have halved since the 1960s: less than 30% of black South Africans (and disproportionately the oldest) are now in wedlock (Hunter 2010). Unemployment levels among black South Africans serve as a key contributor to reduced marriage rates. The decline in marriage for poor people has created a profound sense of distrust between men and women, and helped to structure love as being more entangled with men's support of women through individual gifts – most men, after all, are neither saving money to pay *ilobolo* nor supporting a woman as a wife. The fact that most people's lives do not revolve around a marital home has also contributed to the greater movement of women (below). What needs to be understood therefore is that transactional sex is not just non-marital sex in the sense that it occurs outside of marriage. Rather, just as marriage configured sex and money in a particular way, the reduction in marriage rates today – and yet persistence of the institution in terms of gendered meanings – creates new sex–love–gift connections.

Fourth, geographical shifts

The pattern that characterised much of the twentieth century – migrant men working in urban areas and supporting a rural wife – has diminished. Now, both men and women are very mobile (Posel 2006), and this has important consequences for sexual networks that can stretch between rural and urban areas, with a new intensity. Women arriving in towns face particular difficulties in finding work and can rely on men for material support. These trends are manifested geographically in the tremendous growth of informal settlements since the 1970s, areas that are often the first home for new migrants to towns (Hindson and McCarthy 1994). Significantly, in these marginalised areas of towns, HIV rates are twice as high as in formal urban or rural areas (HSRC 2002, 2005, 2012).

Contemporary relations in South Africa: what has love got to do with sex and gifts?

In the US, we have seen that a culture of 'hooking up' might involve several overlapping partners (depending on how one defines overlapping). However, these encounters' central organising principle is mutual pleasure rather than romantic love – love in this context suggests long-term monogamous relationships with some possibility of eventual marriage. Indeed, some observers argue that sex became progressively delinked from romantic love among the US middle class in the latter part of the twentieth century. We also saw that court-ing gifts, for instance men paying for a meal, do not appear to play as large a role today as they did in the early twentieth century; though some expectations of male chivalry endure, 'going Dutch' is now more accepted, at least for the middle class.

In some respects, South Africa's multi-racial middle class bears some resemblance to the US middle class in terms of being likely to marry; moreover, women's greater ability to demand sexual satisfaction in non-marital relations is tied up with – though in very complex ways – some women's greater economic independence from men (Hunter 2010). What the quite extensive ethnographic literature on poorer (mostly 'African') South Africans makes clear, however, is that sex, love and gifts are now very closely connected (Dunkle et al. 2004; Hunter 2002; LeClerc-Madlala 2003; Selikow, Zulu, and Cedras 2002).

These material boyfriend/girlfriend relations are different from most forms of prostitu-tion because they can endure for some time and embody feelings of 'love'. Of course, the presence of 'love' does not signal equality – almost always it is men who give gifts to women. And neither is there a single meaning of love in existence, especially across a diverse range of South Africans. Love can be represented by a woman's commitment to a lover who is not able to support her, a sense that 'love conquers all' evident in common notions of *romantic love* (Hunter 2010); yet love can also be expressed in men's gifts to girlfriends, a scenario that might be called *provider love* (*Ibid.*). These differ-ent meanings of love overlap in everyday life, and this is one reason why quantitative data on 'transactional sex' is so difficult to gather: whether a person will say that a relationship is based on gifts or love depends on the context of the conversation.

One unfortunate consequence of the recent prominence of the concurrency thesis is that condom use has been somewhat neglected in the AIDS field. But the ethnographic record is clear: 'love' is often an important reason for the non-use of condoms. The most instrumental money/sex exchanges, for instance prostitution, are most likely to lead to condom use (Hunter 2010; Preston-Whyte et al. 2000). Indeed, today both monetary gifts from unmar-ried men to women *and* condomless sex can signal love in important (and dangerous) ways. These meanings are not of course wholly new; they echo long-standing emotional and physical bonds that rested on husbands supporting wives. But while love has always had a material dimension, today it is typically instituted outside of marriage, since economic circumstances make marriage so difficult.

Of course, male–female relations often unfold in unpredictable ways and their trajec-tory depends on a host of factors from whether a couple are cohabiting to the level of phys-ical attraction. Yet, the way in which different concurrent partners are typically differentiated is a good example of the importance of understanding the history of relation-ships. In KwaZulu-Natal, a woman's main lover, described by various terms – *istraight* or *iqonda* (straight), 'number one' or *umkhwenyana* (fiancé, if he has begun to pay *ilobolo*) – is the one with whom the relationship is most serious and might one day lead to marriage. In the rare cases when *ilobolo* payments have been initiated, the status of a woman's main lover is raised substantially. Such payments are the most decisive symbol of commitment and, most residents would say, obligate a woman to be faithful to that man. Importantly, it is in these *istraight* relationships that condoms are least likely to be used.

Secondary lovers – that is, lovers who are not *istraight* – can, at times, be casual partners with whom relationships are brief. Yet although surveys of sexual behaviour commonly distinguish between 'main lovers' and 'casual lovers' – the latter term resonating with a number of English concepts such as 'fling', 'hook-up' and 'one-night stand' – secondary lovers are rarely the same thing as casual lovers; relationships with them can persist for some time. A relationship's secondary status is typically determined not by how long it is expected to last, but by the lesser obligations and expectations it creates and by its more secret nature; for instance, a secondary lover can be called an *ishende* (secret lover) or *umakhwapheni* (also hidden lover, lit. under the armpit). The primary determinant of a relationship's status is not its duration, but the nature of its bond. These secondary relations are more likely to involve condom use but, because of the way that reciprocities change over time, this is by no means certain.

Readers might ask how the boyfriend/girlfriend relationships described above differ from marriage. One difference is that the sense of mutual fidelity is much weaker. Of course, extra-marital relations have long been practised in South Africa as elsewhere (especially by men) and there is certainly no clear association between marriage and HIV in the continent (UNAIDS 2009, 23, 24). Nevertheless, marriage does structure relationships in important ways. As we saw in the case of *ilobolo*, it leads men to save for many years for a single wife. It structures a household as being, to some extent, a shared project geographically located in a physical house. In contrast, unmarried people tend to be more geographically mobile (Posel 2006).

As intimated earlier, while this paper focuses on the 'transactional sex'/concurrency nexus, it is important to note that there are other important processes in which concurrency is entangled, for example decisive recent shifts in masculinities and femininities at the time of chronic unemployment. The fact that there is a high status attached to men having multiple partners talks to both continuities and shifts in masculinities over the twentieth century (Hunter 2005). Similarly, women's ability to have multiple partners has increased significantly in recent decades as men fail to marry and support them.

Nevertheless, for the purposes of this paper, two points need to be emphasised. First, in contrast to accounts of middle-class Americans, sex, love and gifts have become *more* and not less connected among poorer South Africans. This is not to say many relationships in South Africa are not fraught with great tensions – they are – but relationships are still usually framed in terms of love, even the most material and violent ones. Indeed, sexual violence, which I don't consider here, is quite widely reported in South Africa, but cannot be seen as conceptually separate from histories of love. Second, the particular history of relationships means that differentiation tends to take place between lovers in terms of the nature and not simply the duration of the bond (i.e. primary/secondary lover rather than boyfriend/one-night stand).

Conclusion

A certain confidence has surrounded claims over the last decade that concurrency patterns explain high HIV prevalence in Africa. At last, it was thought, an explanation made sense that did not position Africans as being more promiscuous than Westerners (i.e. having more lifetime partners), just partaking in sexual relations that happened to be concurrent. However, in the last few years, this thesis has faced something of a backlash. The evidence for more concurrency taking place in Africa than elsewhere is unproven, critics argue.

The article's contribution is to widen the debate. This means, first, situating concurrency not as a discrete 'cultural' practice that can be studied in isolation. Rather concurrency is embedded in wider social processes, and one process explored here is the growing materiality of sex: gifts from boyfriends to girlfriends.

Instead of there being rigid geographically based differences in sexual behaviour (Africa and the West), some aspects of concurrency in the South Africa and the US, to use this example, are similar and some are very different. We must recognise the ways that race and class engender concurrency, sexuality's constant flux and the fine-grained meanings of intimate relationships. It really does matter if a man is giving several girlfriends Valentine's gifts in a US college, or if a man is supporting one woman with housing and another with food, in southern Africa. In the latter case, relationships might endure for some time, be structured with great inequality and yet have a definitive emotional aspect.

One consequence of viewing concurrency as a series of practices always entangled with wider social structures is that resultant concurrency interventions shouldn't be seen as separate and competing to others, especially condom promotion. Concurrency and condom use are not practices that operate in separate social silos: critically, condoms are much more likely to be used in short-term prostitute relations than in longer-term relations underpinned by gifts. Indeed, the long duration of some concurrent partners clearly has important implications for HIV infection. So too does the history of concurrency raise questions about the social policies that might reduce the dependence of some women on boyfriends, for instance the huge recent increase in state grants in South Africa which now benefit over 16 million South Africans (Khan 2013).

More generally, if AIDS prevalence is ever to be significantly addressed, stronger links must be made between concurrency and underlying structural issues that in South Africa include high unemployment, the growth of shack settlements and reduced marriage rates. Recognising how the political economy of concurrent partners varies in different settings and at different times will enable a more nuanced and contextualised understanding of the relationship between social structure and HIV infection.

Disclosure statement

No potential conflict of interest was reported by the author.

Note

1. The data on South Africa draw from Hunter (2010).

References

Ahlberg, B. 1994. "Is there a Distinct African Sexuality? A Critical Response to Caldwell." *Africa: Journal of the International African Institute,* 64 (2): 220–242.

Akass, H., and J. McCabe, eds. 2004. *Reading Sex and the City*. New York: I.B. Tauris.

Bailey, B. L. 1988. *From Front Porch to Back Seat: Courtship in Twentieth-century America*. Baltimore: Johns Hopkins University Press.

Bogle, K. 2008. *Hooking Up: Sex, Dating, and Relationships on Campus*. New York: New York University Press.

Boily, M. C., M. Alary, and R. F. Baggaley. 2011. "Neglected Issues and Hypotheses Regarding the Impact of Sexual Concurrency on HIV and Sexually Transmitted Infections." *AIDS and Behavior*. doi: 10.1007/s10461-011-9887-0.

Bongaarts, J. 2007. "Late Marriage and the HIV Epidemic in Sub-Saharan Africa." *Population Studies* 61 (1): 73–83.

Bonner, P. 1990. "'Desirable or Undesirable Basotho Women?' Liquor, Prostitution and the Migration of Basotho Women to the Rand, 1920–1945." In *Women and Gender in Southern Africa to 1945*, edited by C. Walker, 221–250. Cape Town: David Philip.

Bourgois, P. 2009. *Righteous Dopefiend*. Berkeley: University of California Press.

Burawoy, M. 2000. *Global Ethnography: Forces, Connections, and Imaginations in a Postmodern World*. Berkeley: University of California Press.

Caldwell, J. C., P. Caldwell, and P. Quiggin. 1989. "The Social Context of AIDS in Sub-Saharan Africa." *Population and Development Review* 15 (2): 185–234.

Castle, S., and M. Konate. 1999. "The Context and Consequences of Economic Transactions Associated with Sexual Relations among Malian Adolescents 1999." Paper Presented at the Third African Population Conference, Durban, South Africa, December 6–10.

Clement, E. 2006. *Love for Sale: Courting, Treating, and Prostitution in New York City, 1900–1945*. Chapel Hill: University of North Carolina Press.

Cole, J. 2004. "Fresh Contact in Tamatave, Madagascar: Sex, Money, and Intergenerational Transformation." *American Ethnologist* 31 (4): 573–588.

Cole, J., and L. Thomas. 2008. *Love in Africa*. Chicago: University of Chicago Press.

Dunkle, K. L., R. K. Jewkes, H. C. Brown, G. E. Gray, J. A. McIntryre, and S. D. Harlow. 2004. "Transactional Sex Among Women in Soweto, South Africa: Prevalence, Risk Factors and Association with HIV Infection." *Social Science and Medicine* 59 (8): 1581–1592.

Dunkle, K., G. Wingood, C. Camp and R. DiClemente. 2010. "Economically Motivated Relationships and Transactional Sex Among Unmarried African American and White Women: Results from a U.S. National Telephone Survey." *Public Health Reports* 125 (Suppl. 4): 90–100.

Engels, F. 1971 [1884]. *The Origin of the Family, Private Property and the State*. New York: International Publishers.

Epstein, H. 2010. "The Mathematics of Concurrent Partnerships and HIV: A Commentary on Lurie and Rosenthal, 2009." *AIDS and Behavior* 14: 29–30.

Epstein, H., and M. Morris. 2011. "Concurrent Partnerships and HIV: An Inconvenient Truth." *Journal of the International AIDS Society* 14 (1): 13.

Farmer, P. 1999. *Infections and Inequalities: The Modern Plagues*. Berkeley: University of California Press.

Foucault, M. 1978. *The History of Sexuality*. New York: Pantheon Books.

Freed, L. F. 1949. *The Problem of European Prostitution in Johannesburg: A Sociological Survey*. Johannesburg: Juta.

Giddens, A. 1992. *The Transformation of Intimacy: Sexuality, Love, and Eroticism in Modern Societies*. Stanford, CA: Stanford University Press.

Groes-Green, C. 2014. "Journeys of Patronage: Moral Economies of Transactional Sex, Kinship, and Female Migration from Mozambique to Europe." *Journal of the Royal Anthropological Institute* 20: 237–255.

Halperin, D. T., and H. Epstein. 2004. "Concurrent Sexual Partnerships Help to Explain Africa's High HIV Prevalence: Implications for Prevention." *The Lancet* 364 (9428): 4–6.

Hart, G. 2002. *Disabling Globalization: Places of Power in Post-apartheid South Africa*. Berkeley: University of California Press.

Hindson, D., and J. McCarthy. 1994. *Here to Stay: Informal Settlements in KwaZulu-Natal*. Dalbridge, South Africa: Indicator.

Human Science Research Council. 2002. *Nelson Mandela/HSRC Study of AIDS*. Cape Town: HSRC Press.

Human Science Research Council. 2005. *South African National HIV Prevalence, HIV Incidence, Behaviour and Communication Survey*. Cape Town: HSRC Press.

Human Science Research Council. 2012. *South African National HIV Prevalence, Incidence and Behaviour Survey, 2012*. Cape Town: HSRC Press.

Hunter, M. 2002. "The Materiality of Everyday Sex: Thinking Beyond Prostitution." *African Studies* 61 (1): 99–120.

Hunter, M. 2005. "Cultural Politics and Masculinities: Multiple-partners in Historical Perspective in KwaZulu-Natal." *Culture, Health, and Sexuality* 7 (4): 389–403.

Hunter, M. 2010. *Love in the Time of AIDS: Inequality, Gender, and Rights in South Africa*. Bloomington: Indiana University Press.

Iversen, A. B. 2005. "Transactional Aspects of Sexual Relations in Francistown, Botswana." *Norsk Geografisk Tidsskrift-Norwegian Journal of Geography* 59 (1): 48–54.

Jochelson, K. 2001. *The Colour of Disease. Syphilis and Racism in South Africa, 1880–1950*. Houndmills: Palgrave.

Kandiyoti, D. 1988. "Bargaining with Patriarchy." *Gender & Society* 2 (3): 274–290.

Kenyon, C., and S. Zondo. 2011. "Why do some South African Ethnic Groups have Very High HIV Rates and Others not?" *African Journal of AIDS Research* 10 (1): 51–62.

Khan, F. 2013. "Poverty, Grants, Revolution and 'Real Utopias': Society Must be Defended by Any and All Means Necessary!" *Review of African Political Economy* 40 (138): 572–588.

Kretzschmar, M., and M. Caraël. 2012. "Is Concurrency Driving HIV Transmission in Sub-Saharan African Sexual Networks? The Significance of Sexual Partnership Typology." *AIDS and Behavior* 16 (7): 1746–1752.

LeClerc-Madlala, S. 2003. "Transactional Sex and the Pursuit of Modernity." *Social Dynamics* 29 (2): 213–233.

Levin, R. 1947. "Marriage in Langa Native Location." MA Thesis, University of Cape Town.

Lurie, M. N., and S. Rosenthal. 2010. "Concurrent Partnerships as a Driver of the HIV Epidemic in Sub-Saharan Africa? The Evidence is Limited." *AIDS and Behavior* 14: 17–24.

Maclin, B., and J. Kelly. 2014. "'They have Embraced a Different Behaviour': Transactional Sex and Family Dynamics in Eastern Congo's Conflict." *Culture, Health & Sexuality* 17 (1): 119–131.

Maganja, R., S. Maman, A. Groves, and J. Mbwambo. 2007. "Skinning the Goat and Pulling the Load: Transactional Sex among Youth in Dar es Salaam, Tanzania." *AIDS Care* 19 (8): 974–981.

Mah, T. L., and D. T. Halperin. 2010. "The Evidence for the Role of Concurrent Partnerships in Africa's HIV Epidemics: A Response to Lurie and Rosenthal." *AIDS and Behavior* 14: 11–16.

Masvawure, T. 2010. "'I Just Need to be Flashy on Campus': Female Students and Transactional Sex at a University in Zimbabwe." *Culture, Health & Sexuality* 12 (8): 857–870.

Morris, M. 2010. "Barking up the Wrong Evidence Tree. Comment on Lurie & Rosenthal, "Concurrent Partnerships as a Driver of the HIV Epidemic in Sub-Saharan Africa? The Evidence is Limited"." *AIDS and Behavior* 14: 31–33.

Morris, M., and M. Kretzschmar. 1997. "Concurrent Partnerships and the Spread of HIV." *AIDS* 11: 641–648.

Morris, M., L. Vu, A. Leslie-Cook, E. Akom, A. Stephen, and D. Sherard. 2013. "Comparing Estimates of Multiple and Concurrent Partnerships Across Population Based Surveys: Implications for Combination HIV Prevention." *AIDS and Behavior* 18 (4): 783–790.

Muchomba, F. 2014. "Colonial Policies and the Rise of Transactional Sex in Kenya." *Journal of International Women's Studies* 15 (2): 80–94.

Parikh, A. S. 2007. "The Political Economy of Marriage and HIV: The ABC Approach, "Safe" Infidelity, and Managing Moral Risk in Uganda." *American Journal of Public Health* 97 (7): 1198–1208.

Parker, R. G., and P. Aggleton. 1999. *Culture, Society and Sexuality: A Reader*. London: UCL Press.

Posel, D. 2006. "Moving On: Patterns of Labour Migration in Post-apartheid South Africa." In *Africa on the Move: African Migration and Urbanisation in Comparative Perspective*, editde by Marta Tienda, Sally Findley, and Stephen Tollman, 217–231. Johannesburg: Witwatersrand University Press.

Preston-Whyte, E., C. Varga, H. Oosthuizen, R. Roberts, and f. Blose. 2000. "Survival Sex and HIV/AIDS in an African City." In *Framing the Sexual Subject: The Politics of Gender, Sexuality, and Power*, edited by R. Parker, R. M. Barbosa, and P. Aggleton, 165–190. Berkeley: University of California Press.

Sawers, L., and E. Stillwaggon. 2010. "Concurrent Sexual Partnerships do not Explain the HIV Epidemics in Africa: A Systematic Review of the Evidence." *Journal of the International AIDS Society* 13: 34.

Sayers, J., M. Evans, and N. Redclift. 1987. *Engels Revisited: New Feminist Essays*. London: Tavistock Publications.

Schoepf, B. 2004. "AIDS, History, and Struggles Over Meaning." In *HIV and AIDS in Africa: Beyond Epidemiology*, edited by E. Kalipeni, S. Craddock, J. Oppong and J. Ghosh, 15–28. Oxford: Blackwell.

Schoepf, B. G., C. Schoepf, and J. V. Millen. 2000. "Theoretical Therapies, Remote Remedies: SAPs and the Political Ecology of Poverty and Health in Africa." In *Dying for Growth: Global Inequality and the Health of the Poor*, edited by J. Yong Kim, et al., 91–126. Monroe, ME: Common Courage Press.

Seidman, S. 1991. *Romantic Longings: Love in America, 1830–1980*. New York: Routledge.

Selikow, T., B. Zulu, and E. Cedras. 2002. "The Ingagara, the Regte and the Cherry. HIV/AIDS and Youth Culture in Contemporary Urban Townships." *Agenda* 53: 22–32.

Shelton, J. 2009. "Why Multiple Sexual Partners?" *Lancet* 374: 367–369.

Smith, J. D. 2006. "Love and the Risk of HIV: Courtship, Marriage, and Infidelity in Southeastern Nigeria." In *Modern Loves: The Anthropology of Romantic Courtship & Companionate Marriage*, edited by J. Hirsch and H. Wardlow, 135–156. Ann Arbor: University of Michigan Press.

Swidler, A., and S. C. Watkins. 2007. "Ties of Dependence: AIDS and Transactional Sex in rural Malawi." *Studies in Family Planning* 38 (3): 147–162.

Tanser, F., T. Bärnighausen, L. Hund, G. P. Garnett, N. McGrath, and M-L. Newell. 2011. "Effect of Concurrent Sexual Partnerships on Rate of New HIV Infections in a High-prevalence, Rural South African Population: A Cohort Study." *Lancet* 378 (9787): 247–255.

Thornton, R. 2008. *Unimagined Community: Sex, Networks, and AIDS in Uganda and South Africa*. Berkeley: University of California Press.

UNAIDS. 2009. *AIDS Epidemic Update, December*. Geneva: UNAIDS.

UNAIDS Reference Group on Estimates, Modelling, and Projections. 2010. "Working Group on Measuring Concurrent Sexual Partnerships. HIV: Consensus Indicators are Needed on Concurrency." *Lancet* 375: 621–622.

Vilakazi, A. 1962. *Zulu Transformations. A Study of the Dynamics of Social Change*. Pietermaritzburg: University of Natal Press.

Von Holt, K., and E. Webster. 2005. "Work Restructuring and the Crisis of Reproduction." In *Beyond the Apartheid Workplace: Studies in Transition*, edited by K. Von Holt and E. Webster, 3–40. Pietermaritzburg: University of KwaZulu-Natal Press.

Wamoyi, J., A. Fenwick, M. Urassa, B. Zaba, and W. Stones. 2011. "'Women's Bodies are Shops': Beliefs about Transactional Sex and Implications for Understanding Gender Power and HIV Prevention in Tanzania." *Archives in Sexual Behavior* 40 (1): 5–15.

Zembe, Y. Z., L. Townsend, A. Thorson, and A. M. Ekström. 2013. "'Money Talks, Bullshit Walks' Interrogating Notions of Consumption and Survival Sex among Young Women Engaging in Transactional Sex in Post-apartheid South Africa: A Qualitative Enquiry." *Globalization and Health* 9: 28. doi: 10.1186/1744-8603-9-28.

Wealthy and healthy? New evidence on the relationship between wealth and HIV vulnerability in Tanzania

Danya Long and Kevin Deane

Using data from the Demographics and Health Surveys for Tanzania in 2003–2004, 2007–2008 and 2011–2012 and borrowing from the methodology used in Parkhurst, the authors analyse the changing relationship between wealth and HIV prevalence in Tanzania. Findings are tabulated, graphed and discussed. The authors find the relationship is multifaceted and dynamic: women are disproportionately affected in all wealth quintiles and experience a stronger 'wealth effect'; some groups experience an increase in prevalence even as population prevalence declines. Relative wealth and poverty are associated with increased prevalence, suggesting that structural drivers create a variety of risk situations – as well as protective factors – affecting different groups. The authors also consider data on testing refusals: wealthier men were consistently more likely to decline testing. Continuing to unpack this complex and shifting relationship is necessary in order to fully understand the structural drivers of HIV transmission and access of testing services, enabling the formulation of appropriate policy responses.

[Riche et sain? Preuve nouvelle de la relation entre richesse et vulnérabilité au VIH en Tanzanie.] En utilisant des données des enquêtes sur la démographie et la santé pour la Tanzanie en 2003-2004, 2007-2008 et 2011-2012 et s'inspirant de la méthodologie utilisée par Parkhurst, les auteurs analysent la relation changeante entre la richesse et la prévalence du VIH en Tanzanie. Les résultats sont mis sous forme de tableaux, de graphiques et sont discutés. Les auteurs aboutissent à la conclusion que la relation est multifacette et dynamique : les femmes sont touchées de manière disproportionnée dans tous les quintiles de richesse et font l'objet d'un « effet richesse » plus fort ; certains groupes font l'objet d'une augmentation de la prévalence même lorsque la prévalence dans la population totale baisse. La richesse et la pauvreté relative sont associées à une prévalence accrue, ceci suggérant que les facteurs structurels créent différentes situations de risque - ainsi que des facteurs de protection - qui affectent différents groupes. Les auteurs considèrent également des données sur les refus d'effectuer des tests : les hommes riches refusent les tests avec une plus grande probabilité. Il est nécessaire de continuer à dénouer cette relation complexe et changeante afin de comprendre les facteurs structurels de la transmission du VIH et l'accès aux services de test du VIH, et permettre la formulation de réponses politiques appropriées.

Introduction

Although there was a general awareness in the early years of the HIV/AIDS epidemic that those of higher socioeconomic status, such as school teachers, had high rates of infection (Hamoudi and Birdsall 2004), HIV/AIDS has long been characterised as a disease of poverty, with explanations for and responses to the epidemic framed within a poverty narrative (World Bank 1999; Hope 2001; Whiteside 2002; Masanjala 2007). The evidence, however, does not necessarily support this narrative, with early acknowledgments that the wealthy were impacted (Chao et al. 1994) supplemented with later findings from nationally representative surveys that emphasise the complexity of the relationships between wealth and prevalence (Wojcicki 2005; Mishra et al. 2007; Fortson 2008) and, in some cases, suggest that it is the wealthiest that have the highest prevalence rates (Msisha et al. 2008; Parkhurst 2010). These recent studies typically use data from representative demographic surveys, an improvement on previous methodological approaches that focused on gathering data at antenatal clinics (Bennell 2004), and in general report a range of different correlations between relative wealth and HIV prevalence in a number of countries in sub-Saharan Africa. The relationship in some cases is seen to be positively monotonic, other times 'U-shaped' with both the wealthiest and poorest segments of the population experiencing higher rates of HIV prevalence. For example, Parkhurst (2010) finds that HIV prevalence increases across wealth quintiles in a number of countries for men and women, though this correlation differs by both GDP per capita and the HIV prevalence rate of the population as a whole. Mishra et al. (2007) find that even when controlling for likely co-factors (for example urban vs rural dwelling), the 'wealth effect' remains significant. The relationship between wealth and HIV is, statistically, experienced differently by gender; typically, relative wealth seems to act more sharply as a 'risk factor' for women than for men. Wojcicki, in a review of 36 studies that specifically focus on the relationship between socioeconomic status (SES) and HIV for women, reported that 'fifteen found no association between SES and HIV infection, twelve found an association between high SES and HIV infection, eight found an association between low SES and infection, and the results from one were mixed' (Wojcicki 2005, 1), again emphasising that relative wealth is often an important factor, though it was noted that the socioeconomic status of male partners is also influential in shaping patterns of infection (*Ibid.*). Whilst the evidence is heterogeneous in that there is no one universal correlation (Parkhurst 2010), it can be said that, contrary to the poverty narrative, 'HIV/AIDS does not disproportionally affect the poorer in sub-Saharan Africa', as Mishra et al. note in their paper of 2007).

There are, however, limitations with the data used for these analyses, as it is all based on panel or survey data and can only give snapshots at a specific point in time, as opposed to longitudinal surveys which track the same population over a sustained period of time and hence can capture changes in incidence rates for different wealth groups. Longitudinal studies are therefore better placed to shed light on how behaviour changes over time, and whether the assumptions noted above are borne out. However, as noted in Johnston (2013), sadly these studies are few and far between, in part inhibited by the cost of repeatedly surveying the same population over a number of years, with the results from the only three available studies portraying a mixed picture (*Ibid.*). Johnston notes that whilst one study reports declining incidence for wealthier men but not women (Lopman et al. 2007), two other studies conducted in South Africa over a similar time period reported different results (Hargreaves et al. 2002; Barnighausen et al. 2007). However, neither of the studies conducted in South Africa found a statistical correlation between increasing incidence and poverty, suggesting that this evidence is broadly supportive of the conclusion that

Mishra et al. (2007) came to with their analysis conducted using prevalence data. Whichever method is used, it seems that the evidence to date consistently contradicts the poverty–HIV narrative.

However, despite widespread acknowledgment of these findings (Fenton 2004; Shelton, Cassell, and Adetunji 2005; Gillespie, Kadiyala, and Greener 2007), the response to the epidemic remains firmly rooted in a poverty narrative, best illustrated by Fenton's conclusion that despite the data, reducing poverty will be at the core of a long-term, sustainable solution to HIV/AIDS (Fenton 2004, 1187). This is echoed across the literature, with a range of other studies emphasising the role of poverty (Booysen Fle and Summerton 2002; Stillwaggon 2002; Freedman and Poku 2005; Kalichman et al. 2006; Dodoo, Zulu, and Ezeh 2007; Kalipeni and Ghosh 2007; Lopman et al. 2007; Weiser et al. 2007; Chaturaka and Senaka 2010; Mufune 2014). Whilst UNAIDS continues to emphasise the need to 'know your epidemic' and for interventions to be evidence based (Wilson and Halperin 2008), this advice is not currently being heeded, and hence the poverty narrative has taken on a paradigmatic quality.

Several factors underpin this lack of consideration of the role of relative wealth, and the continued focus on poverty. First, it was assumed that the wealthy would be the first to change their behaviours in response to the epidemic (Bujra 2006), a view couched in rational behavioural terms; the wealthiest will be more likely to respond to educational campaigns, they can afford condoms and/or treatment and therefore will do so. However, evidence from recent studies shows that risk behaviours are in some cases still correlated positively with wealth (Kongnyuy et al. 2006; Awusabo-Asare and Annim 2008), suggesting that anticipated changes in behaviour have not always materialised.

A second factor is the observation that wealth is often correlated with negative health outcomes simply because the wealthy live longer (Beegle and de Walque 2009). This issue has been prominent in discussions of the correlations between HIV and wealth, with general agreement that as the wealthy have greater access to antiretroviral (ARV) treatment and live longer, prevalence rates for the wealthy are biased upwards and thus this is a statistical anomaly that can be ignored. There is certainly a strong degree of truth to this assumption, as demographic evidence across the continent reports longer life expectancies for the wealthy. However, the issue of biases in the data related to post-infection impacts on household income and wealth is often not addressed, despite evidence suggesting that post-infection morbidity is associated with a reduction in household income. For example, Bachmann and Booysen found that income and expenditure was lower in households which had an HIV-infected member than those that did not (Bachmann and Booysen 2003), whilst a study on a tea plantation in Kenya found that HIV-infected workers earned significantly lower incomes than other workers in the two years before retirement or death (Fox et al. 2004). Studies on the impact of HIV/AIDS-related mortality on households (death rather than illness) emphasise that although households' expenditures/incomes often recover from suffering an HIV/AIDS-related death after a period of around five years (Seeley, Dercon, and Barnett 2010), by inference this suggests that there is a negative morbidity impact to recover from. Although the evidence base for the impact of HIV/AIDS-related morbidity is small and in urgent need of additional research, the limited evidence highlights that households do experience reductions in income post-infection, suggesting that this will bias prevalence data for poorer wealth quintiles.

Third, there is evidence to suggest that positive correlations between wealth and HIV status disappear when samples are divided into rural and urban samples, reflecting that fact that the majority of the wealthy live in urban areas (Beegle and de Walque 2009). An analysis of Demographics and Health Survey (DHS) data available for sub-Saharan countries, using a relative measure of wealth, found that in rural areas poverty was not associated with higher HIV prevalence, but in urban areas the urban poor are disproportionately affected (Magadi 2013). These findings further muddy the picture, illustrating that different forms of poverty may or may not be related to enhanced HIV risk, and that the interaction between poverty and other contextual and structural factors is also important to account for.

A final observation that is often repeated in the literature links HIV and poverty because Africa is both the poorest continent and home to the majority of those living with HIV/ AIDS (Mbirimtengerenji 2007), an analysis that focuses on context, rather than patterns of behaviour and outcomes, reflecting the fertile terrain that Stillwaggon (2002) refers to. However, an alternative view would suggest that Africa is home to the majority of those living with HIV because this was where the epidemic originated (Iliffe 2006).

Whilst there are examples of excellent studies that address the role of wealth in the HIV epidemic (Bujra 2006), there are a number of compelling reasons for revisiting this issue. Prominent amongst them is the availability of new data which enable us to update previous work (Parkhurst 2010) to assess to what extent the optimism around behavioural change and declining prevalence rates for the wealthiest has played out. Second, there are few, if any, policies that incorporate the wealthy (or 'wealthier') within the target population, with recent economic interventions such as microfinance and cash transfers that are becoming increasingly popular in HIV-prevention efforts that seek to address 'structural' drivers (Kim and Watts 2005; Baird et al. 2012) targeted primarily at poor women and girls. The advent of treatment as prevention (Cohen et al. 2011; Thigpen et al. 2012), and the global focus on expanding access to ARVs for those infected (UNAIDS 2013), to some extent at the expense of prevention efforts, are also more recent themes that require attention, and especially concerning the assumptions around enhanced access of these services by the wealthy (Obermeyer et al. 2013). This has not been addressed in great detail in the literature to date yet is a crucial component in the overall debate, especially in relation to the question of whether the prevalence data contain biases. Finally, a very limited number of studies have engaged with this topic previously. Bujra (2006) provides a critical analysis of mainstream economic approaches to transmission, and locates the high rates of HIV seen in wealthy women in Tanzania within the context of processes of class formation and the reinforcement of class identity (Ibid.). Beyond this, convincing explanations are scarce, especially within the economics discipline, which continues to frame transmission within rational terms (Philipson and Posner 1995; Oster 2005, 2007, 2012), emphasising the need for a renewed focus.

The rest of this article is structured as follows. First, we provide a brief introduction to the history of the epidemic in Tanzania, and then present an updated statistical analysis using recent data from Tanzania. We then critically assess competing explanations for these findings, before discussing further implications of our results in relation to the current policy agenda and the structural drivers literature (Gupta et al. 2008; Auerbach, Parkhurst, and Cáceres 2011). It is important to note at this point that we acknowledge poverty will be an important factor in some settings. However, our assertion is that the framing of HIV as a disease of poverty is at best inaccurate, at worst something that diverts attention from the role of wealth, and thus only serves to dilute international efforts to combat the spread and impact of the virus. A renewed focus on the roles of, and interactions between, both wealth and poverty, and how these produce different health outcomes across the population (see O'Laughlin 2015 in this issue), is required.

The Tanzanian epidemic: new evidence on the relationship between wealth and HIV

The first cases of AIDS in Tanzania were recorded in Kagera region in 1983 (Ministry of Health 2003; Iliffe 2006), though it is likely that the virus entered the Uganda–Tanzania border region in the mid to late 1970s (Iliffe 2006). By 1986, just a few years later, the virus had penetrated all mainland regions (*Ibid.*).[1] Whilst it is difficult to build up an accurate picture of prevalence and trends during the 1990s, as prevalence rates were estimates based on measurements taken primarily at antenatal clinics, there is some evidence to suggest that prevalence peaked in Tanzania in 2001 (Asamoah-Odei, Calleja, and Boerma 2004). More recent data, based on the Tanzania HIV/AIDS Indicator Surveys of 2003–2004, 2007–2008 and 2011–2012 (discussed in more detail below), shows a national prevalence rate of 7% in 2003–2004 that declined to 5.1% in 2011–2012 (TACAIDS 2005; TACAIDS et al. 2013). At present, on the mainland, prevalence rates are higher in urban areas in comparison with rural areas, and vary widely between regions, ranging from 11% in Iringa to 2.1% in Dodoma.

The government response[2] to the epidemic commenced as early as 1985 with the establishment of the National AIDS Control Programme (Ministry of Health 1998), and a number of medium-term plans to address the epidemic followed (*Ibid.*). The priorities in the third-year plan included targeting commercial sex workers and vulnerable groups, and also poverty-reduction strategies, amongst the recognition that gender issues, including access to education for girls and an adverse cultural environment for women, were also important issues to address. Following the DHS surveys, which provided greater accuracy on population prevalence rates, the 2008–2012 plan (Ministry of Health and Social Welfare 2007) continued to pursue strategies that acknowledge a broad range of social drivers. With the growing global focus on treatment, the roll-out of antiretroviral therapy (ART) was slow, with the WHO estimating that there were no patients on ART (WHO 2002). By 2005, 19,600 individuals were on ART, though this was less than 7% of those requiring it (WHO 2005). However, supported by large volumes of external funding, ART coverage was estimated to have risen to 69% by 2012 (Global Fund 2013), though a significant funding gap remains if Tanzania is to achieve the 90% treatment coverage by 2020 targets set by UNAIDS in 2014 (UNAIDS 2014).

Tanzania has arguably the most comprehensive nationally representative data available on HIV prevalence, with three HIV/AIDS Indicator Surveys now completed (as noted above). Following Parkhurst (2010), we include the most recent data from the 2011–2012 Tanzanian survey to update his analysis.[3] Below, we conduct a trend analysis over three time periods – 2003–2004, 2007–2008 and 2011–2012. An important qualifier to emphasise is that these data are not cohort, or panel, data: they do not track the incidence of HIV/AIDS transmission within a closed group of respondents – instead, they give three separate 'snapshot' pictures of the prevalence at different intervals. However, it is to be hoped that, with broad population coverage, each snapshot is reasonably representative and can give us some insight into the changing distribution of HIV/AIDS in Tanzania over the last decade.

The measure of wealth in the DHS surveys is based on an 'asset index' incorporating a range of indicators including ownership of certain consumer durables, housing conditions, water access and so on, to meaningfully rank individual respondents' relative wealth in one of five quintiles for the country. This approach tends to correspond poorly with those rankings produced using monetary measures such as income or expenditure and alternative explanations have been put forward for this (Johnston 2013); however, monetary measures can fluctuate particularly dramatically in poorer countries where incomes can be very vola-tile, or come from a mixture of formal and informal economic activity poorly suited to easy ranking. In these circumstances, asset measures seem likely to give a more reliable picture of a household's long-run welfare levels, and indeed have been shown to perform well in predicting health and educational outcomes (Wall and Johnston 2008); this evidence suggests it is suitable for this area. The data available for the first period exclude Zanzibar; for subsequent periods data are available for Zanzibar but in the interest of comparing like with like, we continue to exclude Zanzibar from the analysis.[4]

There are two major criticisms to address before undertaking this quantitative analysis dealing with highly aggregated data. The first comes from Bujra (2006), who correctly points out that wealth groups are not a perfect substitute for 'class', and that much qualitat-ive understanding can be obscured by an overly quantitative, aggregated focus: true, 'wealth quintile' does not adequately capture 'class' – the profoundly social (and sexual) relations upon which the spread of HIV/AIDS is predicated cannot be represented in a headcount which applies these asset-based distinctions and cannot portray interrelations within and between the corresponding groups of people. This detracts from putting forward our results as a *complete* answer; rather, the 'wealth quintile' comparisons should be situated within, and compared against, qualitative studies which look to understand those interrelations; furthermore, this analysis occupies an important middle ground between (irreplaceable) qualitative and theoretical frameworks, and the inevitable top-level analysis of the highest aggregation – it prevents lazy conclusions that since overall prevalence has declined, this decline must be uniform across the population. There can be no single optimal level of analysis which all studies must follow; far greater understanding can emerge from reading across studies conducted at different levels of analysis.

The second major criticism (Gillespie, Kadiyala, and Greener 2007) concerns the inade-quacy of the terms 'rich' and 'poor' in low-income countries where almost all are 'the poor'. This criticism, though important, is in large part semantics: even if three or four quin-tiles of the population come below a given poverty line, this does not imply homogeneity of life quality or prospects among this population majority. The relational terms 'richer' and 'poorer' still apply. For one example, an economically induced decision to sell unsafe sex once or twice during temporary hardship is not equivalent to the economically induced decision to sell unsafe sex repeatedly during prolonged hardship, in terms of life quality or risk of infection.

Below we present data on HIV prevalence rates and testing refusal rates. Table 1 shows HIV prevalence, by gender and wealth quintile, across all three time periods; it also shows the chi-square trend test which is shown to be statistically significant in all cases. Figures 1–3 show the prevalence rates graphically, split by gender and wealth quintile, for each time period, with 95% confidence intervals constructed. Table 2 shows the pro-portion of survey respondents who declined the HIV blood test also by wealth quintile and gender. It is worth noting that overall coverage of HIV testing was influenced by some potential respondents not being interviewed, and also that the measure for refusal to test is different in the first survey.

A number of simple observations regarding the socioeconomic distribution of HIV/AIDS can be made. First, in all cases the chi-square indicates the presence of a trend between wealth quintile and prevalence. It is clear that the overall prevalence is declining; however, there are a number of examples where the prevalence within a wealth quintile rises from one period to the next (for example, among poorer women between 2003–2004 and 2007–2008). It is also evident that prevalence among women is consistently and

Table 1. Tabulated HIV prevalence in Tanzania across three time periods. (All data: DHS/AIS)

	HIV prevalence: 2003–2004			HIV prevalence: 2007–2008			HIV prevalence: 2011–2012		
	Male	Female	Total	Male	Female	Total	Male	Female	Total
Wealth index									
Poorest	4.1%	2.8%	3.4%	3.9%	5.0%	4.5%	3.1%	4.8%	4.0%
Poorer	4.3%	4.6%	4.5%	3.7%	6.6%	5.1%	2.9%	4.8%	3.9%
Middle	4.3%	6.7%	5.6%	4.2%	5.3%	4.8%	4.4%	5.6%	5.0%
Richer	7.7%	11.0%	9.4%	4.7%	6.2%	5.5%	3.6%	7.0%	5.4%
Richest	9.5%	11.4%	10.5%	7.2%	10.1%	8.8%	5.3%	8.6%	7.1%
Total	6.3%	7.7%	7.0%	4.8%	6.8%	5.9%	3.9%	6.4%	5.3%
Chi-square linear association	37.944 ($p <$ 0.01)	91.288 ($p <$ 0.01)		18.579 ($p <$ 0.01)	28.469 ($p <$ 0.01)		11.146 ($p <$ 0.01)	33.984 ($p <$ 0.01)	
N of valid cases	4995	5749	10,744	6897	8006	14,903	7730	9410	17,140

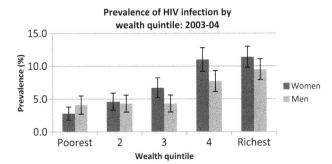

Figure 1. HIV prevalence in Tanzania, 2003–2004. (Data: DHS/AIS).

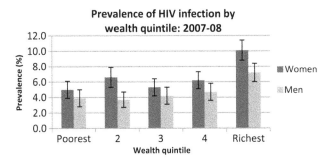

Figure 2. HIV prevalence in Tanzania, 2007–2008. (Data: DHS/AIS).

significantly greater than that among men, by a far greater factor than the 1:1.2 ratio estimated by the earlier UNAIDS data (Bennell 2004).

The results for the earliest period demonstrate a positive monotonic relationship between wealth and prevalence for both sexes which was particularly strong for women, the prevalence of the wealthiest quintile of women being almost four times as great as the poorest. In the second period the relationship between prevalence and relative wealth

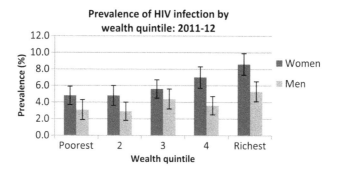

Figure 3.   HIV prevalence in Tanzania, 2011–2012. (Data: DHS/AIS).

Table 2.   The percentage who refused to provide a blood sample for HIV testing, by wealth quintile, for men and women.

	Survey	Poorest	2	3	4	Richest
Male	2003–2004	8.5	11.3	11.0	13.5	23.2
	2007–2008	7.0	5.9	6.0	7.6	11.8
	2011–2012	9.5	9.5	9.0	7.4	10.0
Female	2003–2004	9.8	10.7	9.1	12.0	18.4
	2007–2008	6.1	5.4	4.1	5.2	9.5
	2011–2012	5.3	5.5	4.9	4.9	5.9

becomes less straightforward, in line with the hypothesis that, as an epidemic matures, the brunt of new infections passes to poorer individuals as wealthier and better educated people respond to public health messages; among men, it takes on the U-shaped distribution Parkhurst (2010) finds in a number of other African countries, with the decline more pronounced among the middle and richer quintiles. Among women, the relationship is less clear still: significant decreases in the prevalence for the wealthier and middle-wealth quintiles are matched by increases in the two poorest quintiles. However, a wealthy woman is still more than twice as likely to be HIV-positive as one of the poorest; a notable narrowing of the gap from the previous period, but still a stark contrast.

The shifts in the relationship between relative wealth and HIV prevalence are different again between the second and third data periods. Again, the overall prevalence declines – more significantly for men than for women. For women, declines in the poorer and wealthiest groups, accompanied with slight increases for the third and fourth quintiles, combine to restore the monotonic relationship between wealth and HIV prevalence; however, the gap between the prevalence rate of the wealthiest and poorest women continues to narrow. Whilst not as strongly pronounced as in the earlier distribution, the importance of relative wealth as a risk factor is reiterated, and the hypothesis of maturing epidemics shifting 'down-wards' through the class system[5] is challenged by this finding. The distribution for men in 2011–2012 is less clear: a decline in prevalence is observable for each quintile except the middle (which experiences a very slight rise) and the wealthiest quintile retains the greatest prevalence, but there is no straightforward pattern to the wealth–prevalence relationship. This should not imply that relative wealth or poverty has become irrelevant to the HIV/AIDS epidemic – how could it, when it remains such a clear factor in the female experience of HIV/AIDS? Instead, it again reinforces that our understandings should be nuanced and context-specific, and should consider a number of specific pathways which may seem to negate one another's visibility at this level of analysis.

It is important to reiterate here that 'relative wealth' is not a fixed variable; indeed, both 'common sense' and substantial evidence (Nombo 2007; Hodge 2008) indicate that households affected by HIV/AIDS typically face the double burden of a temporary increase in their necessary expenditure (particularly health care and food) and a decrease in their productivity and income (through loss of labour to disease, death and caring for family members). It is therefore difficult, when considering the increase in prevalence among poorer quintiles and the decrease in prevalence among richer or middle quintiles, to say whether we are primarily seeing a redistribution of disease in accordance with socioeconomic factors, or a redistribution of wealth in accordance with sickness. Mishra et al. (2007) attempt to control for this potential endogeneity problem by excluding households where HIV-positive individuals had reported being 'seriously ill' for three or more months of the previous year, and found this adjustment had virtually no effect on the observed wealth association.

Naturally, neither 'wealth' nor 'poverty' can be, in their own right, a direct *cause* of blood-borne disease: it is thus unsurprising that no firm conclusions can be drawn from this analysis in either direction. However, what does emerge is the existence and relevance of a multifaceted and changing relationship between wealth, poverty and HIV/AIDS, supporting (and supported by) the role of multiple channels and mechanisms in either direction.

Of course, 'prevalence' and 'incidence' are not conceptually interchangeable: it is hard to assess from this non-panel data how much we might attribute the consistently higher prevalence of HIV/AIDS among the wealthiest quintile of Tanzanian society to the risk factors relative wealth induces, and how much must be disregarded as simply representing the greater longevity of wealthier people who are HIV-positive, as compared with their poorer compatriots. This emphasises the importance of the testing refusal. As Table 2 shows, testing refusal rates for every period demonstrate that the wealthiest are not more likely to agree to provide a blood sample for a HIV test. The large differences between the 2003–2004 data and the other two surveys reflect a change in measurement methodology rather than rapid changes in social attitudes towards testing, though this may have been a factor. In general, women are more likely to agree to a test than men, with men in the wealthiest quintile the most likely to refuse a test in all three surveys. There have been significant changes over time for women in the wealthiest quintile, with the refusal rate dropping from 9.5% to 5.9% between the 2007–2008 and 2011–2012 surveys, though this reduction was not observed for men. Again, as with the prevalence data, the evidence reported here would seem to challenge standard assumptions around the behaviour of the wealthy. These data are also telling as they are not based on self-reported data, rather these are data capturing what people actually do, removing any potential biases concerning the wealthy providing more socially acceptable answers, an issue that plagues self-reported data regarding sexual behaviour (Nnko et al. 2004).

Above all, there are four key points to summarise from our analysis. First, that the overall decline in national prevalence rates is not consistently reflected across all population sub-groups. Second, that the dynamic distribution of prevalence is significantly different among women and men. Third, that the shape of the distribution, and the distribution of the overall reduction in prevalence, are shifting through time and the spread may be narrowing, but relative wealth is still clearly of great relevance and it remains deeply inaccurate to characterise HIV/AIDS as a disease of poverty in Africa. Finally, data on testing refusal also pose a major problem for the poverty narrative, with the wealthiest consistently most likely to refuse testing.

Reflections on the evidence

Amongst the studies that focus on poverty, there are some explanations forwarded to explain the prevalence patterns discussed here. These include the notion that the wealthy are more mobile (Fenton 2004), and have more chances to engage in extra-marital sexual encounters, that the wealthy have a greater ability to maintain concurrent relationships (Shelton, Cassell, and Adetunji 2005) and that, owing to a Westernisation of lifestyles and patterns of urbanisation, they have greater access to multiple partners (Gillespie, Kadiyala, and Greener 2007). However, beyond these suggestions, there is little, if any, research on this issue, emphasising the urgent need for this to be corrected in future studies.

Perhaps unsurprisingly, and reflective of the broader policy environment, the initial response by mainstream economics was also predominantly couched in the poverty narrative. Neoclassical analysis (by no means an extensive oeuvre) has failed to produce a convincing explanation for the distribution of HIV prevalence demonstrated in numerous large-scale studies, including this article; this failure has severe consequences for effective policymaking. Problematic assumptions pervade rational-agent models (such as those of Philipson and Posner 1995; Oster 2005; Oster 2012), where sex – or unprotected sex – is treated as a freely negotiated contract, fully abstracted from the other social relations that connect both parties to each other and to wider social networks. Decision-making about sex is reduced to a risk analysis of infection: intimacy, pleasure, childbearing and social/familial relations are conspicuous by their absence. This article does not pretend to conduct a comprehensive rebuttal of this work (Christensen [1998] provides an extensive account of the logical and empirical problems in the assumptions underpinning Philipson and Posner's model, which Gersovitz [2005] corroborates in an African context): suffice to say, it is of no surprise that a framework so narrow and lacking in context is incapable of explaining how wealth persistently correlates with higher prevalence, or why wealthier agents, who consistently demonstrate better knowledge of HIV prevention and report more protective behaviours, do not appear to have a correspondingly higher rate of consent to serostatus testing as part of the AIDS Indicator Survey (AIS). Philipson and Posner's 'shadow price' concept of infection, and Oster's (2012) emphasis on the significant role of non-HIV life expectancy in behavioural responses to a local epidemic, both lead problematically to the perception of longevity as a policy option: this renders the problem of HIV/ AIDS rather circular, as shorter (non-HIV) life expectancy is seen to lead to high levels of HIV prevalence, whilst high prevalence rates contribute to a decrease in overall life expectancy.

The most convincing explanations that address both the roles of wealth and poverty are rooted in the political economy tradition. Bujra (2006) places the AIDS crisis specifically within the context of class formation: the creation of a wage-labour class, with the attendant migration, social upheaval and severing of familial and community ties and norms; the emergence of a parasitic 'political class' intent on consolidating their own power; and around these, other class fractions of professionals, of domestic labourers and of those working in the informal sector, dependent on the functioning of other groups for their own class survival. This creates two particular class-related tendencies which combine to shape 'sexual networking': first, such networks reproduce and reinforce class fractions (marriage and procreation); second, these networks are used to assert power, typically via extra- or non-marital relations. Thus we can consider the specific mechanisms through which high HIV risk is mediated, in this context of major social transformation: migration, changes to family and community structures, and the broader scope for transactional sexual relations are experienced in varied but class-specific ways.

Bujra (*Ibid.*) is scathing about the capacity of indexical accounts to fully capture relational dynamics, and not without reason: quintiles of relative wealth do not properly approximate the power dynamics between and within social classes as identified in the sociological tradition. However, we believe useful insight is also to be found in large-scale quantitative analysis: quantitative studies such as this one do inevitably suffer from some collapsing of analytical categories; we venture it not as an entire foundation of proof, but as one corroborating account. Data alone cannot possibly drive our understanding of social processes, but they can be very instructively discussed alongside relational accounts, and yet there have been very few attempts to combine this particular balancing act. Bujra dismisses indexical findings as so pervasive they are 'taken for granted'; we rather find them – and specifically the insistent correlation between high socioeconomic status and high prevalence – to be widely acknowledged and disregarded.

A significant difference between the neoclassical accounts and a political economy approach is the orientation of the former towards a concept of agent 'choice', and of the latter towards agent 'capacity'. Hunter (2002) and Leclerc-Madlala (2003) both write with reference to South Africa, but a number of their insights should at least give us pause for thought in the Tanzanian context. Characterising 'capacity' should not be construed as perpetuating a 'passive victim' discourse, and indeed both authors strongly acknowledge the agency of women in negotiating sex and relationships within a context of normalised transactional sex (Hunter 2002; Leclerc-Madlala 2003). Much has been made of the role of prostitution in transmission of HIV, but frequently in terms of easily identifiable sex work, loosely correlated with the desperation of poverty, with ignorance about HIV transmission or condom use – an approach which again fails to explain persistently high levels of prevalence among the wealthier members of Tanzanian society. Both authors, however, identify transactional sex as written into the very fabric of social relations: the privileged economic position of men (underwritten by both 'traditional' and capitalist relations), masculine discourses which place high value on men having many sexual partners (likewise with roots or justifications to be found in a wide range of indigenous and Western-imported cultural factors) and the agency of women who recognise a commodity value placed on sex and exploit it to meet their material 'needs' or desires. The materiality of sexual relations is no longer perceived as contingent on desperate poverty, and economic considerations enter into the sexual decision-making of relatively wealthy women; the narrative becomes compatible with our data findings.

Further implications

This can of worms repositioning 'aberrant' sexual behaviour as in fact normal, prevalent among the wealthy and socially sanctioned along multiple cultural lines, opens a discourse in which a high number of relatively wealthy citizens are implicated in 'bad' risky sex; this may well represent too unsettling an introspection to be entertained seriously. However, failure in academic or policy circles to engage with intellectual honesty in discussions about the social relations driving HIV infection is problematic for appropriate research and policy. Following Hunter and Leclerc-Madlala's locating of both toxic masculinities and the commodification of sex in the global context, a similar silence might well be only to be expected from powerful voices in the Global North: the notion of normalised transactional sex and an emphatic belief that fashionable clothes and expensive cell phones are 'needs' rather than luxuries may feel rather closer to home than any 'educated' or 'sophisticated' commentator, African or Western, wishes to feel about an epidemic. The possibility of such implicit concerns does not make for an environment hospitable to frank inquiry into the specific processes leading to persistently high rates of HIV prevalence in spite of education and condom access. In policy, much hinges upon the extent to which the more powerful groups in society (specifically, relatively wealthy men) perceive HIV/AIDS to be a personal threat, and the price they accord that threat as compared with the price of structural change. As Akeroyd (2004) asks, even if female empowerment were to substantially reduce the social risk of HIV infection, how does the loss of male 'power over' necessitated by female empowerment compare to this gain? There are powerful beneficiaries of female precarity in the era of HIV/AIDS, agents and institutions for whom the circular relationship between inequality and HIV/AIDS is a rewarding one.

Such a lack of rigorous engagement undermines the capacity of any approach aimed at unpicking and addressing the structural drivers of HIV: if the behaviour of the wealthy becomes difficult to discuss, the 'structural drivers' agenda melts too easily back into the poverty narrative and leaves us with piecemeal policies such as microfinance and conditional cash transfer schemes – approaches which can only comprehend the transmission of HIV within a context of absolute material deprivation, and within a very specific characterisation of gender and economic power. Whilst the majority of women's economic empowerment programmes include microfinance, it is clear that the notion of empowerment has taken on a distinct concrete form, with wealthy women excluded from this conceptualisation. This helps illustrate the way that structural interventions are being captured by individualised and reduced forms of intervention, with microfinance increasingly being labelled as a 'structural' intervention. Further, this is an approach that focuses on protecting poor(er) women from wealthier men, presented on a range of stylised assumptions about gendered roles (O'Laughlin 2008). A truly structural intervention would address the underlying social structures, processes and relations that shape women's economic dependence on men in general, rather than simply mediating individual impoverished women's economic dependence on men within the existing distribution of (access to) resources. This creeping capture of 'structural' responses illustrates the precarity of Baylies' (2000) optimistic contention that, since the nature of the pandemic so clearly implicates structural inequality, it also makes structural change both possible and necessary; there is no failsafe mechanism to ensure that such structural change will occur.

There are further possible 'losers' from a radical rethink of HIV/AIDS policy. Hunsmann (2012) identifies the political economy of an 'AIDS industry', which forms an effective political constituency for no change to existing infection prevention policies: powerful advocates are concerned to maintain their own funding streams, and 'outsider' groups, potentially pursuing approaches which are more long-term or more appropriate to the changed needs of the changing epidemic, can be disparate and powerless (*Ibid.*). This path-dependency in policy can create tensions between short-run and long-run approaches. The social costs faced by civil society, of both HIV/AIDS and policies targeted at it, may be greatly mismatched with the costs (and benefits) as perceived by policymakers; incentives and timescales in politics can conflict with the long-term interests of the society they govern. For Hunsmann, therefore, a structural response to a structural problem is to focus on reshaping the *context* of policymaking in the hope of this leading to better long-term policies – rather than the common efforts of struggling against the incremental nature of policymaking in search of silver bullets. Whilst it may be difficult to follow up this astute identification of the problem of existing approaches, it points to the challenges of reorienting policy to address the prevalence, behaviour, and testing and counselling habits of wealthy men, in the context in which policy is predominantly being dictated by wealthy men who are likely to divert attention from their own social group, and who have incentives for the perpetuation of the poverty paradigm

The account we put forward is emphatically not one of determinism; it is also not one which provides any easy solution. Above all, our intention is to draw attention to questions barely asked in research and policy, and even less answered: why does policy seem not to target wealthy women, when they are consistently experiencing the highest rates of prevalence? How might it do so? How closely do our 'structural' interventions fit the structural, social processes underlying HIV transmission? The data on testing refusal again recall the limitations of rational agent models for policymakers, because revealed behaviour does not match that anticipated by such models: why are wealthy men least willing to know their serostatus? This is an early result we advance with some caution: it is unclear to what extent these findings can be extrapolated to the general population, as there are a range of other factors which may mean that the wealthy do in fact test more, such as access to testing facilities in urban areas or hospital visits in which patients can be routinely tested for HIV (Obermeyer et al. 2013). Nonetheless, this brings into question whether wealthy individuals may be more likely to test because of similar 'rational' behaviours that are reflected in mainstream economic models, or whether this is just a matter of access. Further, this again challenges stylised negative views of uninformed choices made by poor people. Other issues, such as the stigma around testing for HIV, and concerns over what may happen if the test is positive (Matovu et al. 2014), will not just apply to the poor. The data at least suggest that assumptions around testing and wealth should be treated with caution. This has implications for transmission, as wealthy men have higher rates of HIV and are as likely to refuse a test in comparison to the men in the other four wealth quintiles. Indeed, recent data suggest that men are less likely than women to be on ARVs (UNAIDS 2013). More research is needed urgently on this matter to assess whether these testing refusal patterns are reflective of the general population.

Conclusion

Our findings therefore contribute to, and reflect, the burgeoning understanding of HIV/AIDS as a dynamic and complex phenomenon (Gupta et al. 2008; Auerbach et al. 2010; Auerbach, Parkhurst, and Cáceres 2011), closely related to and strongly influenced by gender and wealth – and more precisely, the specific social relations and structural mechanisms relating these rather abstract concepts to real life in contemporary Tanzania. They reflect the role of both relative wealth and relative poverty as structural drivers of illness, and as mediators of policy responses. They highlight not only the uneven distribution of HIV/AIDS but also the uneven distribution of the headline rate of decline among different groups of the population; and they remind us that the 'progress' of the epidemic is often non-linear (as in the increase in prevalence for some groups, or the revived monotonic wealth–prevalence relationship among women in 2011–2012). Academic and policy responses need to take into account not only the complexity of this nexus, but also its rapid dynamism if they are to offer relevant explanations or solutions. Further, to talk of a 'link' between either, or both, poverty and prevalence or wealth and prevalence, is overly simplistic. This aggregate-level investigation only confirms the relevance of socioeconomic factors to an irreducibly socioeconomic phenomenon. The critical task is to explore the varied channels through which relative wealth and gender shape risk, behaviour and constraints. The broad brush-strokes of 'gender', 'wealth', 'poverty' and even 'class' provide only the crucial backdrop against which context-specific mechanisms can be construed.

Mainstream economic models are consistently failing to help us understand the epidemic. The 'rational' model of behaviour is contradicted by the evidence around testing refusal, undermining the view that we do not need to be concerned about the wealthy. In fact, these findings indicate that more research, and more attention to wealth, is required: in particular, the evidence illustrates that wealthy women are missing from responses to the epidemic and need re-including.

One of the clearest and most repeated inferences from this research is that a significant gap remains between quantitative analysis at the most aggregated level, which can help indicate those social groups most affected, but which is limited in its capacity to explain how this risk is actually embodied; and much closer qualitative analysis which develops nuanced theories of how 'risk groups' and 'risk behaviours' can interact to form 'risk situations' but from which only the most tentative generalisations can be formed.

Bujra (2006) is correct to emphasise that 'relative wealth' is an imperfect proxy for class, and to neglect class relations necessarily renders incomplete any analysis of an epidemic driven almost entirely by social-sexual relations and thus by the power dynamics governing these relations. Further work remains to continue developing a gendered class-based analysis which is structural and non-deterministic, and which is compatible with the observed statistical distribution of prevalence as it changes through time. As HIV/AIDS is long-run and permanent (since infection is irreversible), and policy-sensitive, including in indirect or unanticipated ways, the specifics of context need to play a stronger role in modelling: for example, migration, and the issues it raises and policies it is affected by (labour market, housing, restructuring of communal and familial relations), cuts across gender and class and is profoundly shaped by both, but is also a factor and pathway in its own right.

A further need is primarily methodological: as Johnston (2013) points out, cohort studies enable more reliable data, addressing the difficulties arising from the distinction between 'incidence' and 'prevalence': cohort studies would enable us to say more confidently whether a relative decrease in a given group's prevalence is due to fewer new infections, higher mortality or an income effect whereby households have systematically been reclassified to a different wealth quintile. However, the practicalities involved in such a study are severe, especially at a large scale and with an eye to ensuring broad coverage especially with regard to destitute or highly mobile respondents. Furthermore, as Johnston also notes, the few existing such studies still yield contradictory results across the same region, so it is also clear that such research is no panacea. However, it could still provide an important yardstick for data such as those used here, where incidence has to be estimated from the more easily measurable prevalence.

Disclosure statement

No potential conflict of interest was reported by the authors.

Notes

1. For a thorough assessment of the spread of the virus across Tanzania, see Iliffe (2006).
2. For a detailed view of the response to the epidemic in Tanzania, see Garbus (2004)

3. All data are available from http://www.dhsprogram.com.
4. Incidentally, the inclusion of Zanzibar does not substantially alter the overall impression of the data.
5. Bloom et al. (2001), cited in Bujra (2006); the authors note again that relative wealth is not a perfect proxy for class identity.

References

Akeroyd, A. 2004. "Coercion, Constraints and "Cultural Entrapments": A Further Look at Gendered and Occupational Factors Pertinent to the Transmission of HIV." In *HIV and AIDS in Africa: Beyond Epidemiology*, edited by E. Kalipeni, S. Craddock, J. R. Oppong, and J. Ghosh, 89–103. Oxford: Blackwell.

Asamoah-Odei, E., J. M. G. Calleja, and J. T. Boerma. 2004. "HIV Prevalence and Trends in Sub-Saharan Africa: No Decline and Large Subregional Differences." *The Lancet* 364 (9428): 35–40.

Auerbach, J., J. Parkhurst, and C. Cáceres. 2011. "Addressing Social Drivers of HIV/AIDS for the Long-term Response: Conceptual and Methodological Considerations." *Global Public Health* 6 (Suppl. 3): S293–S309.

Auerbach, J., J. Parkhurst, C. Cáceres, and K. Keller. 2010. "Addressing Social Drivers of HIV/AIDS: Some Conceptual, Methodological, and Evidentiary Considerations." Social Drivers Working Group: Working Papers.

Awusabo-Asare, K., and S. K. Annim. 2008. "Wealth Status and Risky Sexual Behaviour in Ghana and Kenya." *Applied Health Economics and Health Policy* 6 (1): 27–39.

Bachmann, M. O., and F. L. R. Booysen. 2003. "Health and Economic Impact of HIV/AIDS on South African Households: A Cohort Study." *BMC Public Health* 3: 14. doi: 10.1186/1471-2458-3-14.

Baird, S. J., R. S. Garfein, C. T. McIntosh, and B. Özler. 2012. "Effect of a Cash Transfer Programme for Schooling on Prevalence of HIV and Herpes Simplex Type 2 in Malawi: A Cluster Randomised Trial." *The Lancet* 379 (9823): 1320–1329.

Barnighausen, T., V. Hosegood, I. M. Timaeus, and M. L. Newell. 2007. "The Socioeconomic Determinants of HIV Incidence: Evidence from a Longitudinal, Population-based Study in Rural South Africa." *AIDS* 21 (Suppl. 7): S29–S38.

Baylies, C. 2000. "Overview: HIV/AIDS in Africa: Global & Local Inequalities & Responsibilities." *Review of African Political Economy* 27 (86): 487–500.

Beegle, K., and D. de Walque. 2009. "Demographic and Socioeconomic Patterns of HIV/AIDS Prevalence in Africa." In *The Changing HIV/AIDS Landscape*, edited by E. Lule, R. Seifman, and A. David, 81–104. Washington, DC: World Bank.

Bennell, P. 2004. "HIV/AIDS in Sub Saharan Africa: The Growing Epidemic?" ELDIS discussion paper. ELDIS.

Bloom, D. E., A. Mahal, J. Sevilla, and Riverpath Associates. 2001. "AIDS and Economics." Paper prepared for Working Group I of the WHO Commission on Macroeconomics and Health. November.

Booysen Fle, R., and J. Summerton. 2002. "Poverty, Risky Sexual Behaviour, and Vulnerability to HIV Infection: Evidence from South Africa." *J Health Popul Nutr* 20 (4): 285–288.

Bujra, J. 2006. "Class Relations: AIDS & Socioeconomic Privilege in Africa." *Review of African Political Economy* 33: 113–129.

Chao, A., M. Bulterys, F. Musanganire, P. Abimana, P. Nawrocki, E. Taylor, A. Dushimimana, A. Saah, and The National University of Rwanda-Johns Hopkins University AIDS Research Team. 1994. "Risk Factors Associated with Prevalent HIV-1 Infection among Pregnant Women in Rwanda." *International Journal of Epidemiology* 23 (2): 371–380.

Chaturaka, R., and R. Senaka. 2010. "HIV, Poverty and Women." *International Health* 2 (1): 9–16.

Christensen, K. 1998. "Economics Without Money; Sex Without Gender: A Critique of Philipson and Posner's "Private Choices and Public Health: The AIDS Epidemic in an Economic Perspective." *Feminist Economics* 4: 1–24.

Cohen, M. S., Y. Q. Chen, M. McCauley, T. Gamble, M. C. Hosseinipour, N. Kumarasamy, J. G. Hakim, et al. 2011. "Prevention of HIV-1 Infection with Early Antiretroviral Therapy." *New England Journal of Medicine* 365 (6): 493–505.

Dodoo, F. N-A., E. M. Zulu, and A. C. Ezeh. 2007. "Urban-rural Differences in the Socioeconomic Deprivation-sexual Behavior Link in Kenya." *Social Science & Medicine* 64 (5): 1019–1031.

Fenton, L. 2004. "Preventing HIV/AIDS Through Poverty Reduction: The Only Sustainable Solution?" *Lancet* 364 (9440): 1186–1187.

Fortson, J. G. 2008. "The Gradient in Sub-Saharan Africa: Socioeconomic Status and HIV/AIDS." *Demography* 45 (2): 303–322.

Fox, M., S. Rosen, W. MacLeod, M. Wasunna, M. Bili, G. Foglia, and J. Simon. 2004. "The Impact of HIV/AIDS on Labour Productivity in Kenya." *Tropical Medicine and International Health* 9 (3): 318–324.

Freedman, J., and N. Poku. 2005. "The Socioeconomic Context of Africa's Vulnerability to HIV/AIDS." *Review of International Studies* 31 (04): 665–686.

Garbus, L. 2004. *HIV/AIDS in Tanzania*. San Fransisco: AIDS Policy Research Center, University of California.

Gersovitz, M. 2005. "The HIV Epidemic in Four African Countries seen through the Demographic and Health Surveys." *Journal of African Economies* 14 (2): 191–246.

Gillespie, S., S. Kadiyala, and R. Greener. 2007. "Is Poverty or Wealth Driving HIV Transmission?" *AIDS* 21 (Suppl. 7): S5–S16.

Global Fund. 2013. *Program Scorecard: Tanzania HIV/AIDS*. Geneva: The Global Fund.

Gupta, G. R., J. O. Parkhurst, J. A. Ogden, P. Aggleton, and A. Mahal. 2008. "Structural Approaches to HIV Prevention." *The Lancet* 372 (9640): 764–775.

Hamoudi, A., and N. Birdsall. 2004. "AIDS and the Accumulation and Utilisation of Human Capital in Africa." *Journal of African Economies* 13 (AERC Suppl. 1): i96–i136.

Hargreaves, J. R., L. A. Morison, J. Chege, N. Rutenburg, M. Kahindo, H. A. Weiss, R. Hayes, and A. Buvé. 2002. "Socioeconomic Status and Risk of HIV Infection in an Urban Population in Kenya." *Tropical Medicine & International Health* 7 (9): 793–802.

Hodge, M. 2008. "HIV/AIDS, Demographics and Economic Development." In *HIV/AIDS in Africa: Challenges and Impact*, edited by E. M. Omwami, S. Commins, and E. J. Keller, 7–26. Trenton, NJ: Africa World Press.

Hope, K. R. Sr. 2001. "Africa's HIV/AIDS Crisis in a Development Context." *International Relations* 15 (6): 15–36.

Hunsmann, M. 2012. "Limits to Evidence-based Health Policymaking: Policy Hurdles to Structural HIV Prevention in Tanzania." *Social Science & Medicine* 74 (10): 1477–1485.

Hunter, M. 2002. "The Materiality of Everyday Sex: Thinking Beyond 'Prostitution'." *African Studies* 61 (1): 99–120.

Iliffe, J. 2006. *The African AIDS Epidemic: A History*. Oxford: James Currey.

Johnston, D. 2013. *Economics and HIV: The Sickness of Economics*. Abingdon: Routledge.

Kalichman, S. C., L. C. Simbayi, A. Kagee, Y. Toefy, S. Jooste, D. Cain, and C. Cherry. 2006. "Associations of Poverty, Substance Use, and HIV Transmission Risk Behaviors in Three South African Communities." *Social Science & Medicine* 62 (7): 1641–1649.

Kalipeni, E., and J. Ghosh. 2007. "Concern and Practice among Men about HIV/AIDS in Low Socioeconomic Income Areas of Lilongwe, Malawi." *Social Science & Medicine* 64 (5): 1116–1127.

Kim, J. C., and C. H. Watts. 2005. Gaining a Foothold: Tackling Poverty, Gender Inequality, and HIV in Africa.

Kongnyuy, E. J., C. S. Wiysonge, R. E. Mbu, P. Nana, and L. Kouam. 2006. "Wealth and Sexual Behaviour among Men in Cameroon." *BMC International Health and Human Rights* 6 (11). doi:10.1186/1472-698X-6-11.

Leclerc-Madlala, S. 2003. "Transactional Sex and the Pursuit of Modernity." *Social Dynamics* 29 (2): 213–233.

Lopman, B., J. Lewis, C. Nyamukapa, P. Mushati, S. Chandiwana, and S. Gregson. 2007. "HIV Incidence and Poverty in Manicaland, Zimbabwe: Is HIV Becoming a Disease of the Poor?" *AIDS* 21 (Suppl. 7): S57–S66.

Magadi, M. 2013. "The Disproportionate High Risk of HIV Infection among the Urban Poor in Sub-Saharan Africa." *AIDS and Behavior* 17 (5): 1645–1654.

Masanjala, W. 2007. "The Poverty-HIV/AIDS Nexus in Africa: A Livelihood Approach." *Social Science & Medicine* 64 (5): 1032–1041.

Matovu, J. K., R. K. Wanyenze, F. Wabwire-Mangen, R. Nakubulwa, R. Sekamwa, A. Masika, J. Todd, and D. Serwadda. 2014. "Men are Always Scared to Test with Their Partners . . . It is Like Taking them to the Police." In Motivations for and Barriers to Couples' HIV Counselling and Testing in Rakai. Uganda: a Qualitative Study.

Mbirimtengerenji, N. D. 2007. "Is HIV/AIDS Epidemic Outcome of Poverty in Sub-Saharan Africa?" *Croat Med J* 48 (5): 605–617.

Ministry of Health. 1998. *The Third Medium Term Plan (MTP-III) for Prevention and Control of HIV/AIDS/STD's 1998–2002*. Dar Es Salaam. Tanzania: National AIDS Control Programme, Ministry of Health.

Ministry of Health. 2003. *Health Sector HIV/AIDS Strategy for Tanzania 2003–2006*. Dar Es Salaam, Tanzania: Ministry of Health.

Ministry of Health, and Social Welfare. 2007. *Health Sector HIV and AIDS Strategic Plan (HSHSP) 2008–2012*. Dar Es Salaam, Tanzania: Ministry of Health.

Mishra, V., S. B-V. Assche, R. Greener, M. Vaessen, R. Hong, P. D. Ghys, J. T. Boerma, A. Van Assche, S. Khan, and S. Rutstein. 2007. "HIV Infection does not Disproportionately Affect the Poorer in Sub-Saharan Africa." *AIDS* 21: S17–S28.

Msisha, W. M., S. H. Kapiga, F. Earls, and S. Subramanian. 2008. "Socioeconomic Status and HIV Seroprevalence in Tanzania: A Counterintuitive Relationship." *International Journal of Epidemiology* 37 (6): 1297–1303.

Mufune, P. 2014. "Poverty and HIV/AIDS in Africa: Specifying the Connections." *Social Theory & Health Advanced* [online] 29th October: 1–29.

Nnko, S., J. T. J. T. Boerma, M. Urassa, G. Mwaluko, and B. Zaba. 2004. "Secretive Females or Swaggering Males? An Assessment of the Quality of Sexual Partnership Reporting in Rural Tanzania." *Social Science & Medicine* 59 (2): 299–310.

Nombo, C. 2007. *When AIDS Meets Poverty: Implications for Social Capital in a Village in Tanzania*. Netherlands: Wageningen Academic Publishers.

Obermeyer, C. M., S. Bott, R. Bayer, A. Desclaux, R. Baggaley, and the MATCH Study Group. 2013. "HIV Testing and Care in Burkina Faso, Kenya, Malawi and Uganda: Ethics on the Ground." *BMC International Health and Human Rights* 13 (6). doi:10.1186/1472-698X-13-6.

O'Laughlin, B. 2008. *Missing Men Again? Gender, AIDS, and Migration in Southern Africa*. Summary of IGS/CCCRW Commemorative Lecture for Audrey Richards.

O'Laughlin, B. 2015. "Trapped in the Prison of the Proximate: Structural HIV/AIDS Prevention in Southern Africa." *Review of African Political Economy* 42 (145): 342–361.

Oster, E. 2005. "Sexually Transmitted Infections, Sexual Behavior and the HIV/AIDS Epidemic." *Quarterly Journal of Economics* 120 (2): 467–515.

Oster, E. 2007. *HIV and Sexual Behaviour Change: Why not Africa?* Cambridge, MA: NBER.

Oster, E. 2012. "HIV and Sexual Behaviour Change: Why not Africa?" *Journal of Health Economics* (31): 35–49.

Parkhurst, J. 2010. *Understanding the Correlation Between Structural Factors of Wealth and Poverty with HIV in Africa: No Single Correlation*. Geneva: WHO.

Philipson, T., and R. A. Posner. 1995. "The Microeconomics of the AIDS Epidemic in Africa." *Population and Development Review* 21 (4): 835–848.

Seeley, J., S. Dercon, and T. Barnett. 2010. "The Effects of HIV/AIDS on Rural Communities in East Africa: A 20-year Perspective." *Tropical Medicine & International Health* 15 (3): 329–335.

Shelton, J. D., M. M. Cassell, and J. Adetunji. 2005. "Is Poverty or Wealth at the Root of HIV?" *Lancet, Lancet.* 366: 1057–1058.

Stillwaggon, E. 2002. "HIV/AIDS in Africa: Fertile Terrain." *Journal of Development Studies* 38 (6): 1–22.

TACAIDS. 2005. *Tanzania HIV/AIDS Indicator Survey 2003–04*. Dar es Salaam: Tanzania Commission for AIDS.

TACAIDS, Zanzibar AIDS Commission (ZAC), National Bureau of Statistics (NBS), Office of the Chief Government Statistician (OCGS), and ICF International. 2013. *Tanzania HIV/AIDS and Malaria Indicator Survey 2011–12*. Dar Es Salaam, Tanzania: TACAIDS, ZAC, NBS, OCGS, and ICF International.

Thigpen, M. C., P. M. Kebaabetswe, L. A. Paxton, D. K. Smith, C. E. Rose, T. M. Segolodi, F. L. Henderson, et al. 2012. "Antiretroviral Preexposure Prophylaxis for Heterosexual HIV Transmission in Botswana." *New England Journal of Medicine* 367 (5): 423–434.

UNAIDS. 2013. *Access to Antiretroviral Therapy in Africa: Status Report on Progress Towards the 2015 Targets*. Geneva: UNAIDS.

UNAIDS. 2014. *90–90–90: An Ambitious Treatment Target to Help end the AIDS Epidemic*. Geneva: UNAIDS.

Wall, M., and D. Johnston. 2008. "Counting Heads or Counting Televisions: Can Asset-based Measures of Welfare Assist Policy-makers in Russia?" *Journal of Human Development* 9 (1): 131–147.

Weiser, S. D., K. Leiter, D. R. Bangsberg, L. M. Butler, F. Percy-de Korte, Z. Hlanze, N. Phaladze, V. Iacopino, and M. Heisler. 2007. "Food Insufficiency is Associated with High-risk Sexual Behavior among Women in Botswana and Swaziland." *PLoS Medicine* 4 (10): e260.

Whiteside, A. 2002. "Poverty and HIV/AIDS in Africa." *Third World Quarterly* 23 (2): 313–332.

WHO. 2002. *Coverage of Selected Health Services for HIV/AIDS Prevention and Care in Less Developed Countries in 2001*. Geneva: WHO.

WHO. 2005. *Summary of Country Profile for HIV/AIDS Treatment Scale-up*. Geneva: WHO.

Wilson, D., and D. T. Halperin. 2008. ""Know your Epidemic, Know your Response": A Useful Approach, if We get it Right." *The Lancet* 372 (9637): 423–426.

Wojcicki, J. M. 2005. "Socioeconomic Status as a Risk Factor for HIV Infection in Women in East, Central and Southern Africa: A Systematic Review." *Journal of Biosocial Science* 37 (1): 1–36.

World Bank. 1999. *Confronting AIDS: Public Priorities in a Global Epidemic*. New York and Washington, DC: Oxford University Press and World Bank.

Paying the price of HIV in Africa: cash transfers and the depoliticisation of HIV risk

Deborah Johnston

Despite biomedical innovation, HIV incidence remains high in some African countries. HIV-related cash-transfer projects propose a solution. However, the author raises concerns about their success from a political economy perspective. Where structural change is invoked by these projects, it is too narrowly conceived. Some cash-transfer projects focus solely on 'nudging' choices about risky sex, without considering the wider set of factors that increase HIV incidence. Consequently, the promise of HIV-related cash transfers is dangerously exaggerated. Instead they obscure the underlying causes of high HIV prevalence, by focusing on individual behaviour and a limited, neoliberal-friendly menu of options.

[Payer le prix du VIH en Afrique : les transferts de liquidités et la dépolitisation du risque lié au VIH.] Malgré l'innovation biomédicale, les cas de VIH restent élevés dans certains pays africains. Les projets de transfert de liquidités liés au VIH proposent une solution. Cependant, l'auteur émet des réserves quant à leur succès à partir d'une perspective politico-économique. Lorsque le changement structurel est invoqué par ces projets, ils sont conçus de manière trop étroite. Certains projets de transfert de liquidités se concentrent seulement sur les choix « encouragés » sur les relations sexuelles risquées, sans considérer l'éventail plus large de facteurs qui augmentent les cas de VIH. Par conséquent, les impacts potentiels des transferts de liquidités liés au VIH sont exagérés de manière dangereuse. Plutôt, ces transferts dissimulent les causes sous-jacentes de la prévalence élevée du VIH en se concentrant sur le comportement individuel, et sur un menu d'options limité proche du néolibéralisme.

Introduction

Picture the following scene: young men and women line up, waiting to enrol in a lottery in Lesotho. Like people all over the world, they see the chance to win a substantial amount of money which they can use to pay off debts, buy household essentials and possibly some small personal luxuries. However, unusually in this lottery, they are not queuing up to buy a ticket. Instead they are waiting to be tested for sexually transmitted infections (STIs), as getting a clean bill of sexual health is the only way they can take part. Indeed, this lottery is a new breed of cash-transfer scheme that aims to reduce HIV infection –

one that is quite different to our usual image of cash-transfer schemes, and as such is emblematic of a new behavioural economics-inspired approach to HIV risk reduction in Africa.

UNAIDS calls recent biomedical advances in the fight against HIV 'game-changers' (UNAIDS 2011). Innovations such as male medical circumcision, treatment-as-prevention and drugs to prevent mother-to-child transmission appear to slash HIV transmission rates.[1] However, HIV incidence[2] is still high in many southern and eastern African countries, and the human cost in terms of ruined lives continues to build. Consequently, interventions to change sexual behaviour remain important in the HIV policy discourse, and, among them, HIV-related cash transfers have become prominent. These transfers intend to make direct or indirect changes in sexual behaviour, thereby reducing HIV incidence.

Here, I scrutinise the conceptualisation of 'choice' and structure underpinning HIV-related cash-transfer schemes in Africa. The success of cash transfers to reduce HIV incidence has been agreed upon by a range of commentators, as we shall see below. Despite positive reviews, cash transfers have been criticised elsewhere for their questionable ethics and uncertain sustainability. This article confirms and extends previous criticisms, arguing that the analytical foundations of cash-transfer interventions are unconvincing when viewed from a political economy lens. This article is significant in two senses. First, its detailed analysis of the project outcomes suggests success has not been as universal as proponents (and indeed some critics) claim. Second, it highlights the role of new behavioural approaches to HIV risk reduction (some of which result in the lottery style of cash transfer described in the first paragraph), and thereby deepens previous criticisms about sustainability and ethics by linking concerns to a continuing debate about the causes of high HIV incidence.

Below I discuss the various foundations underlying HIV-related cash-transfer interventions, before going on to review projects in sub-Saharan Africa. Finally, I argue that a political economy approach to HIV risk provides a broader perspective to understand high rates of HIV acquisition. Here I will use the concept of political economy based on a radical, materialist interpretation of change in African countries. I am referring to an approach that understands the social relations of production, is historically specific and addresses the issues of class, conflict and power. In particular, I will attempt to show how all variants of HIV-related cash transfers fail to acknowledge the inequities (driven by local and global forces) that have led to high rates of HIV prevalence. As well as a more critical analysis of the kinds of evidence produced by the interventions themselves, this is the new contribution of this article – as previous criticisms of HIV cash transfers have not situated HIV risk in the context of the particular kinds of neoliberal globalisation found in African countries.

This article argues that HIV-related cash transfers obscure and depoliticise the underlying drivers of the HIV epidemics in African countries. In the worst examples, they may even harm those who acquire HIV, as the ethos underlying the new wave of HIV-related projects implies that HIV acquisition is the result of poor choices. This can only add to stigma and blame. However, this scepticism and caution is not widely shared in the policy world, where HIV-related cash-transfer approaches provide attractive and tractable. This article starts by setting out how HIV-related cash transfers became so popular.

The fashion for HIV-related cash transfers in Africa

Before reviewing cash transfers in sub-Saharan African countries, it is important to note that health-related cash transfers are used in other parts of the world, most notably in the now-rich countries to assist in the prevention of disease and in treatment adherence among groups that are seen as difficult to reach through usual methods[3]. In African countries, cash transfers have been used extensively with non-HIV aims, such as for boosting school enrolment and poverty reduction. Programmes have been both universal (available to all) and targeted (available to a selected group), conditional (disbursed only if the recipient follows a particular action) and unconditional (disbursed to anyone in the target group).

Indeed, this review includes examples of projects and programmes whose main aim was not HIV related, but which made HIV-related claims as part of secondary goals or findings. Nine cash-transfer projects or programmes (with HIV-related main or secondary goals) are identified below. The rate of implementation of such programmes may well have been encouraged by the wave of positive coverage from practitioners and international development agencies. For example, on the eve of the International AIDS Society summit in Vienna in 2010, the World Bank released a press statement hailing the success of two HIV-related cash-transfer projects in Malawi and Tanzania. Dr David Wilson, the Bank's Director for its Global HIV/AIDS Program, announced, 'These two studies show the potential for using cash payments to prevent people, especially women and girls, from engaging in unsafe sex while also ensuring that they stay in school and get the full benefit of an education' (http://www.worldbank.org, press release, Vienna/Washington, July 18, 2010). The UNAIDS *2013 Global Report* suggested that:

> [n]ew strategies have emerged to reduce young people's vulnerability to HIV, including social cash transfers that create incentives for safer behaviours. . . . There is clear potential for cash transfers to support HIV prevention for young people, and continued research on the HIV prevention role of such programmes is recommended. (UNAIDS 2013, 18)

In the same year, a joint report by UNAIDS and the Lancet Commission (2013) hailed HIV-related conditional cash transfers as an innovative financial approach (11) and as a proven method to reduce gender inequality (17).

Policy endorsements have been mirrored by academic approval, including two systematic reviews (Pettifor et al. 2012; Heise et al. 2013). Of the 10 studies reviewed by Pettifor et al. (2012), nine showed positive results on sexual behaviour and one showed a reduction in HIV prevalence among young women. The authors concluded that, based on preliminary data, cash payment interventions to reduce HIV risk were effective, especially among young women (*Ibid.*). Heise et al. (2013) were more circumspect as we shall see below, but even they concluded that the emerging evidence suggested that cash transfers could be an important addition to policy.

Praise for a behavioural intervention, especially by key international agencies, is not necessarily at odds with the fact that biomedical innovation currently dominates public health discourse. Cash transfers are seen as complementary to the biomedical advances. Pettifor et al. (2012, 1733) and de Walque et al. (2012a, 6) argue transfers can help with uptake of biomedical interventions, such as antiretrovirals and drugs for prevention of mother-to-child transmission. Pettifor et al. (2012, 1729) also warn that limits to the scale-up and uptake of biomedical interventions mean that behavioural-focused interventions remain important.

Despite wide admiration for cash transfers, critical views do exist. The systematic reviews mentioned above are concerned that cash transfers may not be sustainable (Pettifor et al. 2012; Heise et al. 2013), while Heise et al.'s (2013) more critical review doubts whether cash transfers can change the structural factors causing high HIV risk. Other evidence suggests that the impacts of cash-transfer projects are short-lived. Rigsby et al. (2000) studied the impact of a four-week cash-transfer project on anti retroviral drug adherence among a sample of US veterans. While the use of monetary reinforcement clearly helped treatment adherence during the project, eight weeks after its end adherence in the cash-transfer group had returned to near-baseline levels.

Some commentators raise a wider set of concerns. Harman, for example, proposes that those excluded from the project feel disincentivised to change their behaviour: 'The question of who is left out limits sustained behaviour change ... local communities have increasingly been found not to engage in activities that help themselves and their communities unless they receive financial support to do so' (2011, 876). To provide support for this concern, Deci, Koestner, and Ryan's (1999) meta-review of 128 studies suggests external motivation, such as cash transfers, tends to undermine 'intrinsic' or internalised motivation. Similar concerns emerged in a review of cash interventions in tuberculosis treatment adherence, which were compounded by the observation that transfers created sharp power asymmetries between monitoring staff and clients (Eichler, Levine, and the Performance-Based Incentives Working Group 2009). Harman develops the issue of power beyond that of the project itself, to argue that the use of HIV-related cash-transfer projects, with their frequent requirement of abstinence and/or safe sex, has 'significant implications for individual choice, the family and forms of social engineering that restrict childbirth within specific socio-economic demographics' (2011, 876). These criticisms will be confirmed but also extended by reference to a wider political economy approach in the remainder of the article.

All cash transfers are not created equal

HIV-related cash-transfer schemes have emerged from several theoretical perspectives: social protection, social work and, more recently, behavioural economics (for a review see Heise et al. 2013). Social protection cash transfers can be conditional or unconditional. Where conditional, they are often premised on school attendance. Examples below have been implemented in Kenya and Malawi. Often the link to HIV comes from an attempt to change the structural factors that lead to high HIV risk through education, poverty reduction and women's empowerment. Elsewhere in this special issue, O'Laughlin considers how the term 'structural' is used. Handa et al. (2014, e85473) set out these channels, arguing that 'cash transfers may reduce the risk of HIV by addressing structural risk factors, especially poverty, vulnerability and low human capital.' School attendance might reduce HIV risk directly (as it is argued that sex is less likely to occur in school), and indirectly, as young people will receive HIV education and are more likely to have partners of the same age (rather than older partners who may have already acquired HIV). At the same time, Handa et al. suggest that HIV risk is reduced through a poverty channel, as cash transfers may postpone sexual debut by reducing poverty and making young people less likely to engage in transactional sex, with young women less dependent on male partners, reducing sex generally and unprotected sex acts in particular.

A social work approach (borrowing from the study of anti-social behaviour) is also mobilised in interventions that require school attendance through conditional grants. For example in the Zimbabwe project listed below, school attendance is seen as changing sexual behaviour as it encourages bonding with 'prosocial' adults, peers and institutions, especially important for orphans and other vulnerable children (OVCs) (Hallfors et al. 2011, 1083). Hallfors et al. argue that supporting OVC girls to stay in school will lead to 'greater attendance, ... higher educational aspirations, more positive expectations about the future, more equitable gender attitudes, more protective attitudes about sex, lower self-reported sexual behaviour, and lower rates of marriage and pregnancy' (*Ibid.*).

In contrast, behavioural economics sees people as economic agents, some of whom are myopic, heavily discounting the future benefits of safe sex and focused on immediate reward (the pleasure of unsafe sex). Borrowing from psychologists who use cash transfers to change behaviours such as smoking and substance abuse, these interventions operate through tightly designed frameworks of conditionality and reward. Specifically, conditional cash transfers are seen as changing the balance between short- and long-run benefits so that individuals are more likely to choose safe sex (de Walque et al. 2012b). This specific be-havioural economics approach is conceived within a libertarian paternalist view of chan-ging an individual's 'choice architecture' (Thaler and Sunstein 2008). While individuals are seen as optimisers, some apparently make decisions using poor judgement – and this 'sub-optimal' behaviour is at the heart of HIV spread.

The assumption that some individuals are at risk of HIV acquisition because they cannot account for future risk adequately is the basis for a number of interventions below, but most notably the lottery-style intervention in Lesotho. This intervention, by not guaranteeing a cash payout (but only the chance of one), is quite different from other kinds of cash transfer where participants might expect a certain cash payment should they fulfil any necessary conditions. The designers of the Lesotho lottery, Björkman-Nyqvist et al. (2013), argue that certain people engage in risky sexual behaviour despite a high background level of HIV as they weigh short-term gains more highly than long-term benefits. Similarly, refer-ring to young people involved in the Tanzania RESPECT project, de Walque et al. (2012a, 6) conclude that '[t]hese young people appear to understand their HIV risks and know how to behave to prevent transmission – yet they don't choose to act on that knowledge.'

These different theoretical approaches lead to varying kinds of conditionality. A poverty-focused intervention based on the social protection approach may have no condi-tionality and might target poor households generally, while an education or gender equality project arising from the same social protection approach might be conditional on school attendance and/or may be focused only on households with school-age girls. Projects devel-oped with a social work approach would certainly have conditionality based on school attendance, with payments directly to the school attendee. However, interventions informed by behavioural economics are premised on a far more tailored conditionality in order to incentivise behaviour change. While other cash-transfer designs might be conditional on engaging in an easily monitored behaviour, such as school attendance, the behavioural economics approach requires participants to refrain from complex, private behaviour, such as risky sex. As such, self-reported monitoring is eschewed in favour of 'objective' measures (such as a sexually transmitted infection test), and monitoring and reward transfer are frequent in order maximise incentives for those with a high discount rate (Medlin and de Walque 2008, 3, 5; de Walque et al. 2012a, 9, 14). As such, behavioural economics interventions will have much smaller, more frequent cash transfers than poverty- or edu-cation-focused interventions. Indeed, some behavioural economics projects simply offer the chance of a cash reward, as in the Lesotho lottery, and so are attractive to funders because of their cheapness.

In practice (as we will see below), while some projects recorded HIV prevalence to chart impacts, only a few used it to screen recipients (i.e. requiring a negative HIV result to be a recipient). For those from a social protection or social work perspective, this eschew-ing of HIV status as a conditionality undoubtedly has its roots in ethical concerns about stig-matising and impoverishing individuals who have received a positive test (Heise et al. 2013). However, as Medlin and de Walque (2008, 12–13) illustrate, for behavioural econ-omics interventions, there is an additional set of reasons why HIV is not chosen as an indi-cator. Background HIV rates are low in many settings (meaning that risky sexual behaviour may not always lead to HIV acquisition) and, given the incubation period of HIV, testing positive may be too distant from unsafe sex. Medlin and de Walque (12) argue that it is better to use the absence of other sexually transmitted infections as a condition, if they are prevalent within the population, linked to risky sex and can be tested cheaply and conveniently.

The new behavioural economics approaches are effectively embellishments of a standard micro-economic model of consumer choice, based around the analysis of the choices of a rational and representative consumer who attempts to maximise his/her utility. The decisions of the representative individual are then aggregated up to explain outcomes at the level of the society (Fine and Milonakis 2009, 3). This is reductionist in several ways. The first is that the issue of a 'representative individual' is problematic, as complex and shifting gender- and class-based social norms around sex and relationships exist for different groups within any one country (Johnston 2013).

More generally, these approaches are set up with only limited attention to the broader social context, and more specifically the way that social norms over sexual behaviour are established. For example, a number of authors have pointed to the predominance of male migration in explaining concurrency in some contexts (for example, Marks 2007; Katz 2009), while others have pointed to the delays resulting from inadequate transport infrastructure and border red tape to explain commercial sexual transactions (for example, Stillwaggon 2006). By isolating behaviour from the social norms that affect it, all three of the cash-transfer approaches (behavioural economics, social protection and social work) are treating these norms as exogenous, when in practice they are dynamic and reflect wider social and economic changes (of which more below).

In this way, the approaches above lose any sense of context or historical specificity, and then go on to make very particular assumptions about the way in which decisions are made. The first assumption is that individuals make independent decisions over unsafe sex and HIV risk. Is it really possible to isolate decisions over sex and condom use from other factors, such as pregnancy and trust? To understand this, we might instead want to know more about the role and value of condom use and sex in different kinds of relationship. Further, authors like Marais (2005) and Marks (2007) remind us that both the construction of health information and its acceptance is not a simple matter. Ideology in the form of religious or moral standpoints has an important to role to play. Those who think that education is the sole determinant of take-up of orthodox medical information about HIV transmission are, therefore, fundamentally misguided.

We are also left wondering about the concept of 'choice' in these approaches. Individuals are seen as having a high degree of choice about engaging in or refusing certain kinds of sexual behaviour. This ignores the significant role of coercion in sexual activity by strangers or partners, despite the evidence from a range of studies of its prevalence (Watts and Zimmerman 2002, 1235; WHO 2010, 12; Garcia-Moreno and Watts 2011). Even where coercion is not present, approaches based on free choice are far from applicable. Shula Marks (2007, 867) suggests that many young South African women are 'choice-disabled', being dependent to a large extent on men for economic support and status, thus engaging in risky sexual behaviour to secure their attentions and fatalistically accepting the concomitant risk of HIV and sexual violence as a necessary part of survival. In recognition of the interlinkages of sex, money and social standing, we may then want to think not about sexual choices, with all of the concomitant understandings of 'freedom', but rather about *options* available to particular types of people. These options may be extremely narrow for some, especially for poor women in certain areas who may not always face violent compulsion to engage in sexual relationships, but whose degree of 'choice' is severely limited.

On these grounds we might be sceptical about the likely success of cash-transfer policies, given their construction around concepts of choice and incentives that are divorced from an understanding of the options individuals have. How do cash transfers work in practice?

The practice of HIV-related cash transfers in Africa

Table 1 distils the key characteristics of HIV-related, Africa-based, cash-transfer schemes, evaluated in terms of the evidence that they had reduced HIV risk in both the short and long term. These cases, located through web searches, are listed where either academic articles, project documentation or website information was publicly available. Subsequently, the impact of each project on HIV risk is set out. Of course, the discussion is limited by the availability of information and evidence. All of the evidence presented in the project documentation comes from randomised control trials (RCTs) – i.e. where large-scale quantitative exercises are carried out to investigate the impact on an intervention by comparing the outcomes for participants with those for a 'control' group. Arguably, these exercises wrongly privilege certain kinds of quantitative information, have a narrow focus and are poor at understanding causal links (Deaton 2010; Cartwright and Hardie 2012; Basu 2013), and these concerns are relevant in understanding the impact of cash transfers, as we shall see below.

Before moving to a more detailed assessment of these projects, it is important to initially evaluate their impact on HIV acquisition. And here it is clear that their success has been far more limited than the policy literature would suggest.[4] For those projects measuring HIV status, only a subset reported a reduction in HIV incidence over time or in HIV prevalence among the intervention group compared with the control group. In the Lesotho lottery, for which only medium-term information is available, there was a reduction in HIV incidence rates for the intervention compared with the control. Two years after the project start, HIV incidence was significantly lower among the study participants, especially for women and for the intervention arm facing the highest lottery payments (Björkman-Nyqvist et al. 2013). The Malawi Schooling, Income and HIV Risk (SIHR) project found lower HIV and herpes simplex virus (HSV) rates only for some arms of the intervention, i.e. not for girls who started out as school dropouts and then went on to receive the transfer (Baird et al. 2012).

In two other projects for which HIV data was available, the Malawi Incentive Programme and the Tanzania RESPECT project, there was no change in HIV rates. Both studies raise particular challenges for researchers. In the Malawi Incentive Programme, the authors are shocked to find that male recipients end up with a greater HIV risk. While Kohler and Thornton (2012) report no *overall* impact of the conditional cash transfer on remaining HIV negative, this was averaged over a reduced risk for women and a *higher* risk for men. Male participants were more likely to report having sex than non-participants, and, despite being slightly more likely to report using a condom, this increased their overall HIV risk. In contrast, female recipients were less likely to report having had sex, leading the authors to conclude that conditional cash transfers can be protective for women (*Ibid.*, 169). In the Tanzania RESPECT project, while the risk of the targeted STIs was lower for the treatment group with highest payment, there was no impact on three other, far more serious STIs: HSV, syphilis and crucially HIV (de Walque et al. 2012b).

Some interventions did not measure HIV, instead relying on various indicators of HIV risk (such as sexual debut, pregnancy, early marriage etc.). However, these indicators did not move neatly together. The Kenya OVC intervention changed the overall age of

Table 1.   Key characteristics of HIV-related cash-transfer schemes based in African countries.

Place	Name	Target group	Aim	Conditionality	Design	Source
Kenya – national	Cash Transfer Programme for Orphans and Vulnerable Children (OVCs)	OVCs are 0–17 years old in poor households, with at least one deceased or chronically ill parent/carer	Improving the welfare of OVCs	None	US$20 per month to 'the main care giver' in each participating household.	Handa et al. (2014)
Kenya – two western districts	School Support Through Uniforms and HIV Education	Boys and girls enrolled in Grade 6	Changing sexual behaviour, fertility, and reducing the risk of HIV and herpes simplex virus	School attendance	Three intervention arms which provided school uniforms, HIV education, and both uniforms and HIV education.	Duflo, Dupas, and Kremer (2012)
Malawi – Zomba area	Schooling, Income and HIV Risk (SIHR)	Young women, 13–22 years old, never married	Improve educational attainment, reduce HIV/STD risk, prevention of unwanted pregnancy and early marriage	Mixture of conditional and unconditional transfer, dependent on the intervention arm	Carers received an amount randomly chosen for each enumeration area (ranging from $4 to $10 per month); while the amount given to girls was determined by lottery (ranging from $1 to $5 per month). Those in secondary school had their fees paid.	Baird et al. (2012)
Malawi – rural areas	Malawi Incentive Programme	People, 14 years and above	Assisting individuals and couples to maintain their HIV status	Maintenance of baseline HIV status for one year. For couples, both members must maintain their HIV status	Each individual or couple randomly drew an amount to be paid 1 year later. Individuals received between zero and approx. $16; couples, between zero and $32.	Kohler and Thornton (2012)

(Continued)

Table 1. Continued.

Place	Name	Target group	Aim	Conditionality	Design	Source
Tanzania – rural southwest	The RESPECT study	People aged 18–30	Reducing HIV acquisition	Testing negative for four curable STIs	Two intervention groups, paid either approx. $10 or $20 per four-month testing round.	de Walque et al. (2012b)
Lesotho – rural and peri-urban villages across 5 districts	Evaluating the impact of short-term financial incentives on HIV and STI incidence among youth in Lesotho	Peopled aged 18–30 years	Changing sexual behaviour and HIV incidence	Testing negative for two easily treated STIs	Two intervention groups, with individuals eligible to participate in a lottery, with prizes the equivalent of US$74 or US$147 per four-month testing round. In each round, four lottery winners were drawn (2 men and 2 women).	Björkman-Nyqvist et al. (2013)
Zimbabwe – five rural areas of Manicaland Province	Supporting Adolescent Orphan Girls to Stay in School as HIV Risk Prevention	All Grade 6 girls (ages 12–14) with one or more deceased parent in a selected set of primary schools	Reducing HIV risk	School attendance	School support included: fees, exercise books, uniforms and other school supplies. Girls who were required to board to attend secondary school had assistance with boarding costs. Female teachers were trained as helpers to monitor participants' school attendance and to assist with absenteeism problems, for which a small fund was also available. Participant schools benefited from a feeding programme.	Hallfors et al. (2011)

Table 1. Continued.

Place	Name	Target group	Aim	Conditionality	Design	Source
South Africa – northwest area of Agincourt	Swa Koteka, HPTN 068	Young women aged 13–20 in Grades 8–11 and their parents	Reducing HIV incidence	School attendance	Each month that a girl attends 80% of school days, the family and the young woman will receive a cash-transfer payment (approx. $18 to female carer and $9 to girl). There is also a community education aspect aimed at changing gender norms.	No published results as yet but some information can be found online, e.g. http://www.cpc.unc.edu/.
South Africa – Vulindlela in KwaZulu-Natal	Reducing HIV in Adolescents (RHIVA), CAPRISA 007	Boys and girls aged at least 13 years in Grades 9 and 10 in selected schools	Reducing HIV incidence	School attendance and other educational milestones, such as passing exams	Cash incentives paid to learners – amount unclear at time of writing.	No published results as yet. Some information can be found online, e.g. http://www.caprisa.org/.

Source: Author's extracts from sources listed in final column.

sexual debut but was not able to change any other features of self-reported sexual behaviour. Young recipients (aged 15–25) had a 23% lower rate of sexual debut than others (Handa et al. 2014). However, it is unclear if there was any additional risk reduction from delayed sexual debut, and certainly the transfer had no other impacts on HIV risk, with indicators such as condom use, number of sexual partners, transactional sex etc. being unaffected. The western Kenya project had varied results (depending on which intervention arms participants were in). The uniform subsidy only reduced teen marriage, pregnancy and not HSV, while HIV education only reduced *out of wedlock* teen pregnancy in first three years. When the two were implemented together, fertility fell less than using the education subsidy alone but HSV was lower (Duflo, Dupas, and Kremer 2012). Certainly for the western Kenya project, it could not be argued that the results for the cash intervention were in all ways superior to those for HIV education.

Worryingly, longer-run impact studies exist for both the western Kenya and the Tanzania RESPECT projects. In western Kenya, the impacts of a uniform subsidy on marriage and school dropout were eroded as participants aged, and seven years later these had disappeared. In the Tanzanian RESPECT project, after two years the impact on STI acquisition by women vanished (Heise et al. 2013). For other projects, either there was no long-run impact data or it was not available at the time of writing.

In evaluating HIV-related cash transfers, it is important to note the limited usefulness of evidence coming from the interventions themselves. RCTs have generally been criticised for their inability to understand causal pathways, owing to their reliance on quantified end-results. This general criticism seems specifically relevant here, where few projects were able to discuss the evidence on causal mechanisms (and where those that did were open to challenge). For example, in the Malawi SIHR project, the project team hypothesised that reduced HIV prevalence for some participants relative to the control group came about as participants had younger boyfriends than non-participants (Baird et al. [2012] report that the partners of girls in the treatment group were one year younger on average than those in the control). However, some authors have doubted that lower HIV rates were due solely to the choice of older partners. Heise et al. (2013) note that only 2.5% of girls in the control group versus 0.5% of girls in the intervention groups had older sexual partners, and so the small reduction in age of partners could not explain the difference in HIV prevalence. Moreover, I would argue that the fact that girls in the conditional arm had the same teen pregnancy and marriage rates as the control group suggests that the mechanisms for impact are unclear.

With this caveat about the kinds of evidence available from RCTs, I will now turn to an investigation of the support for each of the theoretical positions that were identified as supporting cash transfers for HIV risk reduction. In the social work approach, anti-social peer-group orientation and low self-esteem lead to poor life choices and raise HIV risk. In the social protection approach, HIV risk is raised by the choices forced on poor people, or specifically on poor women. In behavioural economics, HIV risk is the result of poor discounting of time and risk, leading people to choose immediate pleasure over safe sex or abstinence.

The social work approach hypothesises that school attendance has a risk-reduction effect. Certainly, many of the projects listed above were effective in increasing school attendance for some participants, but the impact on HIV risk has been far more complex. In the Kenya OVC programme, secondary school-age participants were 8 percentage points more likely to be in school than the control and Handa et al. (2014) argue that this was the cause of the delay in sexual debut that was also found. However, as we have noted, while sexual debut was delayed, the indicators of risk for those participants who were sexually active (number of sexual partners, condom use and transactional sex) were unaffected. In the western Kenya project, those in the group receiving uniform subsidies were less likely to have dropped out of school and also less likely to have been married or borne children two years later (Duflo, Dupas, and Kremer 2012). However, there was no impact on HSV incidence and the authors suggest that the impact may have occurred through lower rates of committed partnership, while casual partnership rates remained similar. In the Zimbabwe intervention, Hallfors et al. (2011) report that two years after the start, participants were less likely to have dropped out of school and to have initiated sexual debut. The study did not collect information on HIV or other STIs, and noted that the data they collected on self-reported sexual intercourse was unreliable (*Ibid.*). These three interventions, then, seem to have reduced some kinds of sexual activity but cannot clearly be seen to have reduced HIV risk on all counts.

Importantly, all three made relatively large transfers to the young people they targeted, especially the Zimbabwe and Kenyan OVC projects. In projects with smaller interventions, the tensions in the relationship between school attendance and HIV risk become clearer. In the Malawi SIHR, with its lower cash transfer, setting a condition of school attendance may have had negative effects on teen marriage and pregnancy. Baird et al. (2012) argue that the cost of schooling may have led families to push girls into early marriage. So the interaction between the size of the cash transfer and the implicit cost of the conditionality is important (e.g. fees, uniform, books and transport costs are all incurred when children have to attend school).

Consequently, the social work approach (with its focus on the pro-social effect of school on HIV risk) seems to be making too simplistic an assumption about the role of schooling, without looking at its costs and the social context. This is supported by a wider set of evidence on the relationship between education and HIV. While in most African countries, studies suggest that those with higher education usually have higher HIV prevalence, there is growing evidence that this pattern is changing (Hargreaves et al. 2008). In several settings, Hargreaves et al. (2008) conclude that strong statistical associations suggesting greater HIV risk in the more educated at earlier time points were replaced by weaker associations later. Similar shifts in patterns were found for Tanzania, the only setting with national data at the time of writing (Hargreaves and Howe 2010).[5] What this shows is that the relationship between education and HIV is complex. Taking the case of Zambia, as reported by Hargreaves et al. (2008), for both young, urban men and women education was becoming protective, while this was not true for rural areas, where having some education was still associated with higher HIV prevalence.

The results are more promising for those working from a social protection perspective. Results for interventions with different-size transfers for different treatment arms suggest that larger payments are more likely to have an impact. This was true for the Tanzanian RESPECT and the Lesotho lottery projects (see above). Only in the Malawi SIHR was there no apparent relationship between transfer value and HIV or HSV prevalence (Baird et al. 2012). Even where we do not have project evidence on the impact of different-size transfers, the headline results seem to suggest it is important. In the Malawi Incentive Programme, the authors blame the small size of the transfer ($0–$16 after one year), as well as the lagged reward structure, for the failure to have an impact (Kohler and Thornton 2012, 168, 169). Similarly, the Kenya OVC (with a monthly payment of $20) had a bigger impact on sexual debut than the conditional Malawi SIHR (with a monthly payment to carers of $4–$10 and to girls of $1–$5).

This may be a source of support for those who see poverty or, where funds are targeted to girls, gender inequality as the biggest HIV risk. However, it is also true that the authors of the report on the Malawi Incentive Programme suggest that higher income puts male participants at greater risk of HIV. They speculate that, among other things, the detrimental impact on male HIV risk came about because participants could spend more money on items that made them more attractive (such as new clothes), and that some men were able to use the money to purchase more sex (*Ibid.*, 186). More than that, we have already seen that the impact on HIV risk was itself unclear for most studies, even with the higher payment arms.

This ambiguity about income fits with other studies that show that the relationship between wealth and HIV is far more complex. The vast majority of studies provide a snapshot picture of HIV prevalence and they tend to find either find a clear positive relationship between wealth and HIV status (i.e. the rich are more likely to be HIV positive) or an 'inverted U-shaped' relationship (i.e. the middle wealth groups have the highest HIV prevalence) (Mishra et al. 2007; Parkhurst 2010). Parkhurst (2010, 520) finds a positive correlation is common in poorer African countries, but not in richer countries. The three available longitudinal studies (i.e. where a group of people are followed over time) also produce entirely contradictory results, despite all being drawn from southern Africa. One shows that poor men have the highest incidence, another that it was the middle-income men, while the third finds no relationship between wealth and incidence of HIV (Johnston 2013).

The evidence on female income and HIV risk also challenges simple assumptions that increasing women's relative income will reduce their HIV risk. A systematic review of 35 or so studies found slightly more evidence that women with higher socio-economic status have higher HIV acquisition (Wojcicki 2005). Wojcicki concludes 'there is some indication that access to increased funds for women may put them at increased risk for HIV infection – potentially by giving them access to more partners or opportunities for travel' (19). When projects assume that female poverty increases HIV risk, they seem to be glossing over a complex and possibly contradictory picture.

Based on the discussion above, it is clear that the praise for HIV-related cash transfers has selectively interpreted the evidence. In the following section, we will evaluate the approaches that generated these projects more broadly, using a radical political economy approach.

A critical political economy assessment

Political economy work on health seeks to explain how poor health, or affliction – as O'Laughlin (2013) terms it – is produced, often unintentionally, by the nature of production structures, and the social and political factors that determine health care provision. To fully understand this production of affliction, however, we must differentiate between different forms of disease. With the main mode of HIV in Africa being sex, Hunter's work (2010, 218; and in this issue) convinces us that sex (and other aspects of intimacy, including affection, love, pleasure and fertility) is always linked in multiple ways to making a living. Indeed, Hunter (2010, 11–12) suggests that we must consider intimacy rather than solely sex, defining the broader term to include 'fertility, love, marriage and genital pleasure' (3). Analysing HIV through the political economy of affliction and intimacy places importance on the relationship between capital and labour, and between classes of labour transcribed by gender and social status. Specifically sexual norms and health provisioning reflect the economic and social relations of production, and it is important to expand on this here to explain why.

Using class analysis and linking intimacy to work and livelihoods, we can see how sexual norms are created and change over time. Eschewing a vision of simple sexual norms (of the poor, of the educated … etc.), we instead adopt an approach where norms are varied by social grouping in different settings. Thus in Tanzania, Bujra (2006) explains the creation of class-based sexual networks. In South Africa, Hunter (2010) explains the risks faced by the poor in peri-urban KwaZulu-Natal. At the same time as being complex, sexual norms respond dynamically to changes in patterns of employment and residence.

Here we see how the pattern of uneven development within and between African countries can lead to a restructuring of sexual norms in ways that promote concurrency, transactional and commercial sex. Specifically, authors point to the way in which both local and global forces have led to substantial inter- and intra-country migration, as well as growing inequality. For example, Bujra (2006) has argued that the growing wealth, power and mobility of an elite group in Tanzania led to patterns of sexual networking, including commercial and transactional sex, which raised HIV risk. Hunter (2010) considers how the dismal income-earning opportunities, especially for women, in a peri-urban area of South Africa have changed the nature of intimate relationships. Men are able to adopt a new 'playboy' status, where their relative economic power allows them to have several intimate partnerships with poorer, economically vulnerable women. This pattern of multiple partnership is compounded by the fact that, despite having better economic options than women, employment security for poor black men has also deteriorated in the face of a collapse of employment growth and increased casualisation. Older and more stable patterns of partnership, where a man was able to maintain his wife in a rural homestead, are no longer viable. Hickel (2012) points to similar trends, arguing that bleak income-earning opportunities for poor women in Swaziland, coupled with high inequality, have led to a rise both in transactional and commercial sexual relationships. For him, patterns of partnership can also be explained by male migrancy to South Africa, as this promotes shifting and transient sexual partnerships.

This discussion of the way that intimate partnerships have been affected by rising inequality and uneven economic development across the African region places HIV risk in a new light. While patterns will vary between different countries, classes and genders, it is clear that patterns of intimacy are related to the long run and dramatic changes to the way that individuals reproduce themselves, to the places where they live and work. No longer is it the result of poor decisions by individuals about safe sex, but instead it reflects the long integration of African economies into a globalised economy.

However, HIV risk can only be fully understood if we combine the analysis of intimacy and sexual norms with that of health provisioning. Before taking each of these in turn, we should remind ourselves of the factors that increase both the transmission of HIV and its aggressiveness. There is evidence that the presence of other sexually transmitted infections increases the likelihood both of contracting HIV, and of transmitting it (Stillwaggon 2006; see also CDC 1998). Poor nutrition, parasitic disease and malaria may raise the chances of contracting HIV, and also the onset of AIDS (Stillwaggon 2006). Male medical circumcision appears to significantly reduce HIV transmission from women to men during sex (WHO 2012b), although there are dissenting voices (Perrey et al. 2012). Access to medication is important. Taking antiretrovirals (ARVs) reduces HIV transmission from an HIV-positive person to their HIV-negative partner (WHO 2012a) and drugs are needed to reduce mother-to-child transmission (UNAIDS 2010). Finally, the safety of medical interventions is crucial in reducing medical transmission (Gisselquist 2004).

Thus, public health policy on the treatment of sexually transmitted infections, on circumcision, nutrition, drug access for mother-to-child transmission and ARVs generally will affect both adult and child transmission rates in particular settings. On each of these issues, there are reasons for concern in most African countries. Indeed, until 2003, poor countries were prevented from importing generic ARVs for almost a decade (Hickel 2012, 526) as a result of the WTO's Trade Related Aspects of Intellectual Property Rights. The costs of ARVs were kept at extremely high levels, available only to the wealthiest individuals. Hickel (*Ibid.*) argues that not only were a generation of AIDS sufferers condemned to death, but the lack of effective AIDS mitigation produced a strong disinclination for testing in Swaziland. Thus, barriers to low-cost generic ARVs increased HIV incidence through direct and indirect channels. At the same time, medication to reduce mother-to-child transmission has not been fully accessible to those who need it (UNAIDS 2010).

Many authors have pointed to the limited health services available in sub-Saharan Africa, in terms of both private and public provision. The scale of medical transmission of HIV in many African countries is fiercely debated, with poor historical and current medical practices possibly transmitting HIV far more frequently than usually acknowledged (see Gisselquist 2004, for example). Further, O'Laughlin (2013) suggests that the lack of employment-related health care provision (restricted to the elite of the formally employed) is a key reason for limited health care access, with casual or migrant work having few or no health benefits attached. Hickel (2012, 519) reminds us that many migrants receive particularly poor health provision, taking the case of South African migrants where curable STIs are often endemic (raising HIV risk). As Campbell (2003) and Stuckler, Basu, and McKee (2010) argue, South African mining companies have externalised the health costs of the industry, in terms of AIDS, tuberculosis and other mining-related health conditions. At the same time, the outcome of neoliberal labour market policy has been a greater casualisation and informalisation of work (Whiteside 2005; Hickel 2012; O'Laughlin 2013). Casualisation further reduces employers' commitments to a worker's health, as well as producing extremely insecure employment, forcing women in particular into risky sexual relationships.

In the light of political economy understandings of HIV transmission, the limitations of cash-transfer projects are clear. Let us take each aspect in turn. Can cash transfers change sexual norms? This might depend on the extent to which longer-run patterns of reproduction and residence are changed. To echo other criticisms of cash transfers (such as Ghosh 2011), cash transfers are limited in their ability to fundamentally and significantly change the economic options available, when these are determined by wider financial, trade and industrial policies.

Instead we need an increase in decent employment opportunities (i.e. with stability, benefits and reasonable wages), and opportunities for poor women are crucial. Hickel (2012, 528–529) sets out how these changes could take place for Swaziland, suggesting the creation of local employment options that would slow labour migration rates, and that this would need a wide swath of support for small-scale agriculture: investment in small-scale farmers; tariff barriers to protect the domestic food market from subsidised foreign imports; the sourcing of US food aid from local farmers, instead of American agribusiness; greater integration of small-scale farmers in the sugar industry and other agricultural industries; and the introduction of legislation to allow women equal rights to land and credit. Hickel (529) also suggests that there should be widespread domestic employment creation through state- and donor-funded infrastructure projects, open to both male and female workers.

Alongside substantial changes to the means of reproduction and residence patterns, health provisioning must be improved. Can cash transfers lead to an improvement in health generally? Evaluations of cash transfers generally suggest that they appear to have positive effects on household food consumption and dietary diversity, while conditional cash transfers specifically increase awareness of health messages, immunisation rates, and use of health and nutrition services (Gaarder, Glassman, and Todd 2010; Ranganathan and Lagarde 2012; Ruel and Alderman 2013). However, evidence of effects on health and nutritional outcomes is limited, and the most comprehensive indicator, child anthropometry, suggests there have been no statistically significant effects of either conditional or unconditional transfers overall (Ruel and Alderman 2013). Information for individual programmes supports this, suggesting that only a few programmes have effects on bodily outcomes and these have tended to be for the youngest or poorest children or those on the project for longer (*Ibid.*). Aside from specific impacts on macro- and micro-nutrients, little data has been collected on other health outcomes and even less shows significant changes.

Several reasons have been given for the lack of impact on nutritional and health outcomes, given that health service use increased (*Ibid.*). There may be a statistical basis – that most evaluations use RCT data that comes only from programmes in middle-income countries while programmes in low-income countries might be more effective. More fundamentally, it has been argued that programmes might be poorly designed, too short or not generous enough. Finally, the lack of correlation between increased use of nutritional/health services and improved health and nutritional outcomes implies that health services are poor quality (Ranganathan and Lagarde 2012; Ruel and Alderman 2013).

A political economy approach would consider the issue of health provisioning differently, and as an issue not only for the public sector, but for the private. As O'Laughlin (2013) has argued for South Africa, it is important that there is wider responsibility among employers for worker health, and for ARV provision. Migrant rights to health care must also be improved, and, for international migrants, this will require policy change by host governments. An improvement in employment-based health care rights would be limited to larger employers, however, leaving the majority of African populations dependent on state-provided health care.

The menu for state economic action laid out above requires active trade and industrial policies, massive investment in health and weaker fiscal discipline. Cash-transfer programmes are extraneous to this programme. This critical evaluation confirms the concerns of earlier writers about the sustainability and ethics of HIV-related cash transfers. The intrusiveness of some interventions can only justified by their potential benefits, but we have seen how limited these are. At the same time, for example, very specific ethical concerns are raised by a project which runs a lottery with a group of people who apparently struggle to evaluate risk. The use of the lottery structure in this case seems more to do with affordability than ethical or theoretical issues. Conditionality can also have (unintended) harmful consequences. For example, the CAPRISA 007 RHIVA project is intended to be conditional not only on school attendance but also good exam performance, raising the issue of whether adjustments can be made for different academic abilities. Interventions requiring a negative STI test do not always explain what happens to those who fail the test – given that curable STIs might be chosen, are participants offered treatment if they test positive? These issues become more sensitive as target groups usually start at 14. Often teenage girls are particularly at risk of acquiring HIV, but the issues of power imbalance are never clearer than when young, poor individuals are targeted.

Conclusion: choice and structure in HIV-related cash-transfer projects

Cash transfers are the latest fashion – liked by almost everyone, seemingly effective and potentially cheap. However, above, I concluded that they are far from successful in reducing HIV risk. The behavioural versions also border on the unethical, and certainly in their focus on 'faulty decision-making' they compound the stigma that is attached to HIV acquisition. The contribution of this article is twofold. It provides a critical analysis of existing cash-transfer schemes, providing a more detailed reading than previous assessments and one that recognises the limitations of RCT-generated data. Second, the article provides a radical political economy perspective on the conceptual basis for these interventions. Projects based on social work theory (and centred on the positive effects of education) may fail because they do not recognise the economic and social relations that govern the options that young people face. Projects based on poverty reduction or gender inequality have an equally narrow view. Of course, reductionism is clearest in schemes based on the libertarian paternalist version of behavioural economics. Here the reductionism underlying interventions is one that blames HIV acquisition on faulty discount rates (i.e. the inability to properly respond to HIV risk). These projects set out to change only the way that people make choices. However, a wider set of factors leading to high HIV prevalence is ignored: factors related to the economic and social relations of production. Not only are sexual norms influenced by economic and social factors, but HIV risk itself is related to wider health provisioning. The underlying causes of high levels of HIV are deeply political in nature.

Consequently, readers will not be surprised that cash-transfer projects have had such complex and limited impacts. They may be equally unsurprised that cash transfers remain so attractive to policy makers. After all, the oversimplified premise of these projects edits out politically difficult questions of power, distribution and class. As Harman (2011, 879) argues, 'Cash transfers perform key roles essential to the main paradigm of global health: they are performance oriented, show measurable results, engage in social protection and can be replicated in multiple different contexts.'

A political economy approach to HIV would instead consider the broad factors that affect patterns of intimacy, illness and health provisioning. As HIV risk is produced by these factors, we must consider how those broad factors emerge and are sustained. By recognising the need for a change in the social and economic organisation of the economy, an inherently political analysis is produced, one with very different conclusions to the menu of behaviour change interventions. However, in place of a far-reaching policy agenda to change health risks, instead we indulge in a fashion for cash transfers. Individuals, not states or markets, must change their behaviour. Cash transfers try (with limited degrees of success) to change how people act in situations where deep-seated economic and social factors have led to shockingly high HIV prevalence. Lotteries, sliding-scale transfers and other incentive schemes will be designed, implemented and evaluated – all the time avoiding the bigger, more difficult and politically sensitive questions.

Acknowledgements

I wish to thank Ben Fine and Kevin Deane for discussions on these issues, as well as anonymous reviewers for their comments. I also wish to thank participants at a workshop held in SOAS in 2012, 'The Political Economy of HIV', for their helpful comments on an early draft. All the usual disclaimers apply.

Disclosure statement

No potential conflict of interest was reported by the author.

Notes

1. There are dissenting voices. For example, see Perrey et al. (2012) for a discussion of the contro-versial construction of the public health consensus on male medical circumcision.
2. HIV incidence is a measure of the new acquisition of HIV over time in a given population. It is expensive to measure and HIV prevalence is used in its place, itself being the percentage of people (usually aged 15–49) who are HIV positive.
3. Cash transfers may be perceived to be better than standard methods where there are compounded problems of both a deeply ingrained health problem (e.g. drug addiction, overeating, alcohol abuse and smoking cessation) and the character of the target population (e.g. those with chaotic lifestyles, or suffering a range of social problems) (Medlin and de Walque 2008).
4. The discussion is related only to those projects that have publicly available evaluation material. There was no such material for the two South African projects identified. The Swa Koteka project will have its last evaluation visits only at the end of 2014, but aims to measure HIV, HSV, sexual behaviour, mental health, school outcomes, socio-economic status and other key social factors. The CAPRISA 007 RHIVA project will measure HIV incidence rates, academic performance, substance use, pregnancy rates and contraceptive use in girls, participation in extra-curricular activities and sexual behaviour.
5. There are two small-area studies of HIV incidence in South Africa that also provide relevant evi-dence – the drawback being their limited representation. Bärnighausen et al. (2007), working in one area of South Africa, reported that educational attainment reduced the hazard of HIV sero-conversion. Hargreaves et al. (2007) report on a study in another area of South Africa, finding that HIV seroconversion was negatively associated with education amongst women (but not men).

References

Baird, S. J., R. S. Garfein, C. T. McIntosh, and B. Özler. 2012. "Effect of a Cash Transfer Programme for Schooling on Prevalence of HIV and Herpes Simplex Type 2 in Malawi: A Cluster Randomised Trial." *The Lancet* 379 (9823): 1320–1329.

Bärnighausen, T., V. Hosegood, I. M. Timaeus, and M. L. Newell. 2007. "The Socioeconomic Determinants of HIV Incidence: Evidence from a Longitudinal, Population-based Study in Rural South Africa." *AIDS* 21 (7): S29–S38.

Basu, K. 2013. "The Method of Randomization, Economic Policy, and Reasoned Intuition." World Bank Policy Research Working Paper no. 6722. Washington, DC: World Bank.

Björkman-Nyqvist, M., L. Corno, D. de Walque, and J. Svensson. 2013. "Evaluating the Impact of Short Term Financial Incentives on HIV and STI Incidence among Youth in Lesotho: A Randomised Trial." *Sexually Transmitted Infections* 89 (Suppl. 1): A325. doi:10.1136/sextrans-2013–051184.1017.

Bujra, J. 2006. "Class Relations: AIDS and Socio-economic Privilege in Africa." *Review of African Political Economy* 33 (107): 113–129.

Campbell, C. 2003. *Letting Them Die*. Oxford: James Currey.

Cartwright, N., and J. Hardie. 2012. *Evidence-based Policy: A Practical Guide To Doing It Better*. New York: Oxford University Press.

CDC (Centers for Disease Control and Prevention). 1998. "HIV Prevention Through Early Detection and Treatment of Other Sexually Transmitted Diseases - United States." *Morbidity and Mortality Weekly Report* 47 (RR-12): 1–24.

Deaton, A. 2010. "Instruments, Randomization, and Learning about Development." *Journal of Economic Literature* 48(2), 424–455. doi:10.1257/jel.48.2.424.

Deci, E. L., R. Koestner, and R. M. Ryan. 1999. "A Meta-analytic Review of Experiments Examining the Effects of Extrinsic Rewards on Intrinsic Motivation." *Psychological Bulletin* 125 (6): 627–668.

Duflo, E., P. Dupas, and M. Kremer. 2012. "Education, HIV and Early Fertility: Experimental Evidence from Kenya." UCLA manuscript. Accessed March 17, 2014. http://www.stanford.edu/~pdupas/DDK_EducFertHIV.pdf

Eichler, R., R. Levine, and the Performance-based Incentives Working Group. 2009. *Performance Incentives for Global Health: Potential and Pitfalls*. Washington, DC: Center for Global Development.

Fine, B., and D. Milonakis. 2009. *From Economic Imperialism to Freakonomics: The Shifting Boundaries Between Economics and Other Social Sciences*. London; New York: Routledge.

Gaarder, M. M., A. Glassman, and J. E. Todd. 2010. "Conditional Cash Transfers and Health: Unpacking the Causal Chain." *Journal of Development Effectiveness* 2: 6–50.

Garcia-Moreno, C., and C. Watts. 2011. "Violence Against Women: An Urgent Public Health Priority." *Bulletin of the World Health Organization* 89 (1): 2–3.

Ghosh, J. 2011. "Cash Transfers as the Silver Bullet for Poverty Reduction: A Sceptical Note." *Economic and Political Weekly* 46 (21): 67–71.

Gisselquist, D. 2004. "HIV Transmission Through Health Care in Sub-Saharan Africa." *The Lancet* 364 (9446): 1665.

Hallfors, D., H. Cho, S. Rusakaniko, B. Iritani, J. Mapfumo, and C. Halpern. 2011. "Supporting Adolescent Orphan Girls to Stay in School as HIV Risk Prevention: Evidence from a Randomized Controlled Trial in Zimbabwe." *American Journal of Public Health* 101 (6): 1082–1088. doi: 10.2105/AJPH.2010.300042.

Handa, S., C. T. Halpern, A. Pettifor, and H. Thirumurthy. 2014. "The Government of Kenya's Cash Transfer Program Reduces the Risk of Sexual Debut among Young People Age 15–25." *PLoS ONE* 9 (1): e85473. doi:10.1371/journal.pone.0085473.

Harman, S. 2011. "Governing Health Risk by Buying Behaviour." *Political Studies* 59: 867–883. doi:10.1111/j.1467–9248.2011.00920.x.

Hargreaves, J. R., and L. D. Howe. 2010. "Changes in HIV Prevalence Among Differently Educated Groups in Tanzania Between 2003 and 2007." *AIDS* 24 (5): 755–761.

Hargreaves, J. R., C. Bonell, L. A. Morison, J. C. Kim, G. Phetla, J. Porter, C. Watts, and P. M. Pronyk. 2007. "Explaining Continued High HIV Prevalence in South Africa: Socioeconomic Factors, HIV Incidence and Sexual Behaviour Change Among a Rural Cohort, 2001–2004." *AIDS* 21 (7): S39–S48.

Hargreaves, J. R., C. P. Bonell, T. Boler, D. Boccia, I. Birdthistle, and A. Fletcher. 2008. "Systematic Review Exploring Time Trends in the Association Between Educational Attainment and Risk of HIV Infection in Sub-Saharan Africa." *AIDS* 22 (3): 403–414.

Heise, L., B. Lutz, M. Ranganthan, and C. Watts. 2013. "Cash Transfers for HIV Prevention: Considering their Potential." *Journal of the International Aids Society* 16: 18615. doi:10.7448/IAS.16.1.18615.

Hickel, J. 2012. "Neoliberal Plague: The Political Economy of HIV Transmission in Swaziland." *Journal of Southern African Studies* 38 (3): 513–529.

Hunter, M. 2010. *Love in the Time of AIDS: Inequality, Gender, and Rights in South Africa*. Bloomington, IN: Indiana University Press.

Johnston, D. 2013. *Economics & HIV: The Sickness of Economics*. London: Routledge.

Katz, A. 2009. "Time to Get Beyond the Sex Act: Reflections on Three Decades of AIDS Reductionism." *Social Medicine* 4 (1): 1–7.

Kohler, Hans-Peter, and Rebecca L. Thornton. 2012. "Conditional Cash Transfers and HIV/AIDS Prevention: Unconditionally Promising?" *World Bank Economic Review* 26 (2): 165–190. doi:10.1093/wber/lhr041.

Marais, H. 2005. *Buckling: The Impact of AIDS in South Africa*. Centre for the Study of AIDS, University of Pretoria. Pretoria, South Africa: University of Pretoria. Accessed December 1st, 2012. http://www.sarpn.org/documents/d0001789/index.php

Marks, S. 2007. "Science, Social Science and Pseudo-science in the HIV/AIDS Debate in Southern Africa." *Journal of Southern African Studies* 33 (4): 861–874.

Medlin, C., and D. de Walque. 2008. *Potential Applications of Conditional Cash Transfers for the Prevention of Sexually Transmitted Infections and HIV in Sub-Saharan Africa*. Human Development and Public Services Team. World Bank Policy Research Working Paper 4673.

Mishra, V., S. Bignami-Van Assche, R. Greener, M. Vaessen, R. Hong, P. Ghys, T. Ties Boerma, A. Van-Assche, S. Khan, and S. Rutstein. 2007. "HIV Infection does not Disproportionately Affect the Poorer in Sub-Saharan Africa." *AIDS* 21 (Suppl. 7): S17–S28.

O'Laughlin, B. 2013. "Land, Labour and the Production of Affliction in Rural Southern Africa." *Journal of Agrarian Change* 13 (1): 175–196. doi: 10.1111/j.1471–0366.2012.00381.x.

Parkhurst, J. 2010. "Understanding the Correlations between Wealth, Poverty and Human Immunodeciency Virus Infection in African Countries." *Bulletin of the World Health Organization* 88: 519–526.

Perrey, C., A. Giami, K. R. de Camargo, and A. de Oliveira Mendonça. 2012. "De la recherche scientifique à la recommandation de santé publique: la circoncision masculine dans le champ de la prévention du VIH." *Sciences sociales et santé* 30 (1): 5–38.

Pettifor, A., C. MacPhail, N. Nguyen, and M. Rosenberg. 2012. "Can Money Prevent the Spread of HIV? A Review of Cash Payments for HIV Prevention." *AIDS and Behavior* 16 (7): 1729–1738. doi:10.1007/s10461-012-0240-z.

Ranganathan, M., and M. Lagarde. 2012. "Promoting Healthy Behaviours and Improving Health Outcomes in Low and Middle Income Countries: A Review of the Impact of Conditional Cash Transfer Programmes." *Preventive Medicine* 55: S95–S105.

Rigsby, M. O., M. I. Rosen, J. E. Beauvais, J. A. Cramer, P. M. Rainey, S. S. O'Malley, K. D. Dieckhaus, B. J. Rounsaville. 2000. "Cue-dose Training with Monetary Reinforcement: Pilot Study of an Antiretroviral Adherence Intervention." *Journal of General Internal Medicine* 15 (12): 841–847.

Ruel, M. T., and H. Alderman. 2013. "Nutrition-sensitive Interventions and Programmes: How can they Help to Accelerate Progress in Improving Maternal and Child Nutrition?" *The Lancet* 382 (9891): 536–551.

Stillwaggon, E. 2006. "Reducing Environmental Risk to Prevent HIV Transmission in Sub-Saharan Africa." *Africa Policy Journal* 1: 36–56.

Stuckler, D., S. Basu, and M. McKee. 2010. "Governance of Mining, HIV and Tuberculosis in Southern Africa." *Global Health Governance* 4 (1). Online. Accessed December 1, 2012. http://blogs.shu.edu/ghg/files/2011/11/Stuckler-Basu-andMcKee_Governance-of-Mining-HIV-and-Tuberculosis-in-Southern-Africa_Fall-2010.pdf.

Thaler, R. H., and C. R. Sunstein. 2008. *Nudge: Improving Decisions About Health, Wealth, and Happiness*. London: Penguin Books.

UNAIDS. 2010. *2010 Report on the Global AIDS Epidemic*. Geneva: UNAIDS.

UNAIDS. 2011. *Game-changing Year: 2011*. UNAIDS Briefing. [online] Accessed November 25, 2012 //www.unaids.org/en/resources/multimediacentre/videos/20111213pcb/

UNAIDS. 2013. *Global Report: UNAIDS Report on the Global AIDS Epidemic 2013*. Geneva: UNAIDS.

UNAIDS and Lancet Commission. 2013. "An Opportunity to Make Things New." Report from first meeting of 'The UNAIDS and Lancet Commission: Defeating AIDS – Advancing Global Health', 28–29 June 2013, Lilongwe, Malawi. Accessed February18, 2014. http://www.unaids.org/en/resources/documents/2013/name,82120,en.asp.

de Walque, D., W. H. Dow, C. Medlin, and R. Nathan. 2012a. "Stimulating Demand for AIDS Prevention: Lessons from the RESPECT Trail." National Bureau of Economic Research (NBER) working paper 17865. Cambridge, MA: NBER. Accessed February18, 2014. http://www.nber.org/papers/w17865.

de Walque, D., W. H. Dow, R. Nathan, and R. Abdul. 2012b. "Incentivising Safe Sex: A Randomised Trial of Conditional Cash Transfers for HIV and Sexually Transmitted Infection Prevention in Rural Tanzania." *BMJ Open* 2 (e000747). doi:10.1136/bmjopen-2011–000747.

Watts, C., and Zimmerman, C. 2002. "Violence Against Women: Global Scope and Magnitude." *The Lancet,* 359: 1232–1237.

Whiteside, A. 2005. "The Economic, Social, and Political Drivers of the AIDS Epidemic in Swaziland: A Case Study." In *The African State and the AIDS Crisis*, edited by A. S. Patterson, 97–125. Aldershot, UK and Burlington, VT: Ashgate Publishing.

WHO (World Health Organization). 2010. *Preventing Intimate Partner and Sexual Violence Against Women: Taking Action and Generating Evidence*. Geneva: World Health Organization/London School of Hygiene and Tropical Medicine.

WHO. 2012a. *The Strategic Use of Antiretrovirals to Help End the HIV Epidemic*. Discussion paper for the 2012 International AIDS conference.

WHO. 2012b. *Voluntary Medical Male Circumcision for HIV Prevention*. Fact sheet: July 2012. [online] Accessed September 7, 2012. http://www.who.int/hiv/topics/malecircumcision/fact_sheet/en/index.html.

Wojcicki, J. M. 2005. "Socioeconomic Status as a Risk Factor for HIV Infection in Women in East, Central and Southern Africa: A Systematic Review." *Journal of Biosocial Science* 37 (1): 1–36.

Exploring the complexity of microfinance and HIV in fishing communities on the shores of Lake Malawi

Eleanor MacPherson, John Sadalaki, Victoria Nyongopa, Lawrence Nkhwazi, Mackwellings Phiri, Alinafe Chimphonda, Nicola Desmond, Victor Mwapasa, David G. Lalloo, Janet Seeley and Sally Theobald

This study utilised qualitative research methodology to explore female fish traders' experiences of accessing microfinance in fishing communities in southern Malawi. Microfinance is a tool that has been used to alleviate poverty. People living in fishing communities in the Global South are at an increased risk of HIV and, equally, microfinance has been identified as a tool to prevent HIV. The authors' research found consistent testimonies of overly short microfinance loan-repayment periods, enforced by the threat of property confiscation. These threats, coupled with gendered power dynamics and the unpredictability of fish catches, left some female fish traders vulnerable to HIV.

[Exploration de la complexité de la microfinance et du VIH dans les communautés de pêcheurs sur les bords du lac Malawi.] Cette étude a utilisé une méthodologie de recherche qualitative pour analyser les expériences des négociantes en poissons en matière d'accès à la microfinance dans les communautés de pêcheurs dans le sud du Malawi. La microfinance est un outil qui a été utilisé pour éradiquer la pauvreté. Les personnes vivant dans les communautés de pêcheurs dans les pays du Sud sont exposés fortement au VIH, et la microfinance a été identifiée comme un outil pour empêcher la diffusion du VIH. Les recherches des auteurs aboutissent à des témoignages concordants attestant de périodes de remboursement de prêts de microfinance excessivement courtes, imposées par la menace de confiscation des biens. Ces menaces, en plus des dynamiques de pouvoir en vigueur entre les genres et de l'imprévisibilité des captures de poissons, aboutissent à une vulnérabilité accrue de certaines négociantes en poissons face au VIH.

Introduction

Since the 1980s, microfinance[1] (MF) has become the international community's most prevalent development tool to alleviate poverty in the Global South. Microfinance usually involves the offering of small loans to poor households that have been excluded from the formal banking system because they lack collateral and are therefore deemed to be too high-risk to receive loans (Morduch 2000). The underlying logic of providing financial services to poor people is that this will result in improved capacity to manage money and result in greater investment, acquisition of productive assets and increased development of skills and knowledge (van Rooyen, Stewart, and de Wet 2012).

Microfinance programmes are among the most well-funded development interventions and there have been ambitious claims about the far-reaching impact MF can make on their loan recipients' lives (Visvanathan and Yoder 2011). There is a vast academic literature dedicated to the analysis of microfinance programmes and assessment of their impact on outcomes including poverty, health and well-being, and empowerment (Banerjee et al. 2013; Holvoet 2005; Karlan and Valdivia 2011; Korth et al. 2012; Mersland and Strøm 2010; van Rooyen, Stewart, and de Wet 2012). Microfinance programmes have penetrated almost all regions of the globe but are especially concentrated in the poorest countries of the world, particularly in South Asia and sub-Saharan Africa. Recent academic work that has systematically reviewed the impact of microfinance programmes has found very limited evidence to support many of the ambitious claims made by the microfinance industry (van Rooyen, Stewart, and de Wet 2012). Further, studies have demonstrated the range of negative impacts microfinance can have on loan recipients and at the broader community level (Bateman and Chang 2012).

While there is considerable diversity in the operating practices of microfinance pro-grammes, they often have a number of common features. The first is the practice of group lending, where group members assume the responsibility for repaying the whole loan – this has also been referred to as 'joint liability' (Marr 2012). Second, the grace period between signing the loan agreement and first loan repayment or compulsory saving deposit is typically very short (usually within 2 to 4 weeks). Finally, groups may only graduate to take a subsequent, larger loan once they have successfully completed repayments on their first loan (Sengupta and Aubuchon 2008).

There has been a vast literature dedicated to this work in a number of academic fields. These include international development, gender studies and HIV. To frame our research, we discuss the academic debates about microfinance and women's empowerment, microfi-nance and sub-Saharan Africa, and finally microfinance as a tool to prevent HIV.

Microfinance, women's empowerment and HIV prevention

Globally, the majority of microfinance recipients are women. Microfinance organisations have made ambitious claims regarding the power of microfinance to achieve women's empowerment and poverty alleviation (Mayoux 1999; Visvanathan and Yoder 2011), although academic researchers have often contested these claims. Claims relating to women's empowerment are built on the argument that provision of financial services to poor women (including loans and opportunities for saving) will enable women to generate or support self-employment (Johnson 2005). Further, it is anticipated that the money that women generate through this employment will enhance their role in household decision-making, as well as increasing confidence to negotiate with partners (Johnson 2005; Pan-khurst 2002). The group-based nature of microfinance programmes is also seen as provid-ing women with an opportunity to participate in a wider social network, foster engagement in political activities and provide the opportunity for social change (Kalpana 2011; Pan-khurst 2002).

Despite these laudable aims, a growing body of academic work has challenged the val-idity of microfinance organisations' claims of success in achieving poverty alleviation and empowerment (Cornwall and Edwards 2010; Goetz and Gupta 1996; Kalpana 2011; Mayoux 1999; Pankhurst 2002; Rahman 1999). Visvanathan and Yoder (2011) suggest that microfinance organisations may promote empowerment without sufficiently emphasising either transformation of dynamics within the household, or the social and cultural structures that perpetrate inequality. Cornwall and Edwards (2010) argue that women's empowerment is a complex process that requires more than one simple intervention. In short, by focusing on the individual as a means of overcoming poverty, microfinance programmes fail to address the broader structural factors (both at the local as well as the international levels) that drive poverty and gender imbalances at the household and community levels (Pankhurst 2002).

Further, a number of studies have questioned whether microfinance may actually be harmful for women. Empirical studies mainly undertaken in South Asia have reported disempowering outcomes for female recipients of microfinance. Goetz and Gupta (1996) found that a significant proportion of women's loans were controlled by male relatives in households in Bangladesh. The authors also argued that the preoccupation with 'credit performance', measured primarily in terms of high repayment rates, affects the incentives of fieldworkers dispensing and recovering credit in ways that may outweigh concerns to ensure that women develop meaningful control over their investment activities.

One of the central aims of microfinance organisations is to alleviate poverty in developing countries. However, Matin and Hulme (2003) show that microfinance frequently fails to reach the poorest members of the communities in which they work. This may be a policy that is actively encouraged by some MF organisations because the poorest groups may be less likely to repay their loans (*Ibid.*). Matin and Hulme (2003) also note that microfinance might not be most suitable for the poorest groups. They argue that for households who are trapped in chronic food insecurity and who lack the asset base to protect themselves from shocks to their income and food supply, 'microfinance can be ineffective and sometimes counterproductive' (653). These findings are further supported by Bateman and Chang (2012), who review the impact of microfinance on recipients. They argue that the microfinance model can lock people and communities in a poverty trap and has had catastrophic outcomes in a growing number of microfinance-statured countries such as Bangladesh and some states of India (*Ibid.*).

Rahman (1999) found that the need for timely repayment in loan centres in Bangladesh led to MF loan officers and other lending-group members placing intense pressure on female clients. Many of the borrowers maintained regular repayment through loan recycling that led to considerable increases in the debt liability of the individual households. This in turn led to an increase in tension and frustration in the household and violence against female members (*Ibid.*). Bateman and Chang (2012) presented the case of the Indian state of Andhra Pradesh, where poor households in the state were on average in possession of a total of 9.3 microloans. Households took out loans to cover the repayment of earlier microloans. This led in late 2010 to what the authors describe as 'Andhra Pradesh's microfinance industry effectively collaps[ing]' (16).

Kabeer (2001), however, challenges some of the negative findings relating to women in microfinance programmes (such as those presented in Goetz and Gupta 1996). In her study, which used qualitative and participatory methods, she found that women's access to loans gave them the support to improve their bargaining position within the household.

As noted earlier, much of the research exploring the impact of MF programmes on women's empowerment has been conducted in South Asia. Many feminist scholars have noted that gender power relations are context-specific and there are differences in the social norms that govern women's and men's behaviour in sub-Saharan Africa and South

Asia. These different social norms are likely to have an impact on how men and women can use the loans.

In one study exploring the impact of MF in a range of African countries, Mayoux (1999) argues that the impact of MF in Africa has been mixed. Mayoux used mostly unpublished secondary data analysis from microfinance programmes and her own exploratory research to understand the impact of microfinance on women's empowerment. In this study, African women were generally more widely involved in production and market activities than women in South Asia, and this meant they were more likely to retain and use their own income. The pre-existence of well-developed networks between women meant that microfinance did not necessarily make a considerable contribution to women's social empowerment, as was seen in South Asian programmes. Finally, Mayoux raised the criticism that microfinance programmes in Africa have been far more concerned with financial sustainability than with achieving a broader impact on women's empowerment. This also suggests that the model of microfinance was exported from South Asia to sub-Saharan Africa with very little involvement of local women and men and limited discussion of context. It also means that the design of these programmes could fail to reflect the reality of the lives of participants receiving the loans.

Kabeer (2005) argues that the debate over microfinance has been divided, with those who have an evangelistic zeal for promoting its use being matched by the outright rejection by its opponents. In reality, Kabeer argues that the impact of microfinance is like any development resource and 'represents a range of possibilities, rather than a predetermined set of outcomes' (4709). Kabeer also states that the impact of microfinance is dependent on a wide range of factors including:

> the philosophy that governs their delivery, the extent to which they are tailored to the needs and interests of those they are intended to reach, the nature of the relationships which govern their delivery and – that most elusive of all developmental inputs – the calibre and commitment of the people who are responsible for delivery. (4709)

In the field of HIV prevention there has been an increased focus on the potential MF programmes have to prevent HIV (Dworkin and Blankenship 2009; Kim and Watts 2005). The rationale for this argument is based on the claims that MF programmes automatically empower women. Women's economic dependence on their sexual partner has been identified as a key vulnerability to HIV. This is because women and girls who are economically dependent on their sexual partners have been found to be more likely to engage in sexually risky situations, less likely to leave abusive relationships, more likely to exchange sex for material goods and less able to negotiate safer sex (Dunkle et al. 2004a, 2004b; Dworkin and Blankenship 2009; Epstein 2007). These are all factors that have been identified to increase women's and girls' vulnerability to HIV. Therefore, central to the claim that MF might be a tool that prevents HIV is that if MF provides women with an alternative form of income they will become less dependent on their male partners (Dworkin and Blankenship 2009). In the field of public health, structural interventions (interventions that alter the broader risk environment rather than focusing on the individual behaviour change) have taken a greater prominence particularly in relation to HIV (Seeley et al. 2012). In two countries with very high HIV prevalence, South Africa and Zimbabwe, interventions that use microfinance have been trialled to identify whether microfinance could prevent HIV, the rationale being that MF can support change in the broader social environment by economically empowering women and therefore preventing HIV. The IMAGE Study, which used MF combined with gender training, was conducted in mining communities in rural

South Africa, and found a reduction in gender-based violence but no impact on reductions in HIV transmission. A article based on these findings was published in the *Lancet* (Pronyk et al. 2006). The SHAZ Study, based in Harare, was conducted with young female orphans and combined gender training with microfinance. The study took place in 2004, when Zimbabwe was facing a severe economic crisis and the provision of microfinance loans to this vulnerable group 'increased participants' exposure to physical harm, sexual abuse and coercion' (Dunbar et al. 2010, 158).

Fishing communities, HIV vulnerability and the rationale for this study

Fishing communities in the Global South have been identified as a group particularly vulnerable to HIV (Kissling et al. 2005; Kwena et al. 2013; Tumwesigye et al. 2012). In Malawi, fishermen have also been identified as a group with higher risk of HIV, with prevalence estimates for this group standing at 16.6% (Government of Malawi 2006, 2009). This is higher than the national prevalence rate that stands at 11.7%. Further, in the lakeside district of Mangochi, where the study was situated, prevalence stands at 13.1%, which is higher than other rural Malawian districts.

There are a number of factors that have been identified in the fishing industry particularly in eastern Africa that drive this vulnerability. Fishing often requires frequent travel, both for the men who catch the fish as well as for the men and women who buy, process and sell the fish at markets (Kwena et al. 2013; Seeley, Tumwekwase, and Grosskurth 2009). Travel can lead to men and women having additional sexual partners (for men this is often sex workers, whilst for women this often involves transactional sexual partnerships and receipt of some material benefit). Travel is often combined with high levels of alcohol consumption, which can lead to risky sex (Tumwesigye et al. 2012). However, it is important to note that not all travel leads to higher HIV risk (Deane, Parkhurst, and Johnston 2010). Fishing communities are often located in hard-to-reach areas with poor access to health services and the high levels of mobility can make fisherfolk's ability to access services including HIV testing and treatment services challenging (Seeley and Allison 2005).

Gendered power dynamics also play an important role in shaping vulnerability to HIV. In Malawian fishing communities (like in many other fishing communities in Africa), activities are often highly gendered with men undertaking the fishing and women negotiating access to fish through men. When fish catches are low and competition for fish is high, women engage in sex-for-fish exchanges with fishermen to ensure they have access to fish (MacPherson et al. 2012; Nagoli, Holvoet, and Remme 2010). To date there have been no studies that have explored the role of MF in fishing communities in the Global South. This gap needs to be interrogated to fully understand the opportunities and challenges that are posed by MF in this context.

The primary research objective of this study was to understand how microfinance shaped female fish traders' vulnerability to HIV in two fishing communities in southern Malawi.

Methods

In Malawi, 23% of the land is covered with water (Government of Malawi 2007). Given the large bodies of fresh water covering Malawi's land, fish and the fisheries sector play an important role in providing employment, nutrition and income to Malawians. This study was based in two villages on the southern arm of Lake Malawi in Mangochi District, which is situated in the Southern Region of Malawi. Despite the wide body of water covering Malawi, fishing activities are concentrated in Mangochi District (Hara 2008) because the shallow water found in this area facilitates fish breeding (Darwall and Allison 2002). The Food and Agriculture Organization of the UN estimated that in 2003, 30% of all livelihoods in Mangochi were in the fishing industry (the most recent data the authors could identify). Both villages were selected because of the large fish-landing sites that are situated within the boundaries of the village. Many of the people living in the villages were heavily involved in fishing. However, the presence of large landing sites for boats meant that there was large inward and outward migration of people working within the fishing industry.

As noted above, the HIV prevalence rate in Malawi stands at 11.7%. In keeping with prevalence trends in other southern and eastern African countries, young women are particularly vulnerable to HIV, with the prevalence among women aged 15–19 standing at 4% compared with less than 1% for men of the same age (National Statistical Office 2005).

The dominant form of fishing within the two study villages is *kauni*,[2] which is focused on catching *usipa*, a small cichlid fish. This type of small-scale fishing requires an engine boat, a crew of 10 men, three to four dug-out canoes, lanterns and nets, and takes place at night.[3] The fishing industry in Malawi, like many other countries, is highly gendered with men undertaking the fishing and women buying, processing and selling fish at market. In this role female fish traders are highly mobile, travelling from beaches across the district to access fish, drying them either in their homesteads or in the area they have purchased the fish in, then travelling to the market to sell the fish (MacPherson et al. 2012). Female fish traders need to build and maintain capital for their fish-trading business and spoke frequently of the challenges they face in maintaining their funds (*Ibid.*). The capital is primarily required to buy fish and pay for the transportation (both for themselves to the different beaches and for the fish to the markets once it had been processed). Even when women are able to access capital they often face the challenge of securing access. Social norms within the villages prevent women from undertaking the fishing and therefore any access women have to fish has to be negotiated through men (*Ibid.*). Throughout the process of buying and selling fish, female fish traders face a great deal of economic risk and uncertainty. One key way female fish traders mitigate is through developing sexual relationships with men that can help secure them access to fish (*Ibid.*). Given the transient nature of the fishing communities, these are often transient relationships (particularly for divorced or widowed women).

The men physically undertaking the fishing are often young and socially marginalised. They also face a great deal of danger in their work. This includes the risk of drowning because fishing expeditions usually take place at night and men can and do fall into the water and can be lost quickly, especially when there are strong currents in the lake. The fishing expeditions often entail their spending long periods away from their home villages (sleeping on the beach or in cramped living conditions). Young fishermen are often paid in cash for their work and in poor rural villages this can provide the men with power; they can at times exploit this power by paying women to have sex with them (either for money or fish).

Fish catches in the villages are very unpredictable during the rainy season and winter months. At these times strong winds can prevent the fishing boats from undertaking expeditions, thus limiting the amount of fish that can be caught. During the periods of the month when there was a full moon, the fishing boats did not sail. This means the *usipa* fish trade is subject to temporal and seasonal variation, which can lead to very unpredictable supply. In this situation, even very successful female fish traders face competition with other female fish traders to access fish during periods of low fish catches. This is further exacerbated by the overall decline in fish stocks that Malawi has been experiencing particularly in the last two decades (Jamu et al. 2011).

The topic of this paper emerged out of a larger study exploring gender power relations in fishing communities in southern Malawi and how these relations shaped women's and men's vulnerability to HIV (MacPherson et al. 2012). Throughout the data collection, a wide range of participants (both men and women) discussed both the challenges and benefits of microfinance for women working in the fishing industry. Some participants linked it to providing women with economic independence from their male partners. But others discussed how microfinance created economic vulnerability and put women at risk of HIV. We therefore conducted a second period of data collection that explored women's and men's experiences of using microfinance and how this shaped their lives including their vulnerability to HIV. We focused on female fish traders, as they were a group who had discussed the benefits and the challenges of accessing MF and using it within their businesses. The study used qualitative research methods including in-depth interviews, focus group discussion and structured observation.[4] Qualitative research methods were used because they allow data to be collected in participants' own words (Pope and Mays 1995). The interviews and focus groups were conducted with four research assistants (two men and two women). We used a purposive sampling frame with the aim of capturing the experiences of a range of groups (Lewis 2003). The groups included were older and younger women and men working in the fishing industry and borrowing from a range of microfinance organisations operating in the two villages.

This study ran from January 2011 until April 2012 and had two periods of data collection (January 2011–October 2011 and March–April 2012). In total we conducted 64 interviews and 18 focus groups with a range of participants working inside and outside the fishing industry. For the second period of data collection, we conducted in-depth interviews with 12 additional participants (8 women and 4 men). We conducted one or two interviews with each participant, following up and holding a second interview with participants if we felt there were subsequent questions to explore further.

We purposefully sampled female and male individuals who had received a loan from a range of microfinance organisations. Table 1 provides an overview of the demographic information about the participants we interviewed in the second series of in-depth interviews. None of the real names of participants were used and instead we assigned them a pseudonym. We used the framework approach to analysis the data.[5]

The timing of the fieldwork coincided with a period of time when the Malawian government was struggling to access foreign exchange. The limited access to foreign exchange meant fuel was very difficult to access and the cost of transportation and living costs became very expensive (Cammack 2012). This crisis was due in part to the increasingly autocratic style of President Bingu wa Mutharika, which led to the international donor community freezing large amounts of aid being delivered to the Malawian government. The Malawian economy was facing a severe crisis, however it is important to view these events in context. The Malawian economy is heavily reliant on international aid and commodities such as tobacco and tea which often provide small economic returns, and prices can be unpredictable. The current president, Joyce Banda, is now facing corruption charges and the international community has again suspended aid (Mapondera 2014). There have also been severe food shortages, for instance in 2002 when Malawi faced a famine with hundreds of people dying owing to shortages of maize (the staple diet in Malawi) (Devereux 2002). These events suggest worrying trends in the Malawian social and political context which also suggest that our period of data collection may, sadly, not be unique. In the interviews we asked participants to reflect on their use of microfinance

Table 1. Demographic information relating to microfinance in-depth interviews.

Interview code	Demographic information
M1 Rachel	Female, 30–35, Tumbuka, Anglican, divorced from husband for second time, fish trader, sold fish at distant markets, dropped out of school in S (Standard) 8
M2 Mary	Female, 50–55, Tonga, CAP, widowed in 2005 (married twice), fish trader, sold fish at distant markets, dropped out of school in S4
M3 Marvellous	Female, 30–35, Tonga, CAP, married for a second time still with her husband, a fisherman, trades fish, sold fish at distant market, dropped out of school in S7
M4 Maureen	Female, 36–40, Tonga, Holy Pentecostal Church, widowed and then divorced, trades fish, sells at distant markets, dropped out of school in S8
M5 Annie	Female, 30–35, Chewa, Anglican, married, fish trader, sells fish at distant markets, usually accesses fish from her husband's boat, dropped out of school in S6
M6 Irene	Female, 45–50, Tumbuka, divorced female fish trader (second time), fish trader at distant markets, dropped out of school at S8
M7 Brenda	Female, 30–35, Tonga, Anglican, married but husband left for South Africa in 2008, undertakes small-scale fish trading, dropped out of school in S6
M8 Alinafe	Female, 40–45, Tonga, married for second time, female fish trader, traded larger fresh fish not smaller dried fish, parents owned boats and fishing gear and are well connected, dropped out of school in S8
M9 Gracious	Male, 35–40, Tumbuka, African International Church, married for a second time, fishes and trades fish using MF loan, dropped out of school in Form 3
M10 Richard	Male, 30–35, Tonga, married for second time, fish trader who works with his wife, completed school and trained as an engineer
M11 Wickson	Male, 25–30, Lomwe, CCAP, carpenter and fish trader, married, left school in secondary Form 4
M12 Gift	Male, 35–40, Tumbuka, male fish trader (although also butcher and landlord), married for a second time, completed school

Note: CAP and CCAP are Christian church groupings.

loans over a longer period of time. None of the participants we interviewed were new to borrowing from MF organisations and we therefore do not believe that the results we present are only due to the wider crisis.

Findings

In the following sections we present the findings from this study around three themes: presence of microfinance in the village and the key groups they lent money to; the challenges and opportunities participants faced using microfinance; and how the unpredictability of the fishing industry, the short repayment time frames and threat of property confiscation increased some female fish traders' vulnerability to HIV.

In the two villages, participants identified eight organisations that were currently operating or had previously operated in the villages. Of these, participants most frequently discussed five organisations. Participants perceived the organisations to have slightly different procedures in terms of repayment, saving, deposit required to take the loan, loan size, interest rates and timing for distribution of the loan and these differences are outlined in Table 2. To ensure anonymity of the participants we have not included the names of the MF organisations.

In all the discussions relating to microfinance, participants reported borrowing money in groups rather than as individuals. Participants discussed joining MF organisations in groups of between 10 and 20 and receiving the loan together on the same day. The group then

Table 2.   Reported differences between microfinance organisations.

Organisation	Reported differences

Lender A	Repayment within two weeks of loan disbursement
	    Deposit required
	    Progressively larger loan sizes
	    Viewed to have high interest rates and less flexibility
	    Savings kept within the organisation
	    Provided loans to women and men (although majority women)
	    Non-governmental organisation (NGO)

Lender B	Were seen to be more flexible with a three-month lag between the loan and the first repayment
	    Perceived to have lower interest rates than Lender A
	    Provided smaller loans
	    Slower to distribute the money
	    Hard for participants to get subsequent loans quickly
	    NGO

Lender C	Monthly repayments
	    Seen as requiring a larger deposit
	    Participants discussed losing this deposit when their groups were unable to make the repayments
	    Government owned and run

Lender D	Provides a grace period of approximately a month and a half before repayments began
	    No flexibility once repayments had begun
	    Allowed participants to gain larger loans once they had successfully repaid
	    Provided loans to both male and female participants
	    NGO

Lender E	Only lend to women
	    Repayment due every two weeks
	    Viewed as having higher interest rates
	    NGO

assumed responsibility for repaying the whole loan rather than just their own portion of the money.

All the participants we interviewed who received loans were involved in fish trading. For the female participants, this was their primary mode of income generation although some would use the profits to buy tomatoes or beans and sell them in their local area. All the female participants discussed travelling to buy and sell fish. They often travelled to markets further than their home areas. Male participants also had other businesses that they developed in addition to fish trading. These businesses included carpentry, butchery, and building and renting dwellings in the village.

Participants saw women as the preferred target group for microfinance organisations and they were the group most likely to have taken out a loan. This reflects a number of studies which note women are the primary target for MF loans (Kulkarni 2011; Sengupta and Aubuchon 2008). The male participants we interviewed were all in the minority in their loan groups. One central reason that participants felt the MF organisations focused their activities on women was that they trusted women, but not men, to repay loans. Participants discussed how men could be untrustworthy with money for a number of reasons. Men, particularly fishermen, were not viewed as being serious about the loans and could use them for spending time at the bar drinking and having sex with sex workers. The highly mobile nature of many of the fishing activities meant men could be away from home for long periods of time, which could prevent them from repaying the loan. These views were also reflected in the broader community perceptions about men. Men, particularly young men, who travelled to fish were seen by many participants as being particularly untrustworthy with money. Women and men in the communities discussed how there was a culture of spending on drinking and women rather than on household needs.

Instead women discussed how they were the ones who were viewed as having to use their fish-trading businesses to provide food for the family. Men who went out fishing often faced high levels of risk in their everyday activities. In other studies this has been seen as a reason why fishermen spend more money on sex workers when they travelled (Allison and Seeley 2004).

In the following, Gracious discusses why men were not viewed as trustworthy to receive a loan:

> P: Also, women are the ones mostly interested to do business. That's why they are also mostly involved in taking loans from organizations. Also, most of the organizations trust women more than men. They feel we men are crooks so they prefer women to men.
> I: What do they exactly mean when they say men are crooks?
> P: They say men are crooks because a man could take a loan today and suddenly start thinking about going to a bar to drink. So, as you go out to drink, you will realise you have spent half of the money. But women can't take money to a bar, no. [When they have received a loan], they will directly bring it home. (In-depth interview [IDI], Gracious)

In the quote Gracious is discussing the justification that has been provided by microfinance organisations as to why their activities focused on women and not men.

To overcome this barrier, participants reported that men would use their wives to access the loan and then they took control of the loan for their business. In the following quote Gracious discusses how some men use their wives as a way of overcoming this barrier of access:

> Also, in other households, there are husbands who ask their wives to go and take a loan. They don't want the public to know that they are taking a loan, but they mutually agree in the house that the wife should go and take a loan. (IDI, Gracious)

In this situation the male fish trader described a process that was undertaken with mutual consent. However, evidence from interviews also suggested that in some cases men could pressure women into taking loans on their behalf and then leave them with the responsibility of repaying.

Procedures for repaying the loans

One aspect of the group formation that arose consistently during interviews was that groups required members to register their household property at the start of the loan cycle. Some of the participants discussed groups appointing an auditor to confirm that the property they had registered was in their possession and that it was worth what the participant had claimed it to be. Participants reported registering items such as livestock, kitchen utensils, bedding and furniture. The purpose of this property registration was that if the participants were unable to repay their loans the group could confiscate the property and sell it to recover the money.

Another component of the group formation that participants discussed was the process of vouching for another member. As discussed earlier, there is a high level of inward and outward migration to the villages. Unlike in more stable rural populations, there were often women (and men) wanting to join groups who were not known to the other members. If this scenario occurred, one group member would be asked to vouch for the new member. By vouching for the person they were agreeing to repay the loan, either with money or with the property they had registered. Usually a friend or relative vouched for new members.

The microfinance organisations did not seem to be involved in this process and instead it was the group's members who came up with their own practices for running the groups. However, it did appear that the loan officers were aware of property registrations because some of the participants reported providing the loan officer with written copies of these forms. Also, given how consistently this practice came up, it is likely that the loan officers who worked directly with the groups encouraged the practice. Participants also described at the beginning of the loan cycles being told that they could face arrest by the police if they did not repay their loans. Lamia Karim also discusses the practice of registering property at the commencement of the loan in her monograph documenting microfinance policy and practice in Bangladesh (Karim 2011). In her fieldwork she describes how she witnessed managers within the microfinance organisation compiling these lists and justifying their use by saying that this is a bank and part of ensuring their bank received its money back. This suggests that the policy may be part of broader MF practice.

Experiences of taking and repaying a loan

Participants provided complex narratives around their experiences of taking loans. Some participants found the experience positive but others found it very challenging. While none of the participants reported overwhelmingly positive experiences with microfinance, there were a number of participants who felt their lives had been improved by taking the loans. Examples included the loans allowing them to grow their businesses and improve the economic position of their households, including allowing them to pay for their children's school fees, buy clothes and food, and in some cases build houses. For this reason participants often expressed gratitude at being able to access loans. In the quote below Rachel discusses how MF loans have helped her:

> Borrowing money has helped me. As I don't have a mother or a husband, the money from the organization is what is helping me. It is serving as my mother, father and husband. It assists me in everything I do. (IDI, Rachel)

Rachel discusses using microfinance loans in very positive terms. We have included it because it is illustrative of the high esteem in which some (although not all) participants held microfinance organisations and the personal connections they felt they had with the organisations. The quote also reflects that some female participants felt that microfinance provided economic support when this was absent in their lives. Rachel also went on to discuss how access to loans provided her with financial freedom from male sexual partners and stopped her from engaging in what she termed 'promiscuous behaviour' as a means of accessing money. The positive accounts some female fish traders provided of the MF have been found in other settings. Bauchet et al. (2011) argue that MF can sometimes help loan recipients. However this is dependent on whether the client is able to actually make a profit from the loan (*Ibid.*). A final way that women felt they gained from microfinance was the group aspect of the loans. Some (again, not all) of the participants reported gaining solidarity from being part of the groups. Mary felt that borrowing as a group enabled women to learn good business practices from the other group members.

While participants did speak positively about having access to microfinance loans, there were consistent testimonies from female fish traders that the loans increased economic vulnerability. This economic vulnerability was shaped by both the administration of the loans and the unpredictable nature of the fishing industry. Women faced hierarchies of access where wealthier and socially better connected female fish traders had more secure access to fish. Women who were poor or had fewer social connections found access harder. Processing fish could be challenging particularly during the rainy season, when fish could rot on the drying benches. Traders also faced challenges with realising profit at the market. Hence in this context microfinance was able to temporarily provide women and men with better access to business capital but it did not change the broader structures and gendered inequalities that existed within the fishing industry.

Further, microfinance could at times make fish traders' livelihood strategies more stressful and difficult. The 'grace period', the time between MF organisations providing participants with a loan and the participant having to repay the loan, was very short. For female fish traders, negotiating access to fish, processing it and then selling it were all time-consuming activities. Each point in this process could be time-consuming and fraught with potential challenges. The tight deadlines and the looming fear of property confiscation meant that the microfinance loans placed incredible pressure on fish traders to make a profit. Women also reported that when loans were given to a large number of people in the community on the same day or very close in time, this also increased the competition between fish traders. The increased competition, particularly between female fish traders who struggled to gain access, could drive the price of fish higher. This inflation of prices could mean women struggled to make a profit, particularly if they ended up paying more than they were able to realise at the market. The precarious nature of making profit in the fishing industry could be further exacerbated by the presence of microfinance loans.

In the following quote, the challenges of selling fish at the market are described by this 28-year-old bartender and boat crew member. He emphasises how he saw this affected female fish traders' ability to repay their loans:

> It is true ... fish catches these days change from time to time. They could buy fish but they find the market full of fish when they get there. They also find the price lower than the price at which they bought the fish. When they come back to buy more fish, they find that the price has also gone up. With this, the loan cannot benefit you. Some of them end up having their property forfeited because you initially consent to give your property should you fail to repay the loan. (Focus group discussion, male bartender/boat crew member, 25–30, Chewa, married, dropped out of school in Form 2)

Lender A's very short repayment policies were the most often cited as creating challenges for participants. They required participants to start repaying the loan within two weeks after receiving it and this could create problems, especially during periods of low fish catches. In the following quote a 54-year-old female fish trader described receiving a loan and being unable to repay it because there were low fish catches:

> I once joined Lender A but what was happening was at the time I took the loan there was no catches throughout that time. My children were going to school they needed fees so I just used some of the money I took from Lender A. After some days you hear that Lender A personnel they need the money from us so I just decided to quit Lender A because I was having problems. (IDI, female fish trader and collects firewood, 50–55, Tonga, divorced, dropped out of school at S2)

This was not the only participant who discussed using the loan for household expenses such as school fees and food rather than developing their business. When fish catches were low, some fish traders would use the loan for immediate household expenses that they needed to pay and were then unable to use the loan for income-generation activities, making it difficult to repay the loan. Some participants discussed how these short repayment periods made them feel that taking a loan was not helping them to improve their financial situation or support their families, and at times made them poorer (because of the high interest rates that the organisations charged). If the microfinance organisations were slow to distribute the loan then participants also struggled to access fish. The quote below, taken from a focus group with male fish traders, highlights how some microfinance organisations would be unpredictable:

> Sometimes you plan to get a loan during a period of high fish catches but they [the microfinance organisation] release very late. They release the loan when the season has passed. You feel happy just because you have received the loan but you can't use it for business that time. After three weeks of getting the loan, you are expected to start repaying the loan, but there is no fish to buy. It becomes painful. (Focus group discussion, male boat crew member/fish trader, 35–40, Tumbuka, married, dropped out of school in S6)

As can be seen in the quote above, in the fishing industry fish traders faced tight windows of opportunity when using a loan would enable them to improve their economic position. However, it was not always possible for fish traders to predict when this would occur and if MF organisations were slow to distribute and quick to enforce repayment, fish traders would struggle to repay. When participants were struggling to repay the loan, which in the case of our study was nearly all the participants, they discussed various coping strategies to find money. These included using business capital that they had saved in addition to the loan, using savings they had built up with the microfinance organisation, borrowing from relatives, spouses and friends, borrowing from money lenders, selling their household goods or livestock, and engaging in transactional sex.

Stress and anxiety of meeting repayments

Most of the participants whom we interviewed discussed feeling stress and anxiety when they were trying to repay their loans. This worry was felt regardless of whether the participant had been able to repay their loan or not. Rachel, who in the quote above described microfinance organisations as being a replacement for her husband and family members, also discussed the stress and worry that repaying the loan can cause:

> I did the business frequently trying to make money because you don't sleep if you borrow somebody's money. You always think about returning it ... I managed because I am afraid ... When a repayment day becomes due, or I should say when a repayment day is a week away, you can start looking for the money until you have enough to repay. (IDI, Rachel)

Maureen, who had taken a total of five loans from Lender A, articulated the consequences of this worry for the loan recipient:

> I: What do you think are the challenges associated with taking a loan?
> P: You meet many, so many challenges that you end up hanging yourself because of having so many worries about how to repay a loan. You don't have any relatives to turn to and you start wondering where you are going to find the money to pay back the loan. (IDI, Maureen)

Maureen cited a very extreme reaction to dealing with the challenges of taking a loan and we did not find any participants discussing anyone who had actually killed themselves because they had been unable to repay the loan. Yet, this was not the only female participant who discussed suicide and highlights how worried participants could feel about repaying their loans. There have been reports in the international media of suicides happening in other contexts in the Global South because loan recipients could not repay their loans. One example of this is a spate of suicides that were reported in 2011, in the southeastern Indian state of Andhra Pradesh. This is the same state we discussed in the introduction, where the media reports came at the same time that the MF industry was facing serious crisis (Bateman and Chang 2012). The suicides of young women were seen as directly due to their inability to repay their mounting microfinance debts (Morris 2011).

The stress and anxiety that participants felt about repaying their loans was directly related to the consequences they would face if they were unable to meet their repayments. Confiscation of property, including their houses, was what participants most feared. The group nature of the borrowing created extra pressure for participants to repay. For groups to gain access to further loans (often of a higher value), all their members had to repay and if the group failed to repay then the members who had paid back would not be able to access another loan. It was also the groups and not the microfinance organisations that were responsible for collecting money when repayments were due. If a group member was unable to repay the loan, then other members of the group would often have to provide the shortfall.

Groups were often made up of neighbours, friends and sometimes relatives and the public aspect of failing to repay could be very humiliating for the loan recipients. Groups could also make decisions on whether to help a participant with their repayments on the basis of how the group viewed the participant's behaviour. If the participant was not deemed to be behaving correctly then the groups might not help them with the outstanding repayments. This behaviour was related to how they were seen to be using the money in their homes or in their businesses. How these dynamics played out was very dependent on who was in the groups themselves and how they as a group viewed a participant's behaviour. The power to confiscate property gave the groups power over all their members, yet it tended to be the poorest and least socially connected who had their property confiscated. This was because they were the ones who were least able to find extra money if they were struggling with repayment.

In the following quote, Brenda discusses how some groups could be very aggressive in pursuing participants who were struggling to make their repayments. While, this was a theme that came up across the interviews and focus groups, we included this quote because she was particularly eloquent at discussing this:

> I feel there is always a risk because if someone doesn't have any money to pay the loan back, the kind of punishment they give him/her is too much. Because if the group has a meeting today on Wednesday, and you don't have any money to pay back, you start moving around the community trying to see if you can borrow money from someone. If you don't find the money and when you turn up at the meeting, you are not really respected. Many say 'We are coming to your house.' There is a Lender A group which I usually see gathering under that tree over there. They really show no respect for one another because they might go to somebody's house maybe around 6am and remain there until 10am. They are doing that to you even when you don't have any means of raising the money on that particular day. You may have tried to borrow from people but failed, but they insist that they get money from you so that they can bank it. So, even though people have not done it before, some of them run away from their houses escaping to another place leaving their children behind. They run away because of a challenge like this one which they might have encountered at that particular time. (IDI, Brenda)

These negative experiences of groups harassing each other are also reflected in Marr's (2002, 2003, 2006) studies on the effects of group lending in rural communities. In her research she found that the joint-liability incentive devices produced significant changes in social interactions within groups which 'damaged social cohesion and created negative effects on well-being and group stability' (Marr 2012, 557).

In an interview with Brenda we explored further the process of property confiscation. She said that property confiscation was only done as a final recourse if the participant had been struggling to repay the loan throughout the loan cycle. She described this as occurring at 'injury time' when members of the group had tried to help with all other options and the time had run out for repayment of the whole loan.

Other participants also discussed property confiscation happening at the end of the repayment period rather than something that happened throughout the loan cycle. Gift, who reported not having challenges repaying his loan, described the process of property confiscation by the group. We have included this quote as it provides some insight into how group members who confiscate property come to this decision. This was one of the few incidents in which a participant narrated their role in confiscating other group members' property:

> Well, if I had no money … we encourage every group member to save money with the organization so that if you have problems, the loan officer can write a letter signed by the Chairman and Secretary of the group and send it to the headquarters. At the headquarters, they can then transfer that person's savings to Lender A for the required repayment. If the savings of the person are not enough to meet the repayment, then every group member has to contribute so that the amount being owed to the organization is raised. Or else, we the group members should go to that person's house to take away and sell the property which they registered and declared to the group that could be sold out if they had problems paying back their loan. Not grabbing the property by force and without their consent. When they show the group the property, we ask them, 'Are you willingly surrendering the property from the bottom of your heart? Maybe you have other means of raising the money?' Then they tell you saying, 'No, I have tried several means of raising the money but I am not finding it. I am willingly releasing this property.' That's when we now look for someone to buy the property. If any of the group members wants to buy it, they buy it. We then use the money for meeting the repayment so that we don't owe the organization any money. (IDI, Gift)

In this discussion, Gift emphasises that the person who is having their property confiscated is giving the group their consent, perhaps suggesting that he is not altogether comfortable with this practice. In this description Gift is part of the group who is doing the confiscating and participants who had their property confiscated described how stressful, publically humiliating and economically ruinous it could be. Gift also discussed how other members could buy the confiscated property. In other interviews participants discussed how confiscated property might be sold cheaply to ensure the money was found quickly. This suggests that group members could actually have an economic incentive to confiscate the property of other members.

One challenge that came up in a number of interviews in relation to property confiscation was participants who had their property confiscated because they had vouched for another group member. In this scenario the participants had been able to repay their own loans but had been unable to repay the loan of the participant they had vouched for. In the following quote Irene discusses this scenario:

> I: How much was the money that you failed to repay?
>
> P: I had this property grabbed not because I had failed to repay my loan, but rather because of bearing witness for someone. I bore witness for someone who I had trusted but later ran away and escaped to the northern region. When the person had gone to the northern region, the property which was confiscated was mine, because the person was not reliably settled. She had no house. (IDI, Irene)

In this situation, the person who had given their trust to a relative or friend was economically penalised and by leaving the village and moving to the north there was no other way for the loan to be recovered by the group. When participants discussed having their property confiscated these were items such as bedding, cooking utensils, clothes and livestock. In the household women were responsible for providing food, and having cooking utensils confiscated affected them more than their husbands.

Microfinance, transactional sex and HIV risk

Throughout the data collection, participants reported microfinance as a reason why some women were vulnerable to HIV. In the study villages, some female fish traders used transactional sex as a way to access fish or generate capital for their businesses. Female fish traders' engagement in transactional sexual exchanges was often shaped by the unpredictability of the supply of fish at the lake and the demand for fish at the market. Female fish traders who were poorer or less socially connected could struggle to access fish and lacked economic resources to cushion their income-generation activities if they made a loss either during the processing or the selling of the fish. This situation, particularly when loans were given with very short repayment periods, increased the pressure for women to access fish quickly and to sell fish at a profit at the market. Given that both of these were areas of risk for female fish traders, taking loans could increase the chances of female fish traders engaging in transactional sex. The threat of property confiscation, which was publically humiliating and placed women in a worse economic position, increased the pressure for women to make money and repay the loan. In the study villages, income generation was almost completely dependent on fish catches and there were very few alternative livelihood strategies available for women, therefore generating money outside the fish trade was not an option.

Both women and men discussed how some poor and less well-connected female fish traders engaged in transactional sex as a consequence of taking a loan. When it was discussed it was often seen as a last resort, particularly when a repayment was due. In the following quote Alinafe discusses how this pressure to repay a loan could force women into engaging in transactional sex:

> Agreement is a painful thing. If you promise to pay back K17,500 [£70] by the 30th of a month, you must to do so no matter what. But you will find that you have been to the market three times and made losses on all the trips, and the repayment date may only be a few days away. There you decide to do something unacceptable which cannot help your life. You can put yourself at a certain risk. You will decide to do that so that perhaps you can raise K17,500 [£70] ... You can have sex with any man when you actually don't want it. You can sleep with him thinking that perhaps he can give you K2000 [£8]. You think that if he can give K2000 [£8], and if you could add it with the K2500 [£10] ... that may be left in the house. You take the loan so that you can manage to feed your family, while you are actually selling your life because of taking a loan. (IDI, Alinafe)

Alinafe's quote highlights how women were driven to engage in transactional sex because of the pressure to repay their microfinance loan. In the quote, the pressure that is created by the unpredictability of the fishing industry also comes across with Alinafe describing the continual trips to the market and the inability to sell the fish. She then describes seeking out transactional sex, not because she wants to, but because she feels she has to, to ensure the loan is repaid.

The connection between MF and HIV risk also came up in other focus group discussions and in-depth interviews. In the quote below, a female participant in a focus group discussion discusses the link. What is also clearly articulated is the relationship between taking a loan, engaging in transactional sex and acquiring HIV:

I: What are the problems that arise due to the provision of the loans which require a repayment of 2 weeks?

R3:   What happens is that I went to buy the fish at the Lake and it will take 4 days for me to dry the fish and then I take the fish to the market where the 2 weeks may elapse while at the market due to problems selling the fish. If you are under pressure to pay the loan you can end up having sex for money and coming back home with the disease. That is why we do not want the loan of 2 weeks but it should be at least 2 months. (Focus group discussion, female fish trader, 30–34, Tumbuka, widow, left school at primary S 8)

In the quote below, another female fish trader makes a direct link between MF loans and HIV risk:

When she sees that she has a loan to pay back, she offers to sell her body in order to raise money to pay back to the group, when she actually doesn't know about the health status of the man like whether he is infected or not. If the man is infected, it means she is going to contract the infection (IDI, female fish trader, 30–34, Tonga, married, dropped out of school in primary S 5)

In all three of these quotes, the emphasis by the participants is placed on the pressure that repaying the microfinance loan in a very short period of time can place on female fish traders who are struggling to make a profit.

Discussion and conclusion

We found a complex picture regarding female fish traders' experiences of using microfinance loans in the fishing industry. At times microfinance provided female fish traders with much-needed business capital and access to social networks that allowed them to learn more about successful strategies for the fish trade. The access to business capital also allowed fish traders' economic independence from male sexual partners. Some women reported using the profits they generated from the loans within the household on both food and school fees for children.

However, the fishing industry was highly unpredictable and female fish traders faced multiple uncertainties when trying to make a profit trading fish. Buying, processing and selling fish were all time-consuming and female fish traders with poor social connections and few economic assets were in economically vulnerable positions. This was coupled with the highly gendered environment that meant women had to negotiate access to fish through men. Using microfinance loans, particularly those with short grace periods and a threat of property confiscation, placed further pressure on female fish traders to make a profit. If they made a loss, the consequences were more acutely felt because fish traders had to continue to repay the loan with interest. When women had taken loans and were unable to repay them, engaging in transactional sex was one way of overcoming their need to find money to pay their loans. In a context of high HIV prevalence rates, such as fishing communities, microfinance loans could at times leave female fish traders vulnerable to HIV.

As noted in the introduction, there have been important academic critiques of the way microfinance operates in the field and a number of authors have argued that microfinance can be disempowering for its female loan recipients (Goetz and Gupta 1996; Karim 2011; Rahman 1999). What the testimonies of the participants interviewed highlight is that being given a microfinance loan does not automatically lead to a successful business and alleviation of poverty for those provided with the loan. All the female fish traders discussed the challenges they faced in repaying the loan, even the ones who considered microfinance to be helping their businesses. It therefore challenges the accepted orthodoxy that there is an automatic relationship between the provision of a MF loan and empowerment for women. Critics argue that one of the key reasons for the negative outcomes is the way microfinance organisations view success in their programmes. Principally, success in MF organisations is measured by loan recovery rates rather than in more holistic measures of impact within the household or on participants' lives. In our study some participants reported intense pressure from fellow loan group members. The registering of property by the loan group at the beginning of the loan cycle is likely to be a reflection of the importance that the microfinance organisation placed on recovering their loans. The confiscation and selling of property was both publically humiliating and economically ruinous and lends weight to the argument that microfinance can be disempowering to its borrowers. In her monograph, Karim (2011) describes harrowing cases of loan recipients in Bangladesh having their homes dismantled and the pieces being sold bit by bit to repay their outstanding debt (117–123). This scenario was reflected in the experiences of the female fish traders taking loans in our study and perhaps speaks to a worrying systematic policy across MF organisations to recover their debts.

The group lending process has also attracted criticism, particularly the Grameen Bank's model where groups are responsible for repaying the whole loan rather than just their own proportion (Visvanathan and Yoder 2011). The concern with group lending is that MF organisations use group members as social collateral and exert undue pressure on borrowers to make repayments (Visvanathan and Yoder 2011, 53). This pressure can result in women borrowing money from money lenders and using subsequent loans to repay old debts, creating a spiral of indebtedness that women struggle to break (*Ibid.*). We found this reflected in our research with some participants reporting intense pressure from each other to repay the loan. Participants also described how loan officers would only become involved after participants had tried hard to pressure their fellow loan recipients to repay. The only way participants could default on loans was to leave the village. However, this meant that other participants who had vouched for the member had to clear that group member's debt. This created heavy economic penalties for other group members and tense relationships in loan groups. When participants vouch for other members, it is that participant who experiences a loss if the loan recipient defaults on the loan. If MF organisations are measuring success on the grounds of loan repayments, these dynamics may mask the true success (or lack of it) of programmes.

In the fishing industry, female fish traders required access to business capital to perform their business. In our study all the women we interviewed discussed how they did retain control of their own loans and used the loan for their businesses. However, there were also examples of participants discussing men asking their wives to take loans for them. This reflects the findings in Mayoux's (1999) work on microfinance in a diverse range of African countries including in southern and west Africa. She found that the gender relations in the countries she worked in meant that women often retained control over their loans. This was in contrast to the findings in South Asia where academic studies have reported male relatives taking control of loans (Goetz and Gupta 1996). We also found that if women were able to make a profit from the loan, they also retained control over the money realised from the loan. The loans therefore provided some women with an opportunity to gain financial independence from their partners, providing some weight to the argument that microfinance could be empowering to the women who were included in programmes,

However, while some female fish traders in our study were successful in using their loans to make a profit, they also continued to work in a highly gendered environment. The ability of female fish traders to access microfinance loans did not fundamentally alter these power relations. This provides further support for Cornwall and Edwards' (2010) argument that empowering women is complex and requires more than a single intervention to achieve. It also speaks to the debates about structural interventions that prevent HIV through altering the broader structural factors that place women and men at an increased risk of HIV (Auerbach et al. 2009). As we noted in the introduction, microfinance has previously been identified as a potential structural intervention. However, these findings suggest that MF is unlikely to significantly influence broader gendered power relations and therefore prevent HIV.

Finally, for women, making money in the fishing industry was precarious. Female fish traders required access to money and social connections. For women without these social connections, transactional sex was a way of developing and improving access to money and fish. This form of transactional sex is called sex-for-fish exchange and has been reported in other fishing communities in Africa (Béné and Merten 2008; Merten and Haller 2007). We did not find any literature that explored microfinance in fishing communities. However, in the international literature transactional sex has previously been identified as a risk factor for HIV, particularly in southern and east Africa where prevalence rates are high (Côté et al. 2004; Dunkle et al. 2004a, 2004b; Jewkes et al. 2012; Norris, Kitali, and Worby 2009). This is because when relationships are formed on the basis of material benefit women often have less power to negotiate safer sexual practices (Jewkes et al. 2012). The intense pressure that microfinance placed on female fish traders drove some poorer and less well-connected women to engage in transactional sex in an environment with high HIV prevalence rates, increasing their vulnerability to HIV. For public health programmes that aim to prevent HIV, these findings provide a cautionary lesson.

The findings also provide weight to Kabeer's (2005) and Matin and Hulme's (2003) argument that for microfinance to be successful, the product needs to be tailored to the needs and interests of the recipients. If microfinance is to be used in fishing communities it requires serious modification to reflect the realities of the women and men using it. Oya (2012), drawing on a range of work looking at the impact of MF in rural communities, suggests microfinance could be re-ordinated and used for structural interventions that alter these structural constraints. One example of this could be to use credit to support larger and more viable farms in rural communities that are 'currently starved of appropriate longerterm as well as seasonal production credit' (554).

Female fish traders feared their property being confiscated. Stopping the confiscation of the property by groups would ease pressure on female fish traders. Furthermore, allowing fish traders more flexibility with their repayment schedules, reflecting the unpredictable nature of the fishing industry, would improve women's ability to use their loans. In relation to public health interventions that wish to prevent HIV in high-risk settings in southern Africa where HIV prevalence is high, microfinance is unlikely to be a tool that will be successful in preventing HIV vulnerability.

A key limitation of the study was not including representatives from the MF organisations that the participants discussed. This study was undertaken at the end of the larger study and we did not have time to seek ethical approval to conduct interviews with MF organisations. However, while this is a key limitation much of the themes that were discussed by the participants were also discussed in the international literature and provide weight to the data.

In conclusion, we found a complex picture of the role microfinance played in fishing communities in southern Malawi. Across the dataset, microfinance was seen as increasing female fish traders' economic vulnerability and risk of HIV. Urgent modification of MF products is required to protect highly vulnerable women. Finally, in fishing communities, microfinance should not be used as a tool to prevent HIV.

Acknowledgements

This work was supported by the European & Developing Countries Clinical Trials Partnership (EDCTP) [grant number.CT.2006.33111.011].

Disclosure statement

No potential conflict of interest was reported by the authors.

Notes

1. The term *microfinance* is often used as an umbrella term for a range of financial services including micro-loans, micro-insurance and village banking. In general the term is focused on programmes that provide credit.
2. The term derives from the word *kuunika*, which means to light or give light. The light refers to the lanterns that are used to attract.
3. Ten men usually travel in the engine boat to parts of the lake where they believe there is a large presence of fish. The men then get into the dug-out canoes and use the lanterns to attract shoals of *usipa* fish to the surface and into the nets.
4. Ethical approval was obtained from the College of Medicine Research Ethics Committee, Malawi and the Liverpool School of Tropical Medicine Research Ethics Committee. Further, permission to work in the district and villages was provided by the chiefs of both villages as well as district-level representatives. Written informed consent was obtained from all individuals participating in the interviews and focus groups.
5. To do this, all interviews and focus groups were recorded, transcribed and translated into English by the research assistants. All transcripts were imported into NVivo 9 and the program was used to aid data analysis by coding against the framework. Data analysis began at the beginning of the data collection, continued throughout the data collection and was informed by the framework approach (Ritchie, Spencer, and O'Connor 2003) The framework approach provides a systematic

structure for analysis of qualitative data using both inductive and deductive approaches and entails five stages: familiarisation, identifying a thematic framework, indexing the data, charting and mapping, and interpreting (Pope, Ziebland, and Mays 2000).

References

Allison, E. H., and J. A. Seeley. 2004. "HIV and AIDS among Fisherfolk: A Threat to 'Responsible Fisheries'?" *Fish and Fisheries* 5: 215–234.

Auerbach, J. D., J. O. Parkhurst, K. E. Keller, C. Cáceres, and K. E. Keller. 2009. "Addressing Social Drivers of HIV/AIDS: Some Conceptual, Methodological, and Evidentiary Considerations." aids2031 Working Paper. Massachusetts, US: aids2031.

Banerjee, Abhijit, Esther Duflo, Rachel Glennerster, and Cynthia Kinnan. 2013. "The Miracle of Microfinance? Evidence from a Randomized Evaluation." MIT Department of Economics Working Paper 13–09.

Bateman, Milford, and Ha-Joon Chang. 2012. "Microfinance and the Illusion of Development: From Hubris to Nemesis in Thirty Years." *World Economic Review* 1 (1): 13–36.

Bauchet, Jonathan, Cristobal Marshall, Laura Starita, Jeanette Thomas, and Anna Yalouris. 2011. "Latest Findings from Randomized Evaluations of Microfinance." Access to Finance Forum.

Béné, C., and S. Merten. 2008. "Women and Fish-for-sex: Transactional Sex, HIV/AIDS and Gender in African Fisheries." *World Development* 36 (5): 875–899.

Cammack, Diana. 2012. "Malawi in Crisis, 2011–12." *Review of African Political Economy* 39 (132): 375–388.

Cornwall, A., and J. Edwards. 2010. "Introduction: Negotiating Empowerment." *IDS Bulletin* 41 (2): 1–9.

Côté, A-M., F. Sobela, A. Dzokoto, K. Nzambi, C. Asamoah-Adu, A-C. Labbé, B. Mâsse, J. Mensah, E. Frost, and J. Pépin. 2004. "Transactional Sex is the Driving Force in the Dynamics of HIV in Accra, Ghana." *AIDS* 18 (6): 917–925.

Darwall, W. R. T., and E. H. Allison. 2002. "Monitoring, Assessing, and Managing Fish Stocks in Lake Malawi/Nyassa: Current Approaches and Future Possibilities." *Aquatic Ecosystem Health & Management* 5 (3): 293–305.

Deane, K. D., J. O. Parkhurst, and D. Johnston. 2010. "Linking Migration Mobility and HIV." *Tropical Medicine and International Health* 15 (12): 1458–1463.

Devereux, Stephen. 2002. "The Malawi Famine of 2002." *IDS Bulletin* 33 (4): 70–78.

Dunbar, M. S., M. C. Maternowska, M. S. Kang, S. M. Laver, I. Mudekunye-Mahaka, and N. S. Padian. 2010. "Findings from SHAZ!: A Feasibility Study of a Microcredit and Life-skills HIV Prevention Intervention to Reduce Risk among Adolescent Female Orphans in Zimbabwe." *Journal of Prevention & Intervention in the Community* 38 (2): 147–161.

Dunkle, K. L., R. Jewkes, H. C. Brown, G. E. Gray, J. A. McIntryre, and S. D. Harlow. 2004a. "Gender-based Violence, Relationship Power, and Risk of HIV Infection in Women Attending Antenatal Clinics in South Africa." *Lancet* 363: 1415–1421.

Dunkle, K. L., R. K. Jewkes, H. C. Brown, G. E. Gray, J. A. McIntryre, and S. D. Harlow. 2004b. "Transactional Sex among Women in Soweto, South Africa: Prevalence, Risk Factors and Association with HIV Infection." *Social Science & Medicine* 59 (8): 1581–1592.

Dworkin, S. L., and K. M. Blankenship. 2009. "Microfinance and HIV/AIDS Prevention: Assessing its Promise and Limitations." *AIDS and Behavior* 13: 462–469.

Epstein, H. 2007. *The Invisible Cure: Africa, the West and the Fight against AIDS.* London: Penguin.

Goetz, A. M., and R. S. Gupta. 1996. "Who Takes the Credit? Gender, Power and Control over Loan Use in Rural Credit Programmes in Bangladesh." *World Development* 24 (1): 45–63.

Government of Malawi. 2006. *Behavioural Surveillance Survey Report.* Lilongwe, Malawi: Office of the President and Cabinet.

Government of Malawi. 2007. "The Fish Sector and Its Importance in Malawi." ESA Meeting on Trade and Sustainable Approaches to Fisheries Negotiations under WTO/EPA, The Commonwealth Secretariat, Port Louis, Mauritius, May 2–4.

Government of Malawi. 2009. *National HIV Prevention Strategy and Action Plan.* Lilongwe, Malawi: Office of the President and Cabinet.

Hara, M. 2008. "Dilemmas of Democratic Decentralisation in Mangochi District, Malawi: Interest and Mistrust in Fisheries Management." *Conservation and Society* 6 (1): 74–86.

Holvoet, Nathalie. 2005. "The Impact of Microfinance on Decision-making Agency: Evidence from South India." *Development and Change* 36 (1): 75–102.

Jamu, Daniel, Moses Banda, Friday Njaya, and Robert E. Hecky. 2011. "Challenges to Sustainable Management of the Lakes of Malawi." *Journal of Great Lakes Research* 37 (Suppl. 1): 3–14.

Jewkes, R., R. Morrell, Y. Sikweyiya, K. Dunkle, and L. Penn-Kekana. 2012. "Transactional Relationships and Sex with a Woman in Prostitution: Prevalence and Patterns in a Representative Sample of South African Men." [online] *BMC Public Health* 12: 325.

Johnson, S. 2005. "Gender Relations, Empowerment and Microcredit: Moving on from a Lost Decade." *The European Journal of Development Research* 17 (2): 224–248.

Kabeer, N. 2001. "Conflicts Over Credit: Re-evaluating the Empowerment Potential of Loans to Women in Rural Bangladesh." *World Development* 29 (1): 63–84.

Kabeer, N. 2005. "Is Microfinance a 'Magic Bullet' for Women's Empowerment? Analysis of Findings from South Asia." *Economic and Political Weekly* 40 (29 October): 4709–4718.

Kalpana, K. 2011. "Negotiating Multiple Patriarchies: Women and Microfinance in South India." In *The Women, Gender and Development Reader*, edited by N. Visvanathan, L. Duggan, N. Wiegersma, and L. Nisonoff, 55–63. New York: Zed Books.

Karim, Lamia. 2011. *Microfinance and Its Discontents: Women in Debt in Bangladesh*. Minneapolis, MN: University of Minnesota Press.

Karlan, Dean, and Martin Valdivia. 2011. "Teaching Entrepreneurship: Impact of Business Training on Microfinance Clients and Institutions." *Review of Economics and Statistics* 93 (2): 510–527.

Kim, J. C., and C. H. Watts. 2005. "Gaining a Foothold: Tackling Poverty, Gender Inequality, and HIV in Africa." *BMJ* 331 (7519): 769–772.

Kissling, E., E. H. Allison, J. A. Seeley, S. Russell, M. Bachmann, S. D. Musgrave, and S. Heck. 2005. "Fisherfolk are among Groups Most at Risk of HIV Cross-country Analysis of Prevalence and Numbers Infected." *AIDS* 19 (17): 1939–1946.

Korth, M., R. Stewart, C. van Rooyen, and T. De Wet. 2012. "Microfinance: Development Intervention or Just another Bank?" *Journal of Agrarian Change* 12 (4): 575–586.

Kulkarni, V. S. 2011. "Women's Empowerment and Microfinance: An Asian Perspective." Occasional Paper Rome, International Fund for Agricultural Development, Italy.

Kwena, Zachary A., Carol S. Camlin, Chris A. Shisanya, Isaac Mwanzo, and Elizabeth A. Bukusi. 2013. "Short-term Mobility and the Risk of HIV Infection among Married Couples in the Fishing Communities along Lake Victoria, Kenya." [online] *PLoS One* 8 (1): e54523.

Lewis, J. 2003. "Design Issues." In *A Guide for Social Science Students and Researchers*, edited by J. Richie and J. Lewis, 47–76. Thousand Oaks, CA: Sage.

MacPherson, E. E., J. Sadalaki, M. Njoloma, V. Nyongopa, L. Nkhwazi, V. Mwapasa, D. G. Lalloo, N. Desmond, J. Seeley, and S. Theobald. 2012. "Transactional Sex and HIV: Understanding the Gendered Structural Drivers of HIV in Fishing Communities in Southern Malawi." *Journal of the International AIDS Society* 15 (Suppl. 1): 1–9.

Mapondera, Godfrey. 2014. "Malawi Prepares for $100m 'Cashgate' Corruption Trial." *The Guardian*, Manchester.

Marr, Ana. 2002. "Studying Group Dynamics: An Alternative Analytical Framework for the Study of Microfinance Impacts on Poverty Reduction." *Journal of International Development* 14 (4): 511–534.

Marr, Ana. 2003. "A Challenge to the Orthodoxy Concerning Microfinance and Poverty Reduction." *Journal of Microfinance/ESR Review* 5 (2): 7–42.

Marr, Ana. 2006. "The Limitations of Group-based Microfinance and Ways to Overcome them." *Small Enterprise Development* 17 (3): 28–40.

Marr, Ana. 2012. "Effectiveness of Rural Microfinance: What We Know and What We Need to Know." *Journal of Agrarian Change* 12 (4): 555–563.

Matin, Imran, and David Hulme. 2003. "Programs for the Poorest: Learning from the IGVGD Program in Bangladesh." *World Development* 31 (3): 647–665.

Mayoux, Linda. 1999. "Questioning Virtuous Spirals: Micro-finance and Women's Empowerment in Africa." *Journal of International Development* 11 (7): 957–984.

Mersland, Roy, and R. Øystein Strøm. 2010. "Microfinance Mission Drift?" *World Development* 38 (1): 28–36.

Merten, S., and T. Haller. 2007. "Culture, Changing Livelihoods, and HIV/AIDS Discourse: Reframing the Institutionalization of Fish-for-sex Exchange in the Zambian Kafue Flats." *Culture, Health & Sexuality* 9 (1): 69–83.

Morduch, J. 2000. "The Microfinance Schism." *World Development* 28 (4): 617–629.

Morris, Madeleine. 2011. "Investigating India's Microcredit Crisis." *BBC World Service.*

Nagoli, J., K. Holvoet, and M. Remme. 2010. "HIV and AIDS Vulnerability in Fishing Communities in Mangochi District, Malawi." *African Journal of AIDS Research* 9 (1): 71–80.

National Statistical Office. 2005. Malawi Demographic and Health Survey 2004. Calverton, MD: National Statistical Office of Malawi.

Norris, A. H., A. J. Kitali, and E. Worby. 2009. "Alcohol and Transactional Sex: How Risky is the Mix?" *Social Science & Medicine* 69 (8): 1167–1176.

Oya, Carlos. 2012. "Introduction to a Symposium on Microfinance and Rural Development: Magic Bullet or Blank Bullet?" *Journal of Agrarian Change* 12 (4): 552–554.

Pankhurst, H. 2002. "Passing the Buck? Money Literacy and Alternatives to Credit and Savings Schemes." *Gender & Development* 10 (3): 10–21.

Pope, C., and N. Mays. 1995. "Qualitative Research: Reaching the Parts Other Methods Cannot Reach: An Introduction to Qualitative Methods in Health and Health Services Research." *BMJ* 311 (6996): 42–45.

Pope, C., S. Ziebland, and N. Mays. 2000. "Qualitative Research in Health Care Analysing Qualitative Data." *BMJ* 320: 114–116.

Pronyk, Paul M., James R. Hargreaves, Julia C. Kim, Linda A. Morison, Godfrey Phetla, Charlotte Watts, Joanna Busza, and John D. H. Porter. 2006. "Effect of a Structural Intervention for the Prevention of Intimate-partner Violence and HIV in Rural South Africa: A Cluster Randomised Trial." *Lancet* 368 (9551): 1973–1983.

Rahman, Aminur. 1999. "Micro-credit Initiatives for Equitable and Sustainable Development: Who Pays?" *World Development* 27 (1): 67–82.

Ritchie, J., L. Spencer, and W. O'Connor. 2003. "Carrying Out Qualitative Analysis." In *Qualitative Research Practice: A Guide for Social Science Students and Researchers*, edited by J. Richie and J. Lewis, 219–262. Thousand Oaks, CA: Sage.

van Rooyen, C., R. Stewart, and T. de Wet. 2012. "The Impact of Microfinance in Sub-Saharan Africa: A Systematic Review of the Evidence." *World Development* 40 (11): 2249–2262.

Seeley, J. A., and E. H. Allison. 2005. "HIV/AIDS in Fishing Communities: Challenges to Delivering Antiretroviral Therapy to Vulnerable Groups." *AIDS Care* 17 (6): 688–697.

Seeley, Janet, Grace Tumwekwase, and Heiner Grosskurth. 2009. "Fishing for a Living but Catching HIV: AIDS and Changing Patterns of the Organization of Work in Fisheries in Uganda." *Anthropology of Work Review* 30 (2): 66–76.

Seeley, J., C. H. Watts, S. Kippax, S. Russell, L. Heise, and A. Whiteside. 2012. "Addressing the Structural Drivers of HIV: A Luxury or Necessity for Programmes?" *Journal of the International AIDS Society* 15 (Suppl. 1): 1–4.

Sengupta, Rajdeep, and Craig P. Aubuchon. 2008. "The Microfinance Revolution: An Overview." *Federal Reserve Bank of Saint Louis Review* 90 (1): 9–30.

Tumwesigye, N. M., L. Atuyambe, R. K. Wanyenze, S. P. Kibira, Q. Li, F. Wabwire-Mangen, and G. Wagner. 2012. "Alcohol Consumption and Risky Sexual Behaviour in the Fishing Communities: Evidence from Two Fish Landing Sites on Lake Victoria in Uganda." [online] *BMC Public Health* 12: 1069.

Visvanathan, N., and K. Yoder. 2011. "Women and Microcredit: A Critical Introduction." in *The Women, Gender and Development Reader*, edited by N. Visvanathan, L. Duggan, N. Wiegersma, and L. Nisonoff, 47–54. New York: Zed Books.

Revisiting the economics of transactional sex: evidence from Tanzania

Kevin Deane and Joyce Wamoyi

Transactional sex has been identified as one of the key structural drivers of the HIV epidemic. Mainstream economic analyses of this practice primarily conceptualise transactional sex in the language of rational choice, with the focus on behavioural decisions that women make over whether to engage in transactional interactions (or not). However, whilst providing some important insights in relation to the role of poverty and the importance of acknowledging that women are more than passive agents, these approaches fail to address the social and economic complexities of this practice that are reflected in the broader literature. Further, due to the technical framework used, there is a failure to deal with the broader socio-economic and historical underpinnings of this practice. Using evidence from fieldwork undertaken in Tanzania, the authors revisit the economics of transactional sex, and offer an alternative economic approach to understanding this practice. They explore the notion that transactional sex is an established local sexual norm, and how this norm is creatively applied and reapplied in a range of situations by different actors, including through participation in local value chains. Their analysis has a number of implications for future prevention efforts that differ from the current focus on microfinance as a means of empowering women.

[Revisiter l'économie du sexe transactionnel : témoignage de Tanzanie.] Le sexe transactionnel a été identifié comme un des facteurs structurels clés de l'épidémie du VIH. Les analyses économiques orthodoxes de cette pratique conceptualisent en premier lieu le sexe transactionnel dans le langage du choix rationnel, en se concentrant sur les décisions comportementales que les femmes prennent quant à leur engagement dans des interactions transactionnelles (ou non). Cependant, alors que ces approches fournissent des éclairages intéressants sur le rôle de la pauvreté et l'importance de reconnaitre que les femmes sont plus que des agents passifs, elles ne traitent pas les complexités sociales et économiques de cette pratique qui sont reflétées dans la littérature plus large. Par ailleurs, en raison du cadre technique utilisé, il n'existe pas d'analyse des fondations socio-économiques et historiques plus larges de cette pratique. Sur base d'un travail de terrain en Tanzanie, les auteurs revisitent l'économie du sexe transactionnel et offrent une approche économique alternative pour comprendre cette pratique. Ils explorent la notion selon laquelle le sexe transactionnel est une norme sexuelle locale établie, et la manière dont cette norme est appliquée et réappliquée de manière créative dans une série de situations par des acteurs différents, notamment à travers la participation dans les chaines de valeur locales. Leur analyse comporte un certain nombre d'implications pour les efforts futurs en matière de prévention qui différent de l'accent mis actuellement sur la micro finance comme un moyen d'émancipation des femmes.

Introduction

The response to the HIV/AIDS epidemic has to date been dominated by biomedical and behavioural interventions (Campbell and Williams 1999), with moderate but disappointing progress in relation to sexual behaviour change (Padian et al. 2010). Although it has long been acknowledged that context and social structures have influenced the dynamics of the epidemic (Hahn 1991; Sweat and Denison 1995), it is only more recently that these insights have been fully incorporated into the global policy agenda (UNAIDS 2010), in part as a result of a growing body of literature that has emphasised the structural or social drivers of HIV (Sumartojo 2000; Auerbach et al. 2010; Auerbach, Parkhurst, and Cáceres 2011). This is a much-needed development which transcends early transmission models which are generally individualistic in nature (King 1999). Transactional sex has been identified as one of the most important structural drivers of HIV risk (Jewkes et al. 2012). However, transactional sex has often been defined differently and most of these definitions have not been comprehensive enough to capture the dynamics of the practice in a sub-Saharan African setting. Broadly speaking, the term 'transactional sex' refers to sexual interactions in which something is exchanged or transferred, though on a more informal basis than, and conceptually distinct from, commercial sex work (Hunter 2002; Dunkle et al. 2004; Jewkes et al. 2012). A more formalised definition suggests that transactional sex should be defined as 'a sexual relationship or act(s), outside of marriage or sex work, motivated primarily by the expectation of material gain, where love and trust are also sometimes present (involved/concerned/at play)' (Stoebenau et al. forthcoming).

Whilst having sex is not in itself risky, transactional sex is frequently associated with intimate partner violence, situations in which women are often unable to negotiate condom use, and intergenerational sex which further exacerbates power differentials over the terms and timing of sexual interactions (Dunkle et al. 2004; Jewkes et al. 2012). Statistical work confirms that female participation in transactional sex enhances the likelihood of HIV infection (Dunkle et al. 2004; Jewkes et al. 2012). Although there are some dissenting voices (Stillwaggon and Sawers 2012), the statistical evidence, in light of insights from qualitative work, strongly suggests that this behaviour may be risky and that it needs addressing in current and future prevention efforts. However, despite general agreement that the practice of transactional sex is rooted in unequal and gendered power relations, it is not always clear exactly how transactional sex is conceptualised in a structural way, and how sexual interactions that involve exchange reflect the dynamics of the social system and broader historical socio-economic processes.

Although there are a range of excellent analyses of the social complexities around the practice of transactional sex (Poulin 2007; Swidler and Watkins 2007), mainstream economic attempts to address this issue have to date largely failed to provide useful insights, reflecting a general lack of a substantive contribution by the economics profession to the epidemic (Johnston 2013). In most cases, economic analyses are rooted in the standard microeconomic framework in which individuals make rational decisions over their sexual behaviour, an approach that fails to respond to theoretical and empirical work originating from other disciplines regarding the role of structural drivers, or engages with them to the limited extent permitted by the underlying technical apparatus (Milonakis and Fine 2008). For example, early attempts to model sexual behaviour explained the continued risky sexual behaviour of poor sex workers in light of the epidemic through the prism of the opportunity cost, as sex workers weighed up the perceived probability of infection against the material gains of a given sexual encounter (Philipson and Posner 1995). The opportunity cost is central to later more technical work, though with application to the wider population rather than specific high-risk groups, in which individuals make sexual decisions based on their current and expected lifetime utility, with the immediate lost utility of not having sex related to anticipated future utility (Oster 2012). Transactional sex has also been framed in a similar way (Luke 2006; Robinson and Yeh 2011; De Walque, Dow, and Gong 2013), with attention to the existence of a premium for unsafe sex, and how female decision-making with regards to sexual behaviour responds to external shocks. Whilst these analyses provide some useful insights, overall they fail to address central concerns related to transactional sex, especially unequal and gendered power relations, reflected in the broader literature (Bene and Merten 2008; Jewkes et al. 2012; MacPherson et al. 2012), and which present a strong challenge to models framed in the language of free choice.

Despite these limitations, the mainstream economic framework underpins current interventions such as conditional cash transfers (Baird et al. 2012) and microfinance (Pronyk et al. 2005), which are in part designed to reduce the need for women and girls to engage in transactional sex, and which are currently gaining prominence as 'structural' interventions (see O'Laughlin in this issue). This reductionism of scope and level of analysis, with individualistic economic theory (re)incorporating the social in a limited way (Fine and Milonakis 2009), highlights a pressing need for alternative economic approaches that can address broader concerns around power and gender in relation to transactional sex.

This article will reflect on the economics of transactional sex, using evidence from a research project conducted in Tanzania to develop alternative economic conceptualisations and explanations of this practice. This will complement and add to the growing body of work that roots this practice in the workings of the economic and social system. Our research illustrates the range and complexity of transactional sexual interactions, and illustrates how an alternative economic approach can shed light on the structural dynamics of transactional sex. This enables a critical reflection on current economic approaches to HIV prevention targeted at transactional sex, and implications for a different policy agenda that addresses women's empowerment more generally. The rest of this article is structured as follows. In the next section, we critically assess mainstream approaches to transactional sex, before introducing the study site and fieldwork methods and then presenting evidence from our fieldwork. This enables the formulation of an alternative economic understanding in the following section, and a discussion of the implications for prevention policy that precedes some concluding remarks.

The economics of transactional sex

Mainstream economic approaches to the study of transactional sex, such as Luke (2006), Robinson and Yeh (2011), and De Walque, Dow, and Gong (2013), are articulated in the language of rational choice, in which sex and either money or non-monetary gifts or goods are traded in a market setting (Luke 2006; Robinson and Yeh 2011; De Walque, Dow, and Gong 2013). Typically, survey data is used to statistically test hypotheses that reflect underlying behavioural models. The study of sexual practices that involve some form of exchange using this framework inevitably focuses on the monetary value of whatever has been exchanged for sex, which enables the construction of a market for sex/safe sex, in which the value of the transaction is related to the likelihood that a woman will engage in transactional sex, and/or the likelihood that a condom will or will not be used.

Luke (2006) collected data on informal sexual relationships in urban Kenya, and sought to test whether a market for safe sex existed in which women with given preferences and wealth endowments choose from a range of different possible partnerships 'where each partnership is characterized by a level of transfers and a probability of condom use' (322). The underlying model then tests whether the probability of condom use is related to the size of the transfer, with the hypothesis that condom use will be negatively related to the size of the transfer confirmed as statistically significant. This result is interpreted as evidence that women are active agents in the process of negotiating condom use within transactional settings, and confirmation that informal sexual relationships that involve exchange can be conceptualised as a functioning market for unprotected sex. A further implication of this work is that there is a 'premium' for having sex without a condom, a notion taken up by Robinson and Yeh (2011), who seek to understand whether the existence of a premium for unsafe sex enables women to increase their supply of unsafe sex in times of need. The existence of a risk premium is tested by examining whether the 'price' of a sexual transaction is related to risky sexual activities, which is confirmed as statistically significant, and thus 'it may be rational for women to choose to engage in unprotected sex to capture the risk premium' (*Ibid.*, 50). Having established a clear motivation for women to engage in transactional sex, they then go on to test whether unprotected sex is related to household shocks through two fixed-effects equations that also test whether households maintain consumption after a shock by reducing other expenditures. The statistical results confirm that these women increase their supply of unsafe sex as a reaction to relatively small household shocks, again confirming that sexual interactions involving exchange are underpinned by the logic of the market. These findings echo those of similar modelling exercises that focus on condom use by commercial sex workers (Gertler, Shah, and Bertozzi 2005).

Finally, De Walque, Dow, and Gong (2013) using panel data from rural Tanzania on women whose primary means of survival is agriculture, find that following a negative household shock, both married and unmarried women have more unprotected sex, and are also more likely to have a sexually transmitted infection. In this case, transactional sex is framed as a way of coping with adverse shocks, and this study highlights that this does not just apply to single, divorced or separated women, but is a practice engaged in by the wider population. This study also links unprotected sex to the risk of contracting a sexually transmitted infection, and thus a direct impact on the potential for HIV transmission. As with the other approaches discussed here, women are viewed to increase or decrease the amount of unprotected sex that they have depending on their material needs, and to some degree this captures the notion of 'survival sex', in which poverty and desperation drive women to engage in sex of a transactional nature (Wojcicki 2002).

There are of course some differences between these approaches. In particular, whilst Luke (2006) uses a broader definition of transactional sex that seeks to assess informal relationships and exchange, and De Walque, Dow, and Gong (2013) focus on the general female rural population, Robinson and Yeh (2011) sample women that are 'single, widowed, divorced, or separated woman, aged 18 or older, who had multiple concurrent sex partners' (40), which is not only a very specific target group, but also risks conflating commercial sex work and transactional sex, a blurring of sexual interactions that other authors have been at pains to conceptualise as distinct (Hunter 2002; Leclerc-Madlala 2003; Jewkes et al. 2012).

These economic approaches provide a number of useful insights into the mechanics of transactional sex which echo themes in the broader anthropological and public health literature. Women are not characterised as passive victims, but are ascribed a degree of agency, thus challenging unhelpful negative stereotypes of African women (Hunter 2002; Leclerc-Madlala 2003). The pernicious role of poverty is also brought to the fore, and in particular the vulnerability of fragile households to external shocks. The authors also suggest a number of avenues for intervention that are echoed in the broader literature and that implicitly acknowledge the constrained socio-economic context within which many women live, such as improving access to health care, and especially health care for dependents (Robinson and Yeh 2011), the provision of alternative economic opportunities for women so that they do not have to resort to exchanging sex for survival (Luke 2006), and the need to financially empower poor and vulnerable women (De Walque, Dow, and Gong 2013). These are welcome additions to strategies that go beyond the standard package of biomedical and behavioural interventions (Campbell and Williams 1999).

However, there are a number of limitations associated with these economic approaches that are related to the economic framework employed, which emphasise the degree to which these analyses are at odds with the broader literature. First, whilst there is some acknowledgment of the challenges that women face, it is unclear whether the notion of agency, conceptualised as the ability for women to rationally and freely choose whether or not to engage in transactional sex, reflects the influence of unequal economic and gender relations that frame these decisions. Indeed, the use of the loaded term 'choice' in this context is certainly questionable (Johnston 2011), with the options that poor(er) women face within a constrained socio-economic environment more akin to the frying pan or the fire rather than alternative outcomes that can be regarded in any sense as optimal (Christensen 1998). This narrow formulation of agency ignores issues such as power, force and coercion. A cursory word search of the three papers finds that the term 'coercion' does not appear in any of them; the word 'power' does twice in Robinson and Yeh (2011) and De Walque, Dow, and Gong (2013), though in both papers on one occasion this refers to the power of the statistical test, and the word 'coerce' appears once in a footnote in Luke (2006). Further, the word 'force' only appears in Robinson and Yeh, though not directly in relation to sexual behaviour. These are not linguistic omissions, and represent a systematic failure to address concerns that fall outside of the market framework which explicitly does not engage with questions of unequal power, instead assuming free market entry and, importantly, exit.

This is in stark contrast to the broader literature on transactional sex, in which unequal gender relations, power and coercion are central to the analysis. MacPherson et al. (2012) examined transactional sexual interactions between fishermen and female fish traders in Malawi, finding that fishermen used their economic position to extract sex from traders who were desperate to ensure that they could access fish, particularly in the lean seasons, and in general 'exploit women's economic need by pressuring them into having sex with them' (7). Stoebenau et al. (2011), whilst acknowledging that women actively use their sexuality to extract material goods from men, also note the importance of power, not only in relation to the highly unequal gender relations which provide the backdrop for these sexual interactions, but also 'at the point of the sexual encounter, where men typically determine the terms and, in some cases, do so with violence' (12). These insights emphasise that power and coercion in transactional sex influences both whether women participate, and also the nature of the sexual interaction, two different elements that are conflated in the standard economic framework.

A related concern is the focus on the quantity of money or equivalent value of goods exchanged as the primary motivating factor for women to engage in (unprotected) transactional sex. This is not unsurprising given that these are primarily economic analyses. However, a range of other important factors such as local norms, customs and obligations which shape transactional interactions and emphasise that the value of the exchange can often be a secondary consideration, remain unaccounted for (Hunter 2002; Poulin 2007; Swidler and Watkins 2007). This focus on the exchange element leads to a narrow range of economic interventions, such as conditional cash transfers for schoolgirls which seek to reduce the need for them to engage in transactional sex by providing the income that is seen to be the initial motivator (Baird et al. 2009; Fiszbein et al. 2009), or microfinance, which aims to reduce female reliance on transactional sex as a source of vital income (Pronyk et al. 2005). These approaches fail to incorporate a more nuanced understanding of transactional sex, ignore factors such as norms and conventions which may in fact be a more pertinent point of intervention, and in some cases may make things worse (see MacPherson et al. 2015).

A final limitation is that these approaches are framed implicitly within a poverty narrative, particularly in relation to the response by poor women to adverse household shocks. Whilst this is no doubt an important driver of some transactional interactions, the broader literature emphasises that transactional sex is not just engaged in for basic survival goods, but also for consumption goods or status goods (Hunter 2002; Leclerc-Madlala 2003), and not just by women that are poor (Chatterji et al. 2004). Indeed, it is noted that processes of globalisation, consumerism and the associated expansion of needs that are related to capitalist development may in fact enhance the pressures for women to engage in transactional sex (Hunter 2002; Leclerc-Madlala 2003; Dunkle et al. 2004; Stoebenau et al. 2011), rather than development bringing about a reduction in motivations for transactional sex by fulfilling basic material needs. This highlights the dynamic nature of sexual relations and analytical categories, and also how structural economic processes play an important role in shaping individual behaviours.

This discussion emphasises the limitations and omissions of mainstream approaches to transactional sex, and also how divorced these approaches are from the themes highlighted by the broader public health literature. In particular, transactional sex is viewed in a stylised manner, with little incorporation of issues such as gendered and economic power and coercion, and how transactional sexual interactions are framed by structural dynamics. The economic element is also extremely narrow, reduced to the element of exchange. This ignores the many different forms of transactional sex in practice, and thus presents an incomplete analysis. Despite the dominance of the rational choice framework in the economics profession, there are, however, other approaches which address notions of inequality and power, and which help shed light on an alternative economics of transactional sex.

Fieldwork methods

The evidence presented below is taken from data gathered in a qualitative research project conducted in Mwanza region, northwestern Tanzania, which investigated the relationship between temporary economic population mobility and HIV risk. The main component of the fieldwork was comprised of three interlinked phases. In the first phase, four focus groups were conducted to select the mobile groups to be studied in the rest of the research, using a participatory ranking process that aimed to identify the most important forms of mobility engaged in by the local community. The participants in this stage were men and women from both rural and urban areas within the study site, with focus groups conducted with men and women separately to try and ensure that women's experiences were captured. The mobile groups selected in this stage were mobile farmers, maize traders and *dagaa*[1] sellers. The second phase involved process-mapping exercises with a sample of each mobile group again in a focus group setting, with participants exploring issues of mobility and sexual behaviour, though in relation to the 'general' process, including discussions around the systemic and individual factors that shaped patterns of movement and specific destinations, and the nature of sexual interactions engaged in by mobile individuals. In the third phase, a series of in-depth interviews were conducted with a sub-sample of each mobile group to understand participants' own experiences of engaging in specific forms of mobility, including questions relating to their own sexual behaviour. Owing to emerging themes relating to the issue of transactional sex, two additional focus groups were conducted towards the end of the fieldwork to explore local sexual norms in more detail. All of these activities were conducted in the local languages, Swahili and Sukuma, by local research assistants who were the same sex as the participants.[2] A thorough debrief was conducted after each research activity, and later complemented with translated transcripts for full analysis and triangulation. Other concurrent activities conducted to understand more about the local socio-economic setting, and to contextualise the qualitative component, included interviews with key informants such as local village and government officials, informal discussions with the local research community, the author's own observations and further secondary research.

Whilst transactional sex was not the initial focus of the study, it was a theme that emerged during the research process, and in particular when mobile individuals were talking about their sexual interactions while they were away. Although mobility may have enhanced the opportunities for doing so, it was also clear that transactional sex was not just engaged in by those who were mobile, and indeed this led to a reconsideration of the role of mobility as the project progressed, with the findings suggesting that sexual interactions were strongly influenced by gender relations and local sexual norms rather than mobility. This shed light on how risk was shaped for both mobile and non-mobile populations, and suggested one explanation as to why previous statistical work found few differences in either sexual behaviour or HIV prevalence/incidence between mobile and non-mobile groups (Deane, Parkhurst, and Johnston 2010), hence the focus on transactional sex in this paper. The themes that we present here have important implications for the way that transactional sex is conceptualised in economic terms, discussed in subsequent sections.

Transactional sex in northern Tanzania

Transactional sex as a norm

One key theme reported in both focus groups and interviews was that transactional sex, as we have defined it above, is an established and accepted social norm, with broad agreement within the community that there is an expectation of some form of exchange or transfer when extra- or non-marital sex takes place. For example, male maize traders reported that, in relation to opportunities to have sex whilst they were away, 'when you have ... little amount of money ... you can look for a friend ... but if you have run out completely ... it is impossible,' emphasising that some form of transfer was expected. In later focus groups conducted with male and female adult participants to explore the issue of transactional sex, participants agreed that this was their expectation:

> You can surely tell him and he accepts everything, but in his heart, he says if I say I do not have [money], I cannot go with this woman [to have sex]. (Female focus group participant)

> R: Here ... when a woman expects to have sex with a man, getting money is primary.
> Interviewer: Of primary/importance?
> R: Eeh, it's primary. Even if she's given something else money is the primary thing.
>   (Male focus group participant)

This expectation reflects similar findings in research by Wamoyi et al. (2010, 2011) with young people and their parents, conducted in the same study site, in which parents noted that a girl's private parts are like a 'shop' ('hayo ni maduka'). This expresses the view that nothing is obtained from a shop for free, and hence when applied to sex, women have to be given something in return for satisfying male sexual desires. In fact, fathers argued that sex should never be free as it would make it difficult for men to get women, as no woman would agree to have sex for nothing in return, and parents and grandparents all expressed the view that if a man has sex with their daughter or granddaughter without giving her anything, they will 'have made a fool of her'. Expectations around exchange and casual and informal sexual relationships are also reported in other studies on transactional sex conducted in Tanzania (Maganja et al. 2007).

Operationalising transactional norms

Transactional sexual interactions are engaged in by a wide range of actors in an array of divergent socio-economic contexts, for multiple reasons, and hence avoid neat categorisation. One common theme is that men can utilise transactional norms to stake a future claim on sex by giving gifts upfront, in a sense a down payment which is then followed up on and used to coerce sex at a later time or date. This may involve buying someone a soda, or giving them a few extra tomatoes or fish at the market:

> You may be bought a soda, someone may pass selling mangoes you may be bought and you eat, when it gets to the evening, the one who was buying you those things starts to follow you [ask for sex] because of what he gave you. (Female seller of *dagaa* [small fish, see note 1])

This phenomenon has previously been reported in relation to younger women still at school, with gifts such as sugar cane, *vitumbua*[3] or sweets often received from older men as a means of pressuring them into sex (Wamoyi et al. 2010).

Conversely, men report that they feel targeted by women, who seduce them primarily to gain access to their money. In one example, a male maize trader noted that he is approached by women on buying trips at times when he has available cash to hand, whilst one farmer reported feeling targeted owing to the fact that if his female employee convinced him to have sex with her, he would have to give her something, such as a wage increase or one-off payment:

> Because every woman who sees you will know that ... aah, money has come. (Male maize trader)

> Now if you keep women there must be temptations. Those women will want sex from you so that you can sometime increase the amount of money, you may have agreed, she seduces you so that you may increase the money through sex. (Male farmer)

Whilst these may in part be narratives used by men that seek to absolve themselves of any responsibility for the extra-marital sex that they engage in, this captures the notion that women are often active agents, albeit in a constrained socio-economic gendered context, rather than merely passive victims, in transactional interactions (Hunter 2002). Further, the manner in which transactional interactions are characterised will also depend on who is giving the account.

Sex and local value chains

Transactional interactions were also reported in relation to participation in local value chains, though again there are different accounts of how this takes place. From a male perspective, male fish traders report giving female customers fish in advance on the basis that they will be paid another time, creating the space for women to attempt to pay back the debt through sex.

> Now you may find that someone comes for a loan. You may loan him/her thinking that he/she is a customer but you may find that he/she has some motives. Now in paying he/she may start giving you excuses, now that needs a wise mind, this person is like this and this is his/her motive. (Male *dagaa* seller)

However, men can also use this situation to extract sex by allowing women to come back and pay later on, and once the goods are loaned and the debt created, they have something to negotiate with:

> A man is . . . is . . . you ask for a loan, say lend me *dagaa*, as soon as he lends you, you are tempted. The other day when you send money to him he says just send that money. You meet again later, eeh . . there is no need to pay me back the money, we should just make love. (Female *dagaa* seller)

In a similar vein, transactional sex is related to a local informal credit practice known as *mali kauli*, in which traders provide goods upfront to street sellers who then pay them back from the day's proceeds. This enables the distribution of goods across local value networks without the need for daily cash transactions, and also the space for a degree of negotiation and renegotiation of prices as market conditions change, thus protecting traders and sellers from fluctuations in the market in conditions of mutually beneficial ongoing economic relationships (Ogawa 2006). This is another situation in which sex can ultimately be exchanged in lieu of the debt repayment, but within the structure of local trading practices and credit arrangements. This was reported by local maize traders, tomato intermediary traders and *dagaa* sellers, and is a practice that has parallels with transactional sex related to the workings of the fish value chain observed across sub-Saharan Africa (Gordon 2005; Bene and Merten 2008; MacPherson et al. 2012):

> Now that can find you at times when you are sexually aroused. That means that it tempts you because one can buy maize three or four times, but the fifth she decides to seek for a loan, and tells you many things, now you will find out her intentions for coming, so it mean if you also have directed your thoughts there, that's where the business ends . . . (Male maize trader)

In this situation it is unclear whether sex is engaged in by female sellers because they simply have not managed to sell enough that day to repay the debt, or whether this is a speculative attempt to increase their profits. Further, as with other forms of transactional sex discussed above, the degree of agency and coercion will vary, with some women forced to pay the debt back through sex, whereas some will view these economic relationships as opportunities to supplement their capital. Importantly, it is the gendered nature of these value chains, in which men predominantly sell to women, which provide the circumstances in which gendered and economic power can be expressed. However, it must also be made clear that transactional sex is not always the outcome, as men may not be interested in having sex and will demand repayment through other means such as taking possessions or deferring to a later date.

There are, however, alternative views on the role of sex and exchange and local value chains which reflect unequal gender relations in an entirely different way. One female participant noted that borrowing goods is a way for women to instigate relationships with men in a context in which they are not overtly supposed to do, which emphasises the multiple views and understandings of transactional sex held by those engaging in them:

R: A man hasn't dared to ask for things of love, but she has desires for him, now when she desires him, she will insist on her point that I will go and ask for a loan of something, but today I've got money but I don't want to pay, what I want is …

Interviewer: Love

R: Love. When he comes, 'I want my money,' I will be wandering this and that way while I've got the money, what I am targeting there is sex. But if his blood and mine are attracted, he will just ask that I need you, so let's put aside issues related to that money. That's when love/sex starts. Issues of loan are also put aside. (Female focus group participant)

A final and related category is transactional sex engaged in by female businesswomen of different economic status to increase the capital available to them:

Perhaps when you see that the capital is small you decide maybe I should do this, maybe if you have a big capital you cannot ask for a loan from anyone. (Female *dagaa* seller)

In particular, this quote emphasises that it is not just poor women with little capital who engage in sex for exchange, but also women who are seeking to expand their business. This is a theme that is reflected in other recent work (Hunter 2002; Leclerc-Madlala 2003), and is an extremely important issue if transactional sex is to be better understood, and if prevention efforts are to move away from the poverty narrative that mainstream economic approaches continue to perpetuate.

As noted above, transactional sex has been related to changes in the social system in which pressures for luxury goods and cultures of consumerism, in concert with differential abilities of men and women to fulfil these needs independently, have contributed to the growth of transactional sexual practices. This was again reflected in this study, with focus group participants noting the pressures that women are under in terms of accessing luxury items:

Previously they were just living, today a person may leave here and go somewhere to do her things, meaning living for what … for men, and those men do not have sex with her without bribing, how will she live, how will she eat, what will she wear without being bribed, what makes us being bribed is luxury, thinking of bribery, maybe they were brought by whites. (Female focus group participant)

This further emphasises the need to understand transactional sex as a practice that has specific socio-historical underpinnings, and that, rather than reflecting transactions in an ahistorical 'market' for sex, this practice is not inevitable and reflects changes in the social system, and specifically the penetration of capitalism and the monetisation of economic life.

The economics of transactional sex revisited

The evidence presented here illustrates the array of concrete forms that transactional sexual interactions take, which involve multiple and overlapping explanations, varying degrees of gendered and economic power, a range of different motivations, and are engaged in by women from different socio-economic groups. Whilst these findings corroborate previous work on transactional sex, here we reflect specifically on the mainstream economic approaches reviewed above that are primarily organised around the value of the goods or money that is exchanged.

The conflicting reports that men and women give when talking about transactional sex emphasise that the degree of coercion involved will vary, and that women will enter into these transactions with different degrees of awareness and control over what is expected of them. In some cases women report that men give these gifts without any mention of sex, whereas in others, it is unclear to what extent women have the power or economic security to refuse these gifts. This does not preclude the notion that women can accept these gifts in the knowledge that by doing so there is an expectation of them agreeing to have sex later on, or that they are actively engaging in transactional interactions for material gain. As with other accounts that suggest the exchange is often of secondary importance, we also find evidence to suggest that those engaging in transactional sex do so with contrasting motives and aims, with women using informal credit practices as a way of instigating relationships. These complex and overlapping motivations are not accounted for in mainstream, individualistic approaches, and are at odds with mainstream economic views of the market for informal sex in which both parties enter into the exchange with a common understanding of the specific nature of the transaction. Additionally, the amount transferred, and the frequency, vary across interactions, with exchanges or transfers not required in every instance in ongoing relationships, and nor do 'exchanges' of sex and money/goods always take place at the same time. This presents a challenge for economic analyses that focus on the amount transferred and assume that the exchange is always related to sexual interactions in the same way.

One central issue is the role of social norms, a current focus within the structural drivers literature. In relation to transactional sex, which we have established as a social norm above, it is unclear to what extent economic approaches framed in the language of rational choice are able to incorporate the role of social norms in shaping sexual behaviour. Indeed, one central critique of mainstream economics is that behaviour is often motivated by a range of factors, including not just social norms, but tradition, custom and habit (Davis 2003). Whilst the mainstream economic approaches reviewed above emphasise the role of agency, this agency can be reconceptualised as a form of agency in which men and women creatively utilise, apply and reapply this norm within a specific and changing socio-economic context. As our research suggests, men and women both actively attempt to use this norm to either extract sex (in the case of men) or for material gain (in the case of women), with varying degrees of success and intent. This supports the notion that women are not just passive victims in this process but may utilise their sexuality for material gain, although this must be understood in relation to dominant norms and socio-economic structures.

However, the acknowledged role of social norms raises the question as to whether social norms around transactional sex have any economic content, or whether they should be understood as purely 'cultural' or 'social'. Our research suggests that the development of transactional sexual norms has been influenced by an increasing commodification of social life, with transactional sex linked to the demand for luxury goods that comes with the development of capitalist relations. Lugalla et al. (1999) argue that transactional sexual practices have replaced older forms of reciprocal exchange associated with goodwill, in the light of intensifying poverty (*Ibid.*). Transactional sex also reflects the erosion of patriarchal relations to some extent (Wamoyi et al. 2010), as men who want to have sex with women in non-marital situations are now in a position in which they are required to provide something. Other explanations of transactional sex emphasise the historical institutional roots of these practices, such as *lubambo*,[4] which governs the legitimacy of extra-marital relationships in Zambia and which frames fish-for-sex transactions (Merten and Haller 2007). These narratives suggest that whilst the giving of gifts in exchange for sex is a more recent phenomenon, in part a response to increasing economic liberalisation and change, with transactional sex informed by or replacing local institutions or practices, processes related to development may be enhancing risk. These dynamics are not reflected in mainstream economic approaches, which remain ahistorical, with little concern other than how individuals make optimising decisions. Luke (2006) discusses whether the market for safe sex is a recent phenomenon, and whilst acknowledging that 'the practice of trading money for sex may be a historical occurrence in Kisumu' (344), concludes that this is in fact a response to the HIV/AIDS epidemic, presumably because the epidemic has significantly altered the potential costs of having sex, opening the space for negotiation and optimising agents' responses to different 'prices'. However, this ignores how, as noted above, transactional sex is framed by economic and social processes.

Transactional interactions are also related to participation in local value chains, and the highly gendered nature of these value chains, in which gendered interfaces exist where predominantly men sell to women, creating the space in which gendered and economic power can be expressed. Transactional sex can thus occur in a range of contexts and for different reasons. Men can attempt to extract sex through the extension of credit, whereas women can also use informal credit arrangements as a space in which to repay a debt, either because they have not made enough profit, or to expand their capital. This makes clear that transactions that appear the same can in fact be undertaken for entirely different reasons. However, for some, risk will be experienced owing to participation in value chains in which income and profits are often small, variable and subject to daily fluctuations. In comparison to rational choice economic approaches that frame transactional sex as a response to household shocks, we find that risk can be encountered in the daily undertaking of livelihood activities central to processes of household production and reproduction, owing to participation in fragile economic activities.

Following this, transactional sex, as is alluded to in Luke (2006), has a further consequence in that it structures who has sex with whom, particularly as men are required to have access to the necessary resources for the exchange. Our research finds examples of older men having sex with younger women, employer with employee, trader with street seller, creditor with borrower, and businessmen with hotel worker, to list but a few. This has implications for HIV transmission, particularly as this shapes patterns of intergenerational sex, and thus enhanced risk for women. These partnerships illustrate that transactional relationships reflect power relationships that are rooted in prevailing social relations and the intersection of a range of forms of unequal power. This inequality of power is also expressed in the rare(r) occasions in which women are the ones who are gaining sex through giving money to men, something that was touched upon by participants in our study site and noted in other research projects (Dunkle et al. 2007), adding further nuance, suggesting that in some cases economic power is more important than gendered power. These explanations that address power relations, including the influence of gendered and economic coercion, are in stark contrast to the rational choice models that underpin mainstream economic approaches (Christensen 1998).

This brief discussion enables a reflection on different economic approaches to understanding transactional sex. A political economy approach views the economic content as rooted in the role of women in production and reproduction, and locates transactional sex within the workings of the economic system. The forms of transactional sex reported in our study site also reflect other important economic processes, such as increasing consumerism and peer pressure for status among young women in school, or informal credit arrangements in local value chains that are key to enabling the distribution of goods along complex chains with limited cash transactions. This re-emphasises that an economic approach to transactional sex must look beyond the transaction and the value of the exchange for a more comprehensive economic and structural analysis.

Implications for HIV prevention and public health

Our analysis has a number of implications for future HIV prevention efforts and public health. First, following from the notion that the value of the exchange is not always the primary focus of many transactional interactions, and that transactional sex must be located in local sexual norms around sex and exchange, themselves rooted in broader socio-economic relations, the transaction should not be the primary site of intervention. Programmes such as conditional cash transfer programmes and microfinance programmes that aim to decrease women's reliance on transactional sex by giving them either additional income or the opportunity to earn more income are unlikely to succeed, as they are primarily aimed at what we consider to be the wrong target, and based on a limited individualistic analysis. Some small public health enhancements may be achieved in this way, but the broader social relations remain unaddressed. However, if women are given an expanded access to microfinance and income-generating opportunities, the result may be that rather than rebalancing power, their value to men as productive assets increases, further entrenching current gender relations. The expansion of female income generation may also enhance, rather than fulfil, female consumption possibilities, with increased consumption leading to the creation of new wants and needs, with motivations for transactional sex maintained but in a different form. Further, interventions may need to go beyond reducing individual vulnerability and poverty through moderate expansions of income to trying to ensure that the gains from the sustained rapid economic growth that many sub-Saharan African countries are currently experiencing (IMF 2013) are not exclusively captured by men. A related issue is that, as we have argued above, transactional sex is a social norm, rooted in broader socio-economic processes, and with historical roots. This highlights the limitations of behaviour change programmes, and the challenges encountered by incentive-based approaches that attempt to address institutionalised historical practices.

A second key and related theme of intervention, and one that microfinance and cash transfer programmes aim to address, albeit in a limited way, is women's empowerment. It is widely recognised that female empowerment is an essential component of HIV prevention programmes. Reflecting the suggestions of the economic analyses reviewed above, the broader literature on transactional sex puts forward a similar policy agenda, for example the need to improve education, keep young women in school longer, address parental guidance and enhance income-generating opportunities (Chatterji et al. 2004; Bene and Merten 2008; Jewkes et al. 2012). To some extent, different approaches have yielded similar policy recommendations,. This is an issue that has been grappled with across the developmental arena, embodied in the third Millennium Development Goal (Kabeer 2005). One (but not the only) critical approach to how empowerment is conceptualised, and which offers the potential for a more radical avenue of intervention, emphasises that 'gender inequalities are multi-dimensional and cannot be reduced to some single and universally agreed set of priorities' (*Ibid.*, 23). In this sense, empowerment is not something that can be achieved through a set of isolated interventions, and requires a deeper degree of social change 'in which policy changes are implemented in ways that allow women themselves to participate, to monitor, and to hold policy makers, corporations, and other relevant actors accountable for their actions' (*Ibid.*, 23). For Kabeer, the key issue for international donors is whether they are prepared to fund grassroots women's organisations to mobilise women in the fight for greater equality, a form of collective, not individualistic, notion. This is applicable to

HIV/AIDS-related interventions, with the key to greater autonomy over sexual interactions, and particularly transactional sex, rooted in women's empowerment through collective action.

Reflecting on the structural drivers of HIV, an application of this approach emphasises that better health outcomes for women are a political issue, and involve a collective struggle against entrenched male power. However, mainstream economic approaches consistently fail to engage with this political element, as behaviour is conceptualised at the level of the individual, with little space for incorporating the need for collective action. There are also concerns regarding how these forms of struggle fit into standard public health and epidemiological preventative frameworks, or with donor priorities for measurable outcomes, in which the number of condoms distributed, or the number of people given access to ARVs (antiretrovirals) can be quantified (Hunsmann 2010). The pressure for immediate results also presents a challenge to funding grassroots women's groups, as the degree of social change required will be an inherently uneven process. Further, it is even unclear to what extent grassroots movements can be beholden to external donors, and whether by doing so the overall aims of grassroots movements are compromised (Beckmann and Bujra 2010). This presents a significant challenge in relation to prevention funding that requires more research and attention.

However, the current consensus that unequal gender relations are one of the underlying drivers of HIV suggests that HIV prevention will necessarily involve the transformation of these relations. The debate then becomes whether this is possible through piecemeal interventions that seek to empower women through small transfers of money in the hope that this will give them greater economic autonomy, or other forms of intervention that are more political and collective in nature (Kabeer 2003; Sweetman 2013). The incentives and market-based approach to social engineering is not only misfocused, but also has no historical precedent. It fails to account for the ways in which women in other settings and time periods have struggled for and taken power, and which have frequently involved women as a social group demanding a greater degree of equality. HIV prevention efforts that seek to empower women can, then, learn lessons from the ways in which women have historically struggled for greater freedom. This locates HIV prevention within broader developmental processes of change, but processes of change that are by no means certain, and that involve challenging entrenched male power and dominance. It will also require a significant reorientation of current prevention efforts and the overcoming of institutional resistance to alternative approaches (Hunsmann 2010).

Conclusion

This article has argued that mainstream economic approaches to transactional sex capture only a limited and stylised view of this practice. In particular, we conceptualise transactional sex as a practice that is underpinned by social norms rooted in the historical development of gender relations. Further, the evidence we present illustrates how sexual norms around transactional sex are utilised by a range of actors across different contexts, and also that transactional norms structure who has sex with whom, and thus are located within the context of broader social relations. This alternative, yet admittedly incomplete, economic approach has illustrated the need specifically for improved understandings of social norms that include an analysis of their economic content. This entails understanding economics in a broader sense, rather than the narrow optimisation framework and focus on scarcity and trade-offs that have come to dominate the discipline. We also emphasise that it is necessary to understand how social norms change over time, and how they are related to the development and expansion of the capitalist economic system, and how this influences related processes of consumerism and expanded needs that add to, rather than reduce, the practice of transactional sex, reflecting gendered abilities to access the fruits of development. It is essential that these insights are taken into account in the policy arena, and that development is not seen as a panacea for HIV prevention and the reduction of transactional sex, requiring a move away from the underlying poverty narrative.

We also discussed the implications for potential HIV prevention efforts of different economic approaches. Our analysis questions the transaction as the site of intervention, derived from economic approaches of which this is the focus, particularly in the light of the risk that women can face in engaging in economic activities, and evidence that suggests women from all social strata engage in transactional sex. The current popularity of this intervention is somewhat puzzling, especially as the evidence that microfinance reduces poverty is mixed and inconclusive (Duvendack et al. 2011), let alone expecting microfinance to somehow also tackle prevailing social norms around sex and exchange, or to provide women with more control over their sexual and reproductive lives. Further, this policy is based on a narrow and incomplete economic analysis, and to some extent represents an optimistic and unproven leap of faith. Whether policies such as these that attempt to work within the prevailing economic system (Bateman and Chang 2012) and that focus on small incentive changes without any attempts to engage with structural issues can be challenged, remains to be seen. However, alternative approaches derived from political economy and other economic approaches that are not based on the standard, individualistic, technical apparatus, offer a potential way forward. More research by political economists and those interested in the structural drivers of HIV is needed to better understand the historical, social and economic context of transactional sex, and how this practice evolves over time.

Acknowledgements

The qualitative evidence presented originates from research conducted in northern Tanzania, funded by Bloomsbury colleges and the London International Development Centre. The fieldwork was conducted by and with the support of the National Institute of Medical Research Tanzania, Mark Urassa, Ray Nsigaye, Lucas Boniface, Penina Samwell, Grace Bulugu, Mathius Shimo, Joyce Chuwa and Mpyanjo Chagu.

Disclosure statement

No potential conflict of interest was reported by the author.

Notes

1. Local small fish.
2. For a full discussion of the role of research assistants in this setting, see Deane and Stevano (2015).
3. Rice cakes.
4. *Lubambo* is a customary institution which formalises extra-marital relationships. See Merten and Haller (2007) for a detailed discussion of the meaning of *lubambo*.

References

Auerbach, J., J. Parkhurst, and C. Cáceres. 2011. "Addressing Social Drivers of HIV/AIDS for the Long-term Response: Conceptual and Methodological Considerations." *Global Public Health* 6 (S3): S293–S309.

Auerbach, J., J. Parkhurst, C. Cáceres, and K. Keller. 2010. "Addressing Social Drivers of HIV/AIDS: Some Conceptual, Methodological, and Evidentiary Considerations." Social Drivers Working Group: Working Papers.

Baird, S., E. Chirwa, C. McIntosh, and B. Ozler. 2009. "The Short-term Impacts of a Schooling Conditional Cash Transfer Program on the Sexual Behaviour of Young Women." Policy Research Working Paper, World Bank Development Research Group.

Baird, S. J., R. S. Garfein, C. T. McIntosh, and B. Özler. 2012. "Effect of a Cash Transfer Programme for Schooling on Prevalence of HIV and Herpes Simplex Type 2 in Malawi: A Cluster Randomised Trial." *The Lancet* 379 (9823): 1320–1329.

Bateman, M., and H-J. Chang. 2012. "Microfinance and the Illusion of Development: From Hubris to Nemesis in Thirty Years." *World Economic Review* 1: 13–36.

Beckmann, N., and J. Bujra. 2010. "The 'Politics of the Queue': The Politicization of People Living with HIV/AIDS in Tanzania." *Development and Change* 41 (6): 1041–1064.

Bene, C., and S. Merten. 2008. "Women and Fish-for-sex: Transactional Sex, HIV/AIDS and Gender in African Fisheries." *World Development* 36 (5): 875–899.

Campbell, C., and B. Williams. 1999. "Beyond the Biomedical and Behavioural: Towards an Integrated Approach to HIV Prevention in the Southern African Mining Industry." *Social Science & Medicine* 48 (11): 1625–1639.

Chatterji, M., N. Murray, D. London, and P. Anglewicz. 2004. "The Factors Influencing Transactional Sex Among Young Men and Women in 12 Sub-Saharan African Countries." The Policy Project.

Christensen, K. 1998. "Economics Without Money; Sex Without Gender: A Critique of Philipson and Posner's "Private Choices and Public Health: The AIDS Epidemic in an Economic Perspective." *Feminist Economics* 4: 1–24.

Davis, J. B. 2003. *The Theory of the Individual in Economics: Identity and Value*. London: Routledge.

Deane, K. D., J. O. Parkhurst, and D. Johnston. 2010. "Linking Migration, Mobility and HIV." *Tropical Medicine & International Health* 15 (12): 1458–1463.

Deane, K., and S. Stevano. 2015. "Towards a Political Economy of Research Assistants: Reflections from Fieldwork Conducted in Tanzania and Mozambique." *Qualitative Research*. OnlineFirst, March 24, 2015.

Dunkle, K. L., R. K. Jewkes, H. C. Brown, G. E. Gray, J. A. McIntyre, and S. D. Harlow. 2004. "Transactional Sex among Women in Soweto, South Africa: Prevalence, Risk Factors and Association with HIV Infection." *Social Science & Medicine* 59: 1581–1592.

Dunkle, K. L., R. Jewkes, M. Nduna, N. Jama, J. Levin, Y. Sikweyiya, and M. P. Koss. 2007. "Transactional Sex with Casual and Main Partners among Young South African Men in the Rural Eastern Cape: Prevalence, Predictors, and Associations with Gender-based Violence." *Social Science & Medicine* 65 (6): 1235–1248.

Duvendack, M., R. Palmer-Jones, J. G. Copestake, L. Hooper, Y. Loke, and N. Rao. 2011. *What is the Evidence of the Impact of Microfinance on the Well-being of Poor People?* London: EPPI-Centre, Social Science Research Unit, Institute of Education, University of London.

Fine, B., and D. Milonakis. 2009. *From Economics Imperialism to Freakonomics: The Shifting Boundaries Between Economics and Other Social Sciences*. Abingdon: Routledge.

Fiszbein, A., N. Schady, F. H. G. Ferreira, M. Grosh, N. Kelleher, P. Olinto, and E. Skoufias. 2009. "Conditional Cash Transfers: Reducing Present and Future Poverty." World Bank Policy Research Report. Washington, DC: World Bank.

Gertler, P., M. Shah, and S. M. Bertozzi. 2005. "Risky Business: The Market for Unprotected Commercial Sex." *Journal of Political Economy* 113 (3): 518–550.

Gordon, A. 2005. *HIV/AIDS in the Fisheries Sector in Africa*. Cairo: WorldFish Center.

Hahn, R. A. 1991. "What Should Behaviorual Scientists Be Doing About AIDS?" *Social Science & Medicine* 33 (1): 1–3.

Hunsmann, M. 2010. "Policy Hurdles to Addressing Structural Drivers of HIV/AIDS - A Case Study of Tanzania." Annual Conference of the Norweigan Association for Develpoment Research, Oslo.

Hunter, M. 2002. "The Materiality of Everyday Sex: Thinking Beyond 'Prostitution'." *African Studies* 61 (1): 99–120.

IMF. 2013. *Regional Economic Outlook: Sub-Saharan Africa; Keeping the Pace*. Washington: IMF.

Jewkes, R., K. Dunkle, M. Nduna, and N. Jama Shai. 2012. "Transactional Sex and HIV Incidence in a Cohort of Young Women in the Stepping Stones Trial." *AIDS & Clinical Research* 3 (5): 1–8.

Johnston, D. 2011. "World Bank Research on HIV/AIDS: Praise Where It's Due?" In *The Political Economy of Development: The World Bank, Neoliberalism and Development Research*, edited by K. Bayliss, B. Fine, and E. Van Waeyenberge, 128–145. London: Pluto Press.

Johnston, D. 2013. *Economics and HIV: The Sickness of Economics*. Abingdon: Routledge.

Kabeer, N. 2003. "Gender Equality and Women's Empowerment." In *Gender Mainstreaming in Poverty Eradication and the MDGs: A Handbook for Policymakers and Other Stakeholders*, edited by N. Kabeer, 169–196. London: Commonwealth Secretariat; Ottawa: IDRC/CDRI.

Kabeer, N. 2005. "Gender Equality and Women's Empowerment: A Critical Analysis of the Third Millennium Development Goal 1." *Gender and Development* 13 (1): 13–24.

King, R. 1999. "Sexual Behavioural Change: Where have Theories Taken Us?" *UNAIDS Best Practice Collection*. Geneva: UNAIDS.

Leclerc-Madlala, S. 2003. "Transactional Sex and the Pursuit of Modernity." *Social Dynamics* 29 (2): 213–233.

Lugalla, J. L., M. A. C. Emmelin, A. K. Mutembei, C. J. Comoro, J. Z. J. Killewo, G. Kwesigabo, A. I. M. Sandstrom, and L. G. Dahlgren. 1999. "The Social and Cultural Contexts of HIV/AIDS Transmission in the Kagera Region, Tanzania." *Journal of Asian and African Studies* 34 (4): 377–402.

Luke, N. 2006. "Exchange and Condom Use in Informal Sexual Relationships in Urban Kenya." *Economic Development and Cultural Change* 54 (2): 319–348.

MacPherson, E. E., J. Sadalaki, M. Njoloma, V. Nyongopa, L. Nkhwazi, V. Mwapasa, D. G. Lalloo, N. Desmond, J. Seeley, and S. Theobald. 2012. "Transactional Sex and HIV: Understanding the Gendered Structural Drivers of HIV in Fishing Communities in Southern Malawi." *Journal of the International AIDS Society* 15 (Suppl. 1): 1–9.

MacPherson, E., J. Sadalaki, V. Nyongopa, L. Nkhwazi, M. Phiri, A. Chimphonda, N. Desmond, V. Mwapasa, D. G. Lalloo, J. Seeley, and S. Theobald. 2015. "Exploring the Complexity of Microfinance and HIV in Fishing Communities on the Shores of Lake Malawi." *Review of African Political Economy* 42 (145): 414–436.

Maganja, M., S. Maman, A. Groues, and J. K. Mbwambo. 2007. "Skinning the Goat and Pulling the Load: Transactional Sex among Youth in Dar es Salaam, Tanzania." *AIDS Care* 19 (8): 974–981.

Merten, S., and T. Haller. 2007. "Culture, Changing Livelihoods, and HIV/AIDS Discourse: Reframing the Institutionalization of Fish-for-sex Exchange in the Zambian Kafue Flats." *Culture, Health & Sexuality* 9 (1): 69–83.

Milonakis, D., and B. Fine. 2008. *From Political Economy to Economics: Method, the Social and the Historical in the Evolution of Economic Theory*. London: Routledge.

Ogawa, S. 2006. "'Earning among Friends': Business Practices and Creed among Petty Traders in Tanzania." *African Studies Quarterley* 9 (1 & 2): 23–38.

Oster, E. 2012. "HIV and Sexual Behaviour Change: Why not Africa?" *Journal of Health Economics* 31 (1): 35–49.

Padian, N. S., S. I. McCoy, J. E. Balkus, and J. N. Wasserheit. 2010. "Weighing the Gold in the Gold Standard: Challenges in HIV Prevention Research." *AIDS* 24 (5): 621–635. doi:610.1097/QAD.1090b1013e328337798a.

Philipson, T., and R. A. Posner. 1995. "The Microeconomics of the AIDS Epidemic in Africa." *Population and Development Review* 21 (4): 835–848.

Poulin, M. 2007. "Sex, Money, and Premarital Partnerships in Southern Malawi." *Social Science & Medicine* 65 (11): 2383–2393.

Pronyk, P. M., J. C. Kim, J. R. Hargreaves, M. B. Makhubele, L. A. Morison, C. Watts, and J. D. H. Porter. 2005. "Microfinance and HIV Prevention - Emerging Lessons from Rural South Africa." *Small Enterprise Development* 16: 26–38.

Robinson, J., and E. Yeh. 2011. "Transactional Sex as a Response to Risk in Western Kenya." *American Economic Journal: Applied Economics* 3 (1): 35–64.

Stillwaggon, E., and L. Sawers. 2012. "Power, Race, and the Neglect of Science: The HIV Epidemics in Sub-Saharan Africa." In *Ecologies and Politics of Health*, edited by B. King, and K. Crews, 239–259. London: Routledge.

Stoebenau, K., S. Nixon, C. Rubincam, S. Willan, Y. Zembe, T. Tsikoane, P. Tanga, et al. 2011. "More than Just Talk: The Framing of Transactional Sex and its Implications for Vulnerability to HIV in Lesotho, Madagascar and South Africa." *Globalization and Health* 7 (34): 1–15.

Stoebenau, K., L. Heise, J. Wamoyi, and N. Bobrova. Forthcoming. *Competing Paradigms of Transactional Sex: Clarifying its Meaning for HIV Prevention in Sub-Saharan Africa.*

Sumartojo, E. 2000. "Structural Factors in HIV Prevention: Concepts, Examples, and Implications for Research." *AIDS* 14 (Suppl. 1): S3–10.

Sweat, M. D., and J. A. Denison. 1995. "Reducing HIV Incidence in Developing Countries with Structural and Environmental Interventions." *AIDS* 9 (Suppl. A): S251–257.

Sweetman, C. 2013. "Introduction, Feminist Solidarity and Collective Action." *Gender & Development* 21 (2): 217–229.

Swidler, A., and S. C. Watkins. 2007. "Ties of Dependence: AIDS and Transactional Sex in Rural Malawi."

UNAIDS. 2010. "Combination HIV Prevention: Tailoring and Coordinating Biomedical, Behavioural and Structural Strategies to Reduce New HIV Infections." UNAIDS Discussion Paper. UNAIDS. Geneva: UNAIDS.

De Walque, D., W. H. Dow, and E. Gong. 2013. "Coping with Risk: The Effects of Shocks on Reproductive Health and Transactional Sex in Rural Tanzania." Washington, DC: World Bank Knowledge for Change Impact Evaluation series: no. IE 114.

Wamoyi, J., D. Wight, M. L. Plummer, G. H. Mshana, and D. Ross. 2010. "Transactional Sex amongst Young People in Rural Northern Tanzania: An Ethnography of Young Women's Motivations and Negotiation." *Reproductive Health* 7 (2): 1–18.

Wamoyi, J., A. Fenwick, M. Urassa, B. Zaba, and W. Stones 2011. "Women's Bodies are Shops': Beliefs about Transactional Sex and Implications for Understanding Gender Power and HIV Prevention in Tanzania." *Archives of Sexual Behavior* 40 (1): 5–15.

Wojcicki, J. M. 2002. "'She Drank His Money': Survival Sex and the Problem of Violence in Taverns in Gauteng Province, South Africa." *Medical Anthropology Quarterly* 16 (3): 267–293.

DEBATE

The key questions in the AIDS epidemic in 2015

Alan Whiteside OBE

Introduction

When humans are faced with threats they become inventive. There is particularly rapid scientific development during periods of conflict and tension. The Second World War gave us radar, jet engines and the atom bomb. The Cold War led to the development of satellites and, eventually, GPS systems. In the 1960s the United States' Department of Defense work on getting computers to talk to each other paved the way for the Internet.

Health threats too can lead to innovation, as was seen in the response to HIV. In 1981 the first cases of this frightening, unique, new disease were identified at a time of complacency about progress in health. The development of antibiotics in the 1940s and introduction of mass immunisation programmes in the 1950s and 1960s greatly improved global health. In 1977 the World Health Organization (WHO) was able to announce the elimination of smallpox, the first disease to be eradicated. Polio was confined to sporadic outbreaks in remote areas, and there was significant progress in understanding and combating cancer (Mukherjee 2011).

Globally, life expectancy was climbing steadily, although challenges such as malaria and malnutrition remained. AIDS, the acronym for the Acquired Immune Deficiency Syndrome, burst this bubble.

As the number of AIDS cases rose exponentially there was a period of confusion, blame and denial. There was also rapid and unprecedented global mobilisation and scientific progress. The causal retrovirus, the Human Immunodeficiency Virus (HIV), was identified in 1983. An understanding of how it operated, modes of transmission and disease progression followed quickly. However in the last 30 years, despite progress, AIDS has thrown into stark relief critical questions about the meanings of health, equity and how we value lives.

In this debate I will discuss the key challenges we face in HIV and AIDS in 2015. My perspective is that of an economist who lived and worked in the heart of the epidemic, and has over 25 years' experience writing on and researching the disease. The issues I address include: changing perceptions of HIV and AIDS; issues of prevention and treatment; financing for the response; and the need to understand fundamental drivers of HIV. Each is controversial. I begin with a brief history of the epidemic.

A (very) short history of the epidemic

In the 1980s AIDS grabbed media attention. It was incurable, a horrible way to die, and a number of high-profile people (Magic

Johnson, Arthur Ashe, Rudolf Nureyev and Rock Hudson to name but a few) were among those first affected. Science swung into action; driven, it must be acknowledged, by extraordinary activists who were mainly gay men. Their anger and outrage mobilised attention to the disease, an exceptional event in a field dominated by medical sciences, public health and epidemiology. Understanding what caused the disease, how the virus worked, how it was transmitted and developing treatment were priorities.

By 1985 it was apparent that HIV was not confined to men who had sex with men (MSM) in primarily the major western cities. In Thailand there were significant numbers of cases among commercial sex workers (CSW) and their clients. In Eastern Europe, particularly Russia and Ukraine, infections were seen in intravenous drug users (IDU) and their partners. AIDS was reported from a growing number of African countries, Uganda and Senegal among the first to admit they faced a problem. Everywhere there was a concern that HIV had the potential to spread among general populations, defined as adults aged from 15 to 49, without the specific risk profiles of MSM, CSW or IDU (Fowler 2014). It was further recognised mothers could transmit the virus to their infants, and identifying methods for prevention of mother-to-child transmission was a priority.

In 1987 the WHO established the Global Programme on AIDS, primarily to assist developing countries in the creation of national responses – initially through Short Term, then Medium Term Programmes, known as STPs and MTPs. By the 1990s it was apparent the epidemic would be contained in most rich countries, but it remained uncertain as to what would transpire elsewhere.

This was happening in a context where health was moving up the global political agenda. This began with the Alma Ata Declaration, adopted at the International Conference on Primary Health Care in September 1978, which called for urgent action by governments, health and development workers, and the world community to protect and promote the health of all. This recognised access to health care was a human right. The World Bank's 1980 *World Development Report* endorsed the ideas of health care as a human right and committed to primary health care, however the Alma Ata Declaration did not have much impact outside the health sector, although it did set revolutionary foundations for thinking and policy.

Critically important in the evolution of health care thinking was the 1993 World Development Report *Investing in Health*. This was published as the HIV epidemic took off in much of Africa and was both positive and negative. Under the subheading 'Why health matters', the report stated: 'Good health, as people know from their own experience, is a crucial part of well-being, but spending on health can also be justified on purely economic grounds. Improved health contributes to economic growth … ' (World Bank 1993, 17). This gave reason for investing in health. At the same time it was based on neoliberal and neoclassical principles such as the introduction of user fees, decentralisation and privatisation, all of which were later shown to be controversial. This was also the report where the concept of Disability Adjusted Life Years was unveiled as a way of measuring the economic burden of disease.

In 1996 in Geneva, UNAIDS, the new agency charged with coordinating the United Nations' response to the epidemic, began operations. It argued for comprehensive responses to AIDS, and that these multi-faceted (social, economic, behavioural, developmental, medical) responses had to reach beyond 'health'. This approach did not last. At the XI International AIDS Conference in Vancouver in the same year, the development of effective drugs to treat AIDS was announced. The medical discourse became dominant again, although the initial price of US$12,000 per person per year meant treatment was confined to patients in the wealthy world. In 1996 there was $300 million available for HIV/AIDS in low- and middle-income countries, enough money to treat just 25,000 patients at the prevailing prices (and do nothing else).

In 2000 the Millennium Development Goals (MDGs) were established following the Millennium Summit of the United Nations. Goal six was specifically to combat HIV/AIDS, malaria and other diseases. In the same year the UN Security Council passed Resolution 1308, stating 'the HIV/AIDS pandemic, if unchecked, may pose a risk to stability and security.'

The theme at the International AIDS Conference in Durban in 2000 was 'Breaking the Silence'; this covered 'silences' on access to treatment and care; prevention of HIV transmission; governmental and private-sector support of education and resources; human rights; access to appropriate and meaningful information; and support for people living with HIV (The Body 2001). Health and especially AIDS was firmly on the agenda, including in South Africa (despite the denialism of Thabo Mbeki, the country's president at the time).

In 2001 the WHO released the report of the Commission on Macro-Economics and Health (CMH) (WHO 2001). It argued: 'Improving the health and longevity of the poor is an end in itself, a fundamental goal of economic development. But is also a *means* to achieving other development goals' (*Ibid.*, emphasis in the original). Its third key finding (of ten) was: 'The HIV/AIDS pandemic is a distinct and unparalleled catastrophe in its human dimension and its implications for economic development. It therefore requires special consideration' (*Ibid.*, 16). There were extensive critiques of the work and underlying ideology. For example, Katz wrote: 'Clearly the era of hidden agendas is over. The purpose of the CMH report is explicitly to promote and legitimize corporate-led globalisation of capitalism' (Katz 2005). However, there

was incontrovertible increased global attention to health and AIDS was one of, if not the, key driver of this.

Health was not just desirable on an individual and national economic level, but the absence of health (and the AIDS epidemic) was seen as a threat to development. This was evidenced when, in 2003, the UN Secretary-General Kofi Annan established The Commission on HIV/AIDS and Governance in Africa, with its secretariat at the Economic Commission for Africa. I was a member of this Commission and our task was to clarify the impact of HIV/AIDS on state structures and economic development, and examine design and implementation of policies and programmes to govern the epidemic.

The rhetoric was, unusually, matched by resources. In 2001 Annan called for spending on AIDS to be increased tenfold in developing countries, and the Global Fund for AIDS, TB and Malaria was established. In 2003 US President George W. Bush pledged $15 billion toward the Presidential Emergency Program for AIDS Relief (PEPFAR), and the WHO launched the '3 × 5' campaign to have 3 million people on treatment by 2005.

The first decade of the new century saw an unprecedented increase in funding. According to the Kaiser Foundation, at the peak, in 2011, HIV assistance commitments were $8.8 billion, falling to $8.3 billion in 2012 and $8.1 billion in 2013 (Kates, Wexler, and Lief 2013). Although the amount of *new* money decreased, disbursements, the amount of money being 'moved out of the doors' of agencies, was at the highest recorded level in 2013. The cost of drugs plummeted dramatically, falling to US$115 per person per year for first-line antiretroviral therapy (ART) (WHO 2014a). As a result the numbers on treatment rose rapidly and, at the end of 2013, stood at 11.7 million people in low- and middle-income countries.

The environment in which AIDS was spreading, being responded to and being funded was complex. The IMF and World Bank influence on domestic policies meant there were simply no new domestic resources because tax bases were not growing (Rowden 2009, 2010). At the same time, the sheer cost of the disease meant foreign assistance was essential if prevention and treatment programmes were to be put in place. The confluence of neoliberalism and the spread of HIV were unfortunate in the extreme.

The challenges to the HIV and AIDS response

In 2015 there are significant challenges facing those working in and on HIV and AIDS. Some are new while others have been brewing for the past decade and more. We know where the disease is located, how it is transmitted, and have a good idea of the numbers that are and will be infected. The doomsday scenarios of 1990s, fears of uncontrolled spread and that, in the worst affected countries, it would lead to economic collapse and political implosion, have not come to pass. However, AIDS has not gone away. The remainder of the debate addresses the key challenges. Table 1 provides selected data for a sample of the worst affected countries and helps illustrate the issues.

Adult HIV prevalence ranged from 6.2% in Kenya to a shocking 26.5% in Swaziland. The actual per person government health expenditure is, in some settings, much lower than the cost of AIDS treatment. In Uganda in 2011 the government was only spending $11 per person per year and the country is heavily dependent on donors. By contrast South Africa's per capita expenditure was $329, and here external funding accounted for just 2.1% of the health budget. The percentage of HIV and AID funding from external sources is larger, reaching 97 and 99% in Mozambique and Malawi respectively.

Many countries face what UNAIDS has called the 'AIDS dependency crisis', the situation where countries are reliant on external funds (UNAIDS 2012b). However, this dependency is more than financial. There is an erosion of state sovereignty. Citizens are reliant on external governments and agencies for the drugs that keep them alive. Their governments have no choice but to accept even though the programmes may distort their priorities (Šehović 2014). The thoughtful analysis by Rowden into why governments are, and feel, hampered in increasing public expenditure, points to a dominant development model promoting policies that work

Table 1. Government expenditure on health and HIV prevalence in 2011.

Country	Adult HIV prevalence 2011 (in %)	Actual per capita govt health exp. 2011 in US$	External funding as % of total health exp. 2011	External HIV funding as % of total HIV exp. 2011
Botswana	23.4	263	9.2	23
Kenya	6.2	14	38.8	81
Lesotho	23.1	105	25.2	51
Malawi	11.0	23	52.4	99
Mozambique	11.2	15	69.8	97
South Africa	17.8	329	2.1	12
Swaziland	26.5	184	19.4	59
Uganda	7.2	11	27.0	87
Zambia	13.0	52	27.2	85

Data sources: Bradshaw and Whiteside (2014), McIntyre and Meheus (2014), Médecins Sans Frontières (2011), UNAIDS (2012b, 2013b), WHO (2014a), World Bank (2014).

against building up strong health systems (Rowden 2010). It is against this background that we now turn to the challenges.

Challenge 1. Keeping AIDS on the agenda

AIDS is no longer a discourse-defining health emergency. It is not a global issue. In wealthy countries, and most of Latin America, North Africa and the Middle East, the epidemic is concentrated and stable. This means HIV prevalence is below 1% in the general population. It may exceed 5% in specific 'at-risk' populations but, as will be discussed, these are people on the margins. In Asia the feared extensive epidemic has not materialised.

This raises the issue of who is infected and how much of a voice they have. In most of the world the epidemic is primarily located in 'at-risk' groups: socially and politically marginalised populations including injecting drug users, men who have sex with men, and commercial sex workers. AIDS is generally worst in areas on the global margins whether they be geographic, social or political.

There are places and populations where HIV must be a priority. Two-thirds of global HIV infections are in sub-Saharan Africa. Here the worst epidemic is in east and southern Africa where between 5% and 30% of adults are infected. Of the estimated 21,800,000 million people living with HIV here, 12,800,000 are women (UNAIDS 2014a). In Africa, particularly women and especially younger women are most likely to be infected. Gender relations are such that violence against women is common. This ranges from 'corrective rape' to physical and psychological abuse. In 2013 the WHO released its estimates of violence against women (WHO 2013). When data for intimate partner violence (IPV) are grouped by the regions used for Global Burden of Disease (BOD) assessments, the highest prevalence is in central sub-Saharan Africa. Here 65.6% of ever-partnered women have experienced IPV. All of sub-Saharan Africa is above the global average of 26.4%. In Western Europe and North America the rates are 19.3% and 21.3% respectively.

Gay men and drug users are discriminated against, criminalised and targeted in many countries. Legislation against homosexuality was inherited in much of Africa, but rather than repealing or at least ignoring it, some countries have introduced new and more restrictive laws. Drug use is criminalised across Africa. In only two African countries is sex work legal and regulated – Senegal and Côte d'Ivoire (Wikipedia 2014). Those bearing the burden of AIDS have the least voice and seeking help or identifying need may result in prosecution and persecution. In addition, despite the higher prevalence in these groups, there is, at best, an attitude that they are not important and deserving of services, and at worst the view that they 'deserve it' for 'unnatural' and immoral practices.

Keeping AIDS in the spotlight is made more difficult because internationally health is no longer a priority. Of the eight MDGs three are directly related to health, and goal six was specifically to combat HIV/AIDS. Post-2015 there will be 17 sustainable development goals (SDGs) and 169 targets. Only SDG number three mentions HIV/AIDS, and it is just one of the targets within the goal.[1] Economic development and growth, and environmental sustainability are the dominant themes. The first SDG is to 'End poverty in all its forms everywhere' (UN 2014). This switch of focus is partly a function of attention spans, but also reflects the new challenges humankind faces. Global environmental change is, correctly, very high on the international agenda.

Even within the health sector there are other issues competing for consideration. The BOD study shows in 1990 the top three causes of BOD were lower respiratory infections, diarrheal disease and preterm birth complications. In 2010 they were ischemic heart disease, lower respiratory infections and stroke (Institute for Health

Metrics and Evaluation 2014). In 2011 the United Nations held the first high-level meeting on non-communicable disease prevention and control. These diseases are more relevant to both global populations and leaders than infectious diseases generally and AIDS specifically. The possible exception is Ebola (Quammen 2014). In the second half of 2014 the world was gripped by the emergence of Ebola in southeast Guinea and its subsequent spread to Liberia and Sierra Leone. The WHO declared an 'international public health emergency' in August 2014, with the US-based Centers for Disease Control (CDC) warning that 'the Ebola outbreak in West Africa is unlike anything since the emergence of HIV/AIDS' (BBC 2014). By early 2015 it seemed that Ebola was under control. It is ironic that the lack of HIV in these countries may have partly led to an unpreparedness that is 'a direct consequence of years of insufficient public investment in underlying public health infrastructure' (Rowden 2014).

Finally, it is ironic that the availability of treatment has compounded the perception that the epidemic is over. There is a view that people who are infected can simply take drugs (this generally involves just one pill a day, similar to hypertension or statins, not the complex multi-tablet regimens that were the case), and live regular healthy lives.

Challenge 2. The prevention: treatment tension

In the absence of treatment, an HIV-infected person can expect to live for between 8 to 12 years. They will experience periods of illness that increase in severity, duration and frequency until they die. The advent of antiretroviral therapy changed this. Today a person receiving and adhering to early treatment will have a near-normal life span (UNAIDS 2014b).

In recent years incontrovertible evidence has emerged that a person on treatment is extremely unlikely to infect any one with whom they have sex. Treatment prevents HIV transmission. The HPTN052 trial showed a 96% reduction in new infections in couples where the infected individual was taking antiretrovirals (ARVs) (Cohen et al. 2011). In KwaZulu-Natal each 1% increase in treatment coverage gives a 1.1% decrease in HIV incidence (Tanser et al. 2013).

Other biomedical prevention interventions are medical male circumcision, condoms and microbicides. Circumcision is a one-off intervention which, in trials, showed a 60% reduction in transmission. This intervention brings its own challenges: how to ensure uptake; the risk that men, thinking they are protected, might be complacent; and the fact that it protects men not women. Condoms are a barrier protection, but making sure they are used consistently and correctly is critical. Microbicides have limited effectiveness and are relatively new.

Behaviour change interventions such as reducing the number of partners, using condoms properly, delaying sexual debut and so on are all critically important. At the moment available evidence suggests they are less effective, complicated, require individual and societal change and may be costly. These interventions are not easily evaluated by science's gold-standard randomised control trials. Some would argue that it is easier to simply treat those who have the misfortune to become infected, intervening when they are identified and perhaps even seeking them out.

The current WHO guideline is that ARV treatment should be initiated once a patient's CD4 count falls below 500 cells per cubic millimetre of blood. Pregnant women should be placed on therapy for the rest of their lives, as should the infected individual in discordant couples, those with active TB, and HIV+ children (WHO 2014b). There is pressure from a number of health professionals and activists for all infected people to be put on treatment as soon as they are identified. It is believed the earlier HIV-infected people get treatment, the better they will do. The evidence of prevention benefits is seen as the clinching argument. The view of this camp is we have the drugs, so all we need to do is fund the roll-out.

This prevention: treatment dichotomy should not be a debate, but it is, as prevention is often put in opposition to treatment. A basic public health tenet is prevention is better than cure. We would prefer people to never start smoking and not become obese, rather than have to deal with long-term health consequences of these behaviours. It is exactly the same with HIV. The challenge is to put behavioural prevention back on the HIV and AIDS agenda, make sure it is given the priority it deserves and the resources it needs.

One way is to point to the costs. Treatment is expensive and for life. The July 2014 Médecins Sans Frontières report on prices put the average cost of drugs alone, for first-line treatment, at $136 per person per year (Médecins Sans Frontières 2014). The UNAIDS 2011 estimate of the average annual per patient cost was $177 for established patients and $354 for newly initiated patients (UNAIDS 2014b). The long-term nature of the disease can be illustrated by thinking of a young adult infected in 2014. That individual will need treatment by 2022 (or before) and can expect to live, taking drugs until 2054, assuming a conservative 60-year life expectancy.

Mead Over, of the Center for Global Development in Washington, DC, developed the concept of the AIDS Transition. Put simply:

> The rate of new infections outpaces the rate of AIDS related deaths,[2] the number of people living with AIDS – and therefore the number of people needing treatment – is growing faster than the funding needed to treat them. ... Only by sustaining recent reductions in mortality and bringing down the number of new infections will the total number of people with HIV finally decline. (Over 2011, 1).

Until the transition happens, health ministries are looking at a long-term increase in the number of people who need to be initiated and maintained on treatment. The finance ministers know they will have to provide the budgets to pay for this as donor funding falls. The number of people needing treatment continues to grow; drugs are for life and come with considerable financial and human resources costs. The long-term response necessary to bring the epidemic brought under control is prevention, and treatment is a part of this.

Challenge 3. Funding the fight

There is a gap between what is available and what is required. The UNAIDS Smart Investments document states:

> ... despite the leadership shown by low and middle-income countries, the US$18.9 billion available for HIV programmes in 2012 was well below the target of $22–24 billion of annual investment required in 2015 set forth in the 2011 United Nations Political Declaration. (UNAIDS 2013b)

The Global Fund (GF) collaborated with partners (UNAIDS, WHO, Stop TB Partnership and the Roll Back Malaria Partnership) to estimate the total resources required over the 2014–2016 period. The assessment was that $87 billion was required to reach all vulnerable populations in eligible low- and middle-income countries. It was projected $24 billion would come from international funding; $37 billion from domestic funding ($23 billion from existing sources with a further $14 billion to be raised). The GF hoped to contribute $15 billion (as of August 2014 they had raised $12.4 billion) (Whiteside and Bradshaw 2014). A prominent slogan at the International AIDS Conference in Melbourne in 2014 was to 'fully fund the Global Fund'. It remains to be seen how this develops

The size of the international contribution is significant for two main reasons. Firstly, it gives rise to a mindset of dependence. A Results for Development review of 12 PEPFAR countries noted, 'deeply ingrained perceptions by finance and other senior government officials that "donors will take care of the AIDS programme", as indeed donors have done over the past decade' (Results for Development Institute 2013, 1). This observation, linked to the lack of voice of the majority of HIV-infected people, may give rise at best to a shortage of domestically raised resources and, at worst, a lack of response and abnegating of responsibility in some countries.

Furthermore, as discussed above, there may be imposition of donor-determined strategies and priorities that do not reflect local needs or conditions. A prime example was the abstinence 'earmark' in the PEPFAR funding. An economic 'golden rule' is 'the people who have the gold make the rules.' Even if the donor does not impose on the recipient country, they may write their proposals in order to satisfy the donor or, even more insidiously, what they believe the donor wants.

The cost of treatment could be crippling in some high-prevalence countries. Writing in 2014, Wilson and Fraser said: 'application of current costs to estimates suggests that initiating treatment at a CD4 count of 500 cells/μL could equal South Africa's entire health budget and 'treatment as prevention' (TasP) could equal 10% of Nigeria's health budget' (Wilson and Fraser 2014, S30). The South African national health budget in 2012–2013 was R27.5 billion; the cost of putting everyone with a CD4 count of 500 or less on treatment would be R35.5 billion. Treatment for all would cost R43.5 billion. Clearly this is unsustainable in high-burden countries.

The funding of the response in Africa varies. In general there is a good understanding of funding flows, shares and needs. There is work and analysis being carried out by, among others, the World Bank, UNAIDS, Results for Development, the Clinton Health Access Initiative and the Economic Reference Group of the World Bank and UNAIDS. In a few richer countries, domestic resources cover the majority of the costs with some supplementation by international donors. This is far from the norm. In most settings external funding covers the bulk of the HIV budget. The proportion of the financial contributions by national governments and donors varies and depends on domestic availability of funding, international commitments and the size of the resource gap in each country. There is an indication of this in Table 1.

The challenge is to ensure sufficient sustained funding from all sources. This is becoming increasingly difficult as the numbers on treatment increase and international development assistance declines. The mantra of 'value for money' is increasingly heard. Resources must be spent in the best possible manner. Linked to this are the macro-economic policies. If economies can grow then there is more potential for taxes, and a critical constraint is removed. However, then the challenge is to allocate more to health, and often, even before this is done, to make sure health money is spent.

Challenge 4. Understanding the drivers of the epidemic

Why is Africa the worst affected continent? Why does Lesotho have an adult prevalence rate of 22.9% while in Angola it is 2.4% and in Ethiopia just 1.2% (UNAIDS 2014b)? There have been various attempts to answer this – ranging from the distinguished scholar of Africa John Iliffe to my own work (Iliffe 2006). These range from arguing for biological factors, and social, political and cultural factors. The subtype of the virus, the genetics of the population and the interplay may be partly a cause. Not all southern African tribal groupings circumcise, a proven protector. The brutal history of the region with the repressive exploitative colonial regimes, especially in Mozambique, the illegal Rhodesian government and apartheid in South Africa, all created fertile ground for the spread of the virus. This was well documented decades ago for syphilis in a seminal paper by Sidney Kark (1949). What Kark described in the 1940s was just as relevant up to the end of the minority rule, and indeed the militarisation and conflict of the 1970s and 1980s all contributed further to the spread of HIV.

Those were the drivers of the spread of HIV. Today, while the governments are for the most part democratic and accountable (there are exceptions – Swaziland, the last absolute monarchy, is one), there are still critical drivers. Urbanisation means more people are living in cities, often in squalid conditions. There is a crisis of formal employment; young men especially find themselves without incomes and a role in the world (this is not just a problem in Africa, of course). In 2015 in a globalising world the challenge is to get to grips with the links between poverty, inequality and health. In a comment in the *Lancet* and University of Oslo Commission on Global Governance and Health, Charles Clift notes that 'the essential point is that globalisation has promoted growth but exacerbated inequality. Inequalities in power and economic status drive poor health outcomes for those at the bottom of the pile' (Clift 2014). This is magnified in the case of HIV and AIDS.

The relationship between poverty, inequality, marginalisation and HIV was the focus of the Structural Drivers meeting in Cape Town in 2013. In January 2014 UNAIDS and the World Bank convened a meeting to discuss HIV and AIDS, and global health and development agendas. Under the title 'Action on Social Drivers to End AIDS', the meeting programme noted 'social, economic and legal disadvantages increase vulnerability to HIV, worsen the epidemic's impact and undermine the effectiveness of biomedical tools.' The effects of the epidemic are entangled not

only with social drivers but also with other diseases, especially TB. There is no bandaid fix; this will take decades, social change and possibly even revolution, to address the causes of the HIV epidemic.

Unfortunately, while ART is lifesaving, there is an increased risk for many non-communicable diseases in HIV patients compared with age-matched uninfected people (Frieberg et al. 2013; Schouten et al. 2014). These include cardiovascular disease, non-AIDS malignancies, liver and kidney disease, and osteoporosis. Questions about how the health sector will respond, be prioritised and be funded remain to be addressed.

A critical part of the complexity is the long-term nature of the epidemic. The epidemic has been growing and evolving over more than 30 years. The evidence is that, despite the many interventions, the response in parts of Africa and certainly in southern Africa has been insufficient. Furthermore, even where prevalence and incidence rates are low, long-term commitment must be maintained to ensure transmission rates stay close to zero.

The consequence of HIV infection is illness and death, unless people receive treatment. The mortality shows up in various international indicators from life expectancy to maternal mortality. Two examples show this. Swaziland's life expectancy rose steadily from 46 at independence in 1968 to a peak of 58.98 in 1992. As a result of the AIDS epidemic it fell precipitously to 45.74 in 2004 and had only climbed to 48.85 in 2012 (World Bank 2014). South Africa's maternal mortality rate rose from 230 deaths per 100,000 live births in 1990 to a shocking 410 in 2008, far above the 2015 target of just 58 (WHO 2012). It is quite baffling that the cause of this deterioration in indicators is not explicitly recognised as HIV. The stigma of this epidemic still, it seems, extends to the data. In turn it means politicians and policy makers have manifestly failed to get to grips with the causes and consequences of the epidemic, the greatest challenge Africa has faced in the last 30 years.

Conclusion: the politics of HIV and AIDS

Health and therefore HIV and AIDS are no longer high on the global agenda.[3] This is understandable; there are many new and pressing concerns. There is a need for careful strategising around the epidemic to ensure resources are available. One key way to do this will be to show that the needs are time-bound – that prevention is working and treatment will not consume an ever-increasing share of the money.

The scientific advances and increased funding are astonishing. Commitments have come from Africa. In 2001, the Abuja Declaration bound African heads of state to allocate at least 15% of their annual budgets to the health sector by 2015. Although this target has not been achieved, progress has been made. At the Abuja+12 Special Summit, leaders committed to take action towards the elimination of HIV and AIDS, tuberculosis and malaria in Africa By 2030' (African Union 2013). There is a need to monitor the money and make long-term plans.

The drivers of the epidemic talk to development, equity and equality. In the early years of the epidemic we saw HIV as a lens through which we could see the fractures and schisms in society. This is as true now as it was then. The HIV epidemic is a long-wave event that will need to be managed for decades, even once numbers start falling and it is no longer considered an emergency anywhere. There are few other examples of things to be considered on the same scale as this epidemic (global environmental change is one). The timeline for dealing with it is therefore far longer than most governments, politicians, strategists and donors are willing to consider, even in their 'long-term' plans.

Health and development is ultimately political. The HIV epidemic showed this up starkly. The challenges for those concerned with this are to keep the epidemic on the agenda – and recognise that it has slipped off it; ensure sufficient resources are available – and that they are spent in the best possible ways; face the apparent conflict between treatment and prevention – and show they are complementary but in the long term prevention (which may be treatment) is essential; and finally understand what drove the epidemic – at a social but also personal level. The response to AIDS will driven by political economy questions. This is, above all, an epidemic that is crying out for deeper and better political analysis, and this special issue is an important beginning.

Disclosure statement

No potential conflict of interest was reported by the author.

Notes

1. The global health theme is universal health coverage with access to safe, effective and affordable essential medicines.
2. This is slightly misleading. It does not matter what people die of; as long as the number of deaths of HIV-infected people is lower than the number of new infections, the pool of people requiring treatment will grow.
3. This may change with the Ebola epidemic, but it is unlikely.

References

African Union. 2013. "Special Summit of the African Union on HIV/AIDS, Tuberculosis and Malaria, Abuja, Nigeria." African

Union. http://au.int/en/content/special-summit-african-union-hivaids-tuberculosis-and-malaria-abuja-nigeria.

BBC. 2014. "Ebola: Mapping the Outbreak." *BBC*. http://www.bbc.com/news/world-africa-28755033.

The Body. 2001. "The XIII International AIDS Conference." *The Body*. http://www.thebody.com/content/art16083.html.

Bradshaw, S., and A. Whiteside. 2014. "Responding to Health Challenges: The Role of Domestic Resource Mobilization." CIGI Policy Brief, No. 48.

Clift, C. 2014. "Tackling the Political Origins of Health Inequity." [online] Expert comment. 11 February. London: Chatham House/The Royal Institute of International Affairs. https://www.chathamhouse.org/media/comment/view/197318

Cohen, Myron S., Ying Q. Chen, Marybeth McCauley, Theresa Gamble, Mina C. Hosseinipour, Nagalingeswaran Kumarasamy, James G. Hakim, et al. 2011. "Prevention of HIV-1 Infection with Early Antiretroviral Therapy." *New England Journal of Medicine* 365 (5): 493–505.

Fowler, N. 2014. *AIDS: Don't Die of Prejudice*. London: Biteback Publishing.

Frieberg, M., C-C. H. Chang, L. H. Kuller, M. Skanderson, E. Lowy, K. L. Kraemer, A. A. Butt, et al. 2013. "HIV Infection and the Risk of Acute Myocardial Infarction." *JAMA Internal Medicine* 173 (8): 614–622. http://archinte.jamanetwork.com/article.aspx?articleid=1659742

Iliffe, J. 2006. *The African AIDS Epidemic: A History*. Oxford: James Currey.

Institute for Health Metrics and Evaluation. 2014. "Global Burden of Disease (GBD)." *Institute for Health Metrics and Evaluation*. http://www.healthdata.org/gbd.

Kark, S. L. 1949. "The Social Pathology of Syphilis in Africans." *South African Medical Journal* 23: 77–84.

Kates, J., A. Wexler, and E. Lief. 2013. *Financing the Response to HIV in Low- and Middle-income Countries: International Assistance from Donor Governments in 2012*. Washington, DC: Henry J. Kaiser Family Foundation.

Katz, A. 2005. "The Sachs Report: Investing in Health for Economic Development – or Increasing the Size of the Crumbs from the Rich Man's Table? Part II." *International Journal of Health Services* 35 (1): 171–188.

McIntyre, D., and F. Meheus. 2014. *Fiscal Space for Domestic Funding of Health and Other Social Services*. Chatham House, Centre on Global Health Security Working Group Papers. Paper 5.

Médecins Sans Frontières. 2011. *Reversing HIV/AIDS? How Advances Are Being Held Back By Funding Shortages*. Médecins Sans Frontières Briefing Note.

Médecins Sans Frontières. 2014. *Untangling the Web of Antiretroviral Prices*. 17th ed. Médecins Sans Frontières. www.msfaccess.org/utw17.

Mukherjee, S. 2011. *The Emperor of All Maladies: A Biography of Cancer*. London: Fourth Estate.

Over, M. 2011. *Achieving an AIDS Transition: Preventing Infections to Sustain Treatment, Center for Global Development*. Washington, DC: Brookings Institution Press.

Quammen, D. 2014. *Ebola: The Natural and Human History of a Deadly Virus*. New York: WW Norton.

Results for Development Institute. 2013. *Financing National AIDS Responses for Impact, Fairness, and Sustainability a Review of 12 PEPFAR Countries in Africa*. Washington, DC: Results for Development.

Rowden, R. 2009. *The Deadly Ideas of Neoliberalism: How the IMF has Undermined Public Health and the Fight against AIDS*. London : Zed Books.

Rowden, R. 2010. "Why Health Advocates Must Get Involved in Development Economics: The Case of the International Monetary Fund." *International Journal of Health Sciences* 40 (1): 183–187.

Rowden, R. 2014. "West Africa's Financial Immune Deficiency." [online] *Foreign Policy*. http://foreignpolicy.com/2014/10/30/west-africas-financial-immune-deficiency/

Schouten, J., F. W. Wit, I. G. Stolte, N. A. Kootstra, M. van der Valk, S. E. Geerlings, M. Prins, P. Reiss, AGEhIV Cohort Study Group. 2014. "Cross-sectional Comparison of the Prevalence of Age-associated Comorbidities and their Risk Factors between HIV-infected and Uninfected Individuals: The AGEhIV Cohort Study." *Clinical Infectious Diseases* 59 (12): 1787–97. doi:10.1093/cid/ciu701.

Šehović, A. 2014. *HIV/AIDS and the South African State: Sovereignty and the Responsibility to Respond*. Farnham, UK: Ashgate Publishing.

Tanser, F., T. Barnighausen, E. Grapsa, J. Zaidi, M-L. Newell. 2013. "High Coverage of ART Associated with Decline in Risk of HIV Acquisition in Rural KwaZulu-Natal South Africa." *Science* 339: 966–971.

UN. 2014. "Open Working Group proposal for Sustainable Development Goals." United Nations Sustainable Development Knowledge Platform. http://sustainable development.un.org/focussdgs.html.

UNAIDS. 2012a. "Lesotho: Global AIDS Response Country Progress Report." UNAIDS. http://www.unaids.org/en/data analysis/knowyourresponse/countryprogress reports/2012countries/ce_LS_Narrative_ Report[1].pdf.

UNAIDS. 2012b. "AIDS Dependency Crisis: Sourcing African Solutions." UNAIDS Issues Brief. http://www.unaids.org/en/ media/unaids/contentassets/documents/ unaidspublication/2012/jc2286_sourcing-african-solutions_en.pdf.

UNAIDS. 2013a. "Delivering Results toward Ending AIDS, Tuberculosis and Malaria in Africa: African Union Accountability Report on Africa–G8 Partnership Commitments." UNAIDS. http://www.unaids.org/en/media/ unaids/contentassets/documents/document/ 2013/05/20130525_AccountabilityReport_ EN.pdf.

UNAIDS. 2013b. "Smart Investments." Geneva Report, 17.

UNAIDS. 2014a. "The Gap Report." UNAIDS. http://www.unaids.org/en/dataanalysis/ knowyourepidemic/ Source: UNAIDS GAP Report - 2014

UNAIDS. 2014b. "Ambitious Treatment Targets: Writing the Final Chapter of the AIDS Epidemic." UNAIDS Discussion Paper, Geneva, 22.

UNAIDS. 2014c. "Countries." UNAIDS. http://www.unaids.org/en/regionscountries/ countries/

Whiteside, A., and S. Bradshaw, 2014. "Responding to Health Challenges: The Role of Domestic Resource Mobilisation." CIGI Policy Brief No 48.

WHO. 2001. *Macroeconomics and Health: Investing in Health for Economic Development.* Geneva: WHO.

WHO. 2012. "Countdown to 2015: Maternal, Newborn, and Child Survival: South Africa." WHO. http://www.who.int/woman_ child_accountability/countries/south_africa. pdf?ua=1.

WHO. 2013. *Global and Regional Estimates of Violence against Women: Prevalence and Health Effects of Intimate Partner Violence and Nonpartner Sexual Violence.* Geneva: WHO.

WHO. 2014a. "Access to Antiretroviral Drugs in Low- and Middle-income Countries: Technical Report." WHO. http://apps.who. int/iris/bitstream/10665/128150/1/9789241 507547_eng.pdf?ua=1&ua=1.

WHO. 2014b. "March 2014 Supplement to the 2013 Consolidated Guidelines on the Use of Antiretroviral Drugs for Treating and Preventing HIV Infection: Recommendations for a Public Health Approach." WHO. http://who.int/hiv/pub/guidelines/arv2013/ arvs2013upplement_march2014/en/.

Wikipedia. 2014. "Prostitution in South Africa." Wikipedia. http://en.wikipedia.org/wiki/ Prostitution_in_Africa.

Wilson, D., and N. Fraser, 2014. "Who Pays and Why? Cost, Effectiveness and Feasibility of HIV Treatment as Prevention." *Clinical Infectious Diseases* 59 (Suppl. 1: Controlling the HIV Epidemic with Antiretrovirals): S28–S31. Oxford Journals.

World Bank. 1980. *World Development Report.* New York: Oxford University Press.

World Bank. 1993. *World Development Report 1993: Investing in Health.* New York: Oxford University Press.

World Bank. 2014. "Swaziland Life Expectancy." World Bank. https://www. google.co.uk/search?sourceid=navclient& aq=&oq=life+expectancy+swaziland&hl= en-GB&ie=UTF-8&q=life+expectancy+ swaziland&gs_l=hp . . . 0j0i22i30l4.0.0.0. 10166 . . . . .0.aV1dGfj8_tc&gws_ rd=ssl.

DEBATE

15 years of 'War on AIDS': what impact has the global HIV/AIDS response had on the political economy of Africa?

Sophie Harman

At the turn of the millennium, multiple leaders across sub-Saharan Africa declared a total war against HIV/AIDS.[1] For many, such a declaration of war against HIV/AIDS was a turning point in the political response to the disease on the continent. With the exception of a handful of countries such as Uganda, few leaders or governments had taken an active role in publicly addressing the spread of the disease in their countries up to this point, with the majority of leaders remaining silent over high HIV prevalence rates, and some, perhaps most famously Thabo Mbeki in South Africa, denying the relationship between HIV and AIDS (Youde 2007). The declaration of war against the disease at this point was perhaps in part because of wider recognition by African governments of the impact of the disease on the death and suffering of millions of Africans and the associated consequences for the economies and societies of sub-Saharan Africa. For some, it was also a consequence of the United Nations Security Council declaring HIV/AIDS as a threat to peace and security in Africa (UNSC Resolution 1308 2000) that made it an exceptional health issue (McInnes and Rushton 2013, 122–123). However, it was also in part due to the increase in international attention and finance pledged towards combating

HIV/AIDS. In 2000, 'Combat HIV/AIDS, Malaria and other diseases' became MDG6 of the eight United Nations Millennium Development Goals (MDGs) (UN 2000). The World Bank launched its Multi-Country AIDS Program, one of the first projects of its kind to require the formation of new government agencies to address the epidemic and for governments to commit 40% of the project to civil society organisations (World Bank 2007). In 2002, the international community came together to set up the Global Fund to fight AIDS, Tuberculosis and Malaria (Global Fund), a finance mechanism that was designed specifically to raise and disperse funds to support governments around the world, but particularly in Africa in the fight against HIV/AIDS. Multiple international, regional and local non-governmental and faith-based organisations mobilised to work with government and international institutions to assist with HIV prevention, treatment, care and support of people living with HIV/AIDS. Bilateral government aid commitments towards the disease grew, most notably with US President George W. Bush pledging US$15 billion in 2003 in support of his President's Emergency Plan for AIDS Relief (PEPFAR), the result of which was a groundswell of activity towards combating HIV/AIDS across sub-Saharan Africa.

The last 15 years were in many respects 'the good times' for HIV/AIDS in terms of the finance earmarked towards combating the disease and its elevation to high-level policy status both within African and international public policy arenas. However, as finance towards HIV/AIDS has now begun to decline and the international community shifts its focus towards the Sustainable Development Goals and emergency health crises such as pandemic flu and Ebola, it is important to question not only the impact the 15-year total war on HIV/AIDS has had on containing the spread and impact of the disease, but also the lasting impact it has had on the political economy of Africa. The purpose of this debate article is to reflect on this wider question. The article does so by first reviewing the positive narrative that has been built around the global HIV/AIDS response to suggest that the last 15 years have been a success both in the achievements gained in efforts to contain and reduce the spread of the disease, and in how multiple actors have mobilised and worked together to do so. The article then suggests such gains have been overstated. Second, the article reflects on the wider impact of the global response on the political economy of Africa by looking at the impact of the war against HIV/AIDS on the health sector and wider governance structures of the state. The article concludes by arguing that the war on HIV/AIDS has been notable in the funding and actors mobilised, the gains in treatment and the normalisation of the disease in parts of Africa. However, such progress has also had external consequences for health sectors and the state across sub-Saharan Africa marked by the embedding of market practices of health delivery and a hollowing-out of many African health sectors. The positive narrative associated with the HIV/AIDS response ignores the negative externalities of disease-specific interventions on the wider health system and the intrusive reform of the African state. While there have been some positive gains in the war on HIV/AIDS, such gains are undermined by questions over the longevity and sustainability of the response that have significant

consequences for how African states organise future health systems and respond to health crises.

The positive-progress narrative and evoking HIV/AIDS

The common narrative on the global response to HIV/AIDS is one of progress and positivity. Such progress is shown in two main ways: results and governance. The progress narrative associated with the response to HIV/AIDS in Africa is commonly associated with the results and gains in access to treatment and new infection rates. The Joint United Nations Programme on HIV/AIDS (UNAIDS) releases an annual report on the global HIV/AIDS response to coincide with World AIDS Day on 1 December, which acts as a progress report on the epidemic, a source of data and an advocacy tool for what will shape the HIV/AIDS agenda in the coming year. These reports are launched with press releases stressing the gains and results achieved in the fight against disease, often citing a growth in numbers of people living with HIV/AIDS accessing care and treatment, while raising notes of caution with regard to complacency over such progress. The overarching message is that the global response to HIV/AIDS, particularly in Africa, has generated positive change in combating the disease, but more of the same is needed to continue such progress.

The positivity surrounding such flagship reports is perhaps unsurprising: global institutions have to demonstrate to member states, partner states and the wider public that their activities and initiatives are working as a means of eliciting support and money; and the data monitoring global progress on HIV/AIDS does show some good global outcomes. New infections have declined by 50% between 2001 and 2012; 15 million people living with HIV/AIDS are now accessing treatment, 9.7 million of whom live in low-

and middle-income countries (UNAIDS 2013a). However, whilst new infection rates in many African countries have declined, as of December 2012 only 7.6 million people living with HIV/AIDS in Africa were accessing treatment out of the 21.2 million deemed eligible (UNAIDS 2013b). It remains the case that 71% of people living with HIV/AIDS live in Africa (WHO 2014). Hence, while there has been some progress with regard to provision and uptake of treatment and a decline in new infection rates particularly when looking at the global pandemic, progress in Africa has not been so great, with treatment still failing to reach over 50% of people living with HIV/AIDS. This is particularly disconcerting when considering that the majority of funds towards HIV/AIDS efforts go to treatment initiatives and treatment is increasingly cited as a means of prevention (UNAIDS 2012).

Measurable progress and results are a minor part of the progress and positive narrative; most of the positivity around the war on HIV/AIDS is associated with rhetoric of how a global HIV/AIDS community raised the profile of the disease and positioned it as a global emergency in need of a global response. This narrative is commonly asserted by UN agencies such as UNAIDS and the United Nations Development Programme, non-governmental organisations, and leading individuals involved in global health and HIV/AIDS such as Peter Piot. HIV/AIDS is often evoked at times of global health crisis: for example, the spread of Ebola in West Africa has been commonly compared to the spread of HIV/AIDS in Africa as a means of provoking international condemnation and the need for action (see for example US Secretary of State John Kerry in Watt et al. 2014); when needing more effort in combating Ebola, the type of effort required is again likened to that seen in the global HIV/AIDS response. HIV/AIDS is evoked both as an example of how the global community can take action against a global, or increasingly

African, health crisis, and as a model of global governance to be replicated when addressing other concerns such as noncommunicable diseases on the continent. The supposedly multi-sectoral, multi-level way in which the global response to HIV/AIDS was organised is often evoked as an effective model of global health governance (see for example Sidibe and Buse 2013) – with civil society actors and people living with HIV/AIDS sitting on the executive board of institutions such as the Global Fund, money earmarked for community responses, celebrity-endorsed, high-profile, advocacy campaigns against stigma or prevention of mother-to-child transmission, the Treatment Action Campaign of South Africa, and cross-sector working in government and presidential leadership. Increasingly, it is not the actual progress against HIV/AIDS that is presented as the positive narrative, but the efforts or governance of HIV/AIDS that becomes the main part of the positive-progress story.

However, there is much to suggest that such a positive narrative and the evocation of HIV/AIDS as a means of eliciting wider action towards a health issue overlook several limitations associated with the global response. Global advocacy campaigns did make the international community and African leaders take action on HIV/AIDS. Most people living in sub-Saharan Africa are aware of HIV/AIDS. New institutions were created at the global level and in Africa. However, treatment remains costly, people continue to become infected with HIV, the stigma of people living with HIV/AIDS persists and funding towards HIV/AIDS is now declining. In addition, the governance of HIV/AIDS has not been marked by collaboration and consensus but competition among international institutions, co-optation of key civil society organisations, and the creation of local HIV/AIDS markets where civil society organisations compete for resources (Harman 2010). Despite research highlighting the shortcomings of the recent global war on HIV/AIDS (see for example Harman 2010; Johnston 2013; Seckinelgin 2012), the need to develop a positive narrative around its governance is sustained as a means of justifying further investment and attention from the international community. The positive, progressive narrative associated with the global HIV/AIDS response is misleading and evoking HIV/AIDS is not the solution to the wider health problems of sub-Saharan Africa. As the section below demonstrates, this is particularly the case when considering the impact of the global war on HIV/AIDS on the political economy of African health systems and the African state.

HIV/AIDS and the health sector

The war on HIV/AIDS in sub-Saharan Africa has had three notable impacts on the political economy of the health sector in the subcontinent: it has skewed health policy and planning around HIV/AIDS, particularly in aid-dependent countries; it has introduced a new layer of international consultants and accountants to the management of health programmes; and it has led to a preoccupation of vertical, disease-based interventions to the detriment of wider health system strengthening. Combined, such processes have embedded the use of the market as the guiding principle upon which health policy is decided and created a new, non-health specialist, management-accountancy class within the health sector. The introduction of the market to health sector policy and planning in sub-Saharan Africa is not new and can be traced to the flawed structural reforms of the health sector in the 1980s. However, as shall be discussed below, the finance and models on which HIV/AIDS projects were based since 2000 have accelerated this process.

Financing for HIV/AIDS through international aid programmes has 'flat-lined' to an average of US$7.6–7.8 billion (Kates, Wexler, and Lief 2013), 47% of which

goes to HIV/AIDS programmes in sub-Saharan Africa. The majority of this money comes not from multilateral financing mechanisms such as the Global Fund, but from the US government's PEPFAR project. In addition to aid assistance, African governments such as Kenya, Togo, Zambia, Sierra Leone, Chad and Guinea have increased domestic spending towards HIV/AIDS (AVERT 2014). South Africa tends to be the exception to the majority of African countries with high rates of HIV/AIDS prevalence in that it funds most of its own response with domestic funds and is thus less aid dependent (*Ibid.*). Measurement of Development Assistance for Health (DAH) is fraught with complications; however, as a general measure as of 2010, it can be said to be around US$28 billion (Ottersen et al. 2014), the majority of which is allocated to low- and middle-income countries. Data on DAH includes development assistance to HIV/AIDS projects, hence HIV/AIDS spending makes up over a quarter of all global aid towards health, most of which is spent in Africa.

The scale of such financing towards HIV/AIDS has a notable impact on the political economy of health sector planning and financing, particularly in aid-dependent, low- and middle-income, African countries. The amount of money towards HIV/AIDS and the high-level political status afforded to it have created distortions in African health sectors (Biesma et al. 2009), where policy and planning is organised around HIV/AIDS rather than the wider needs and concerns of a specific country's health sector. Money earmarked for HIV/AIDS does not go into a wider spending pot for public health spending by African state systems but comes with specific conditionalities or targets and performance criteria. For example, in the majority of aid-dependent African countries with high prevalence rates, multilateral funding for HIV/AIDS is agreed upon and disbursed through the Ministry of Finance and stand-alone national AIDS councils or coordinating functions such as the Global Fund's Country Coordinating Mechanisms. Some bilateral funding for HIV/AIDS may be channelled through the Ministry of Health but this tends to be the exception rather than the rule (Harman 2010). The last 15 years have been marked by a rise in vertical health spending, where development assistance is allocated to specific diseases (predominantly HIV/AIDS, malaria, tuberculosis, maternal and newborn child health) rather than horizontal efforts such as health system strengthening. This has several important consequences. As HIV/AIDS receives more international assistance than any other health issue in Africa, it dominates health sector targets. Such financial commitment generates significant political will towards proving the impact of such finance in reversing the trend of the epidemic. Thus significant parts of the health sector – health ministries, local government authorities, presidential officers, health practitioners – are specifically organised around fulfilling international criteria attached to aid and reaching MDG6 above other health concerns that may be important to a specific country but lack the finance to back initiatives or the political exposure to make them a worthwhile endeavour. Hence the first consequence is distortion in the planning and priorities of African health sectors around HIV/AIDS to the detriment of other health concerns (see for example Biesma et al. 2009; Pfeiffer et al. 2010). This is particularly pertinent to the underinvestment in health systems across the continent.

The second consequence is that finance earmarked to HIV/AIDS has given rise to specialist units and care and treatment centres to the neglect of more general health services in Africa. For example, the last 15 years have seen a growth in new care and treatment centres, and maternity and newborn child units at the regional and district level in many African countries. Whilst welcome, the introduction of these units has not occurred at the same time as an increase in regional and district health centres that address a range of other health concerns that affect the health of the African population.

The third consequence is that in recognition of such trends, health authorities align wider health objectives to HIV/AIDS targets rather than HIV/AIDS targets to health objectives (see for example Barnes, Brown, and Harman 2015). The understanding that, over the last 10 years, one of the only ways to get financing is to align a health issue (or even educational, gender, labour or agricultural issues for that matter) to HIV/AIDS as a means of diverting sources to where you want them to go, has led to a rise of HIV/AIDS add-ons such as the Pink Ribbon Red Ribbon (AIDS + Cervical and Breast Cancer) Campaign, or HIV/AIDS and neglected tropical disease. HIV/AIDS thus affects the political economy of the health sector with regard to how HIV/AIDS finance organises the way in which African health authorities have developed health policy and planning so that health policy is oriented around the disease and where the money is, rather than the wider needs of the health service or a particular country's population where HIV/AIDS is one among many health concerns.

It is not only the amount of money towards HIV/AIDS that has had a distorting impact on the political economy of African health systems, but how disbursal of the funds has been organised. Contemporary financing mechanisms for HIV/AIDS do not include the conditionalities of old, but instead refer to performance targets, indicators and results. Targets are mostly associated with the MDGs and measures of how progress in reaching these targets is linked to indicators such as uptake of antiretroviral treatment, or the number of people undergoing voluntary counselling and testing. The performance or results element comes in when key targets are met and actors are thus seen to be performing. The introduction of such targets and indicators has been a significant part of how both the Global Fund and PEPFAR disburse funds. The purpose of targets and indicators is to show measurable results and progress in the war on HIV/AIDS, to show that development assistance money works and to provide transparency and accountability over how aid money is spent. For some, the introduction of performance targets and indicators has been a welcome development in the health sector (Eichler 2006). However, the introduction of such targets and indicators has created confusion and an additional layer of bureaucracy with regard to how such indicators are managed and adjudicated. Different donors have different indicators and targets that are sometimes drawn from a country's health management information system set of indicators and targets for the health sector, but often are not, or include additional indicators. This leads to overlap and the health authorities having to manage competing sets of indicators depending on the donor (Barnes, Brown, and Harman 2015).

One of the most striking trends of the war on HIV/AIDS in Africa is that it has been a war administered by global accountancy firms. Finance for HIV/AIDS in Africa from the Global Fund is not managed by the government but principally the accountancy firm PriceWaterhouseCoopers.[2] PriceWaterhouseCoopers acts as the local fund agent for the Global Fund, which means it is responsible for overseeing the institution's operations in Africa, verifying performance by the recipients of Global Fund money and acting as the Fund's in-country representative. As local fund agent, such accountancy firms participate in government and donor partnership meetings and policy planning processes. Notably, they act as an interlocutor between government health authorities and donors (*Ibid.*). The role and presence of such accountancy firms has specific repercussions for the political economy of the health sector. The

priorities of the health sector around HIV/AIDS become that which can be measured and that which demonstrates the best performance according to accountancy models of performance rather than public health models of performance. Here the emphasis is not on how public health can be delivered to all regardless of quantity of people reached or cost, but how health interventions can demonstrate a return on investment either by scale of the intervention or its ability to produce a result on a spreadsheet. New public management models of performance are embedded into the health sector through the use of targets and indicators by international accountancy firms. These changes in the health sector introduced as part of the wider machinery of the war on HIV/AIDS in Africa are an extension of the market-based approach to health that emphasises return on financial aid investment and rewards measurable impact to the detriment of that which cannot be measured.

HIV/AIDS and the African state

The impact of HIV/AIDS interventions on the political economy of the health sector has wider ramifications for those states in Africa with high incidence rates. The war on HIV/AIDS introduced new agencies and processes at the national and local levels of government and embedded multi-sectoral working at the highest level of office. New agencies such as national AIDS councils and decentralised district and community AIDS councils became the institutional core of national HIV/AIDS strategies and responses in Africa over the last 15 years. In a few cases such as Uganda, these councils predated the MDGs and the scaled-up global war on HIV/AIDS of the new millennium; however, most councils became reinvigorated or introduced across sub-Saharan Africa as a result of the World Bank's Multi-Country AIDS Program, which partly funded the establishment, salaries and institutional support of these agencies.

The Global Fund contributed to such agencies by housing its Country Coordinating Mechanisms in the national HIV/AIDS councils in countries such as Tanzania. HIV/AIDS councils operate outside of the Ministry of Health and tend to fall under the umbrella of the office of the president or prime minister. The establishment of these bodies has clear implications for the African state. The most apparent is the fragmentation of the health sector in African states where specific health issues such as HIV/AIDS and now, increasingly, maternal and newborn child health become removed from the health sector as a means of affording such issues special political status. Removing an issue from the health sector to the office of the president or prime minister can be interpreted as both a statement of political will and a suggestion that the health sector is somehow failing or inadequate. The result of which is a divide between the health sector and HIV/AIDS programmes, an embedding of health silos across the machinery of government, and the exacerbation of competition and mistrust across ministerial portfolios and between civil servants between health ministries, HIV/AIDS councils and the finance ministries that manage international aid. Such practices embed preconceived notions of 'big man' leadership on the continent, where issues are only addressed or afforded political will when they are elevated to the office of the president or prime minister. The elevation of HIV/AIDS from the health sector to the office of the president or prime minister was often not led by the leaders themselves but by the donors that established the national AIDS councils as part of their funding criteria (Harman 2009, 2010).

The establishment of new agencies to take the lead in the war on HIV/AIDS and the accompaniment of certain standards have wider impacts on the processes of state and government practice. A clear example of this is the criteria that civil society actors are brought in to multiple levels of the state in responding to HIV/AIDS. Such criteria are justified by the notion that HIV/AIDS is an exceptional health issue (Lisk 2010) requiring a multi-sectoral response. On the one hand, such criteria of international funding are an acknowledgment of the significant role civil society actors have had on the global response to the epidemic. On the other hand, such requirements can be used as tools to make the government more open and plural to non-state-based activities. Such interventions are not just about changing how states approach the issue of HIV/AIDS but are changing state practices as to how policy is made and implemented by opening government processes up to non-state actor participation and influence. In this sense, HIV/AIDS interventions are as much about reforming state processes and participation in government structures to be more pluralist as they are about creating a national response to HIV/AIDS (Harman 2009, 2010). In responding to HIV/AIDS, international donors such as the World Bank and Global Fund have created models for states to replicate that require a restructuring of how the African state works to be inclusive and open to non-state actors and influences. Such models have created a market in which civil society organisations compete for government and donor contracts and positions in decision-making structures. For some authors such as Seckinelgin (2008), the global war of HIV/AIDS has led to an institutionalisation of the agency of non-governmental organisations which presents a disjuncture between the presumed roles of such actors – e.g. feeding in to the policy arena, delivering on international policy preferences – and what they do in practice. HIV/AIDS has provided justification for international programmes that engage in wider processes of state–society and government reform in Africa. Such reforms would not be so easily countenanced under a programme of good governance, but are somehow permissible or overlooked because of the specialist status afforded to the disease by both international donors that are keen to promote good governance and the international non-governmental organisations and state agencies that normally decry such practices.

Conclusion

The war against HIV/AIDS launched by civil society, international institutions and key states at the start of the millennium has claimed some victories in Africa. More people living with the disease in the continent have access to antiretroviral treatment, people are aware of AIDS and how to prevent HIV transmission, and government leaders from across the continent have taken an active and public role in acknowledging the scale of HIV/AIDS and the need to take efforts to address it. The response to the epidemic has led to an increase in the number of actors at the global, regional, national and local levels from the public, private, health and non-health sectors dedicated to responding to the disease – the result of which is for many to claim that the war waged on HIV/AIDS is a successful example of how the global community and African societies can come together to tackle health problems and turn a health crisis into a manageable, chronic disease. However, this article has argued that such a positive progressive framing of the war on HIV/AIDS overlooks the wider impact the global response has had on the health sector and state in African countries.

The war on HIV/AIDS has led to health sectors being organised around HIV/AIDS, an obsession with performance measurement and results to the detriment of wider public health concerns and investment in health systems, and the introduction of new models of management that have dispersed the authority of the health sector. HIV/AIDS has fundamentally altered the political economy of health in Africa in three key ways. First, it has expanded the

role of the market in the delivery of health indicators and results. It has established a market in the health sector made up of donor and government contracts to be competed for and won by a range of public sector actors – the Ministry of Health, the Ministry of Finance, the Office of the President/Prime Minister – and private sector actors drawn from civil society, management consultancies and accountancy firms. This has removed health concerns, policy and delivery away from central planning within the health sector and generated a system of health planning that is dependent on international targets. Second, the health sector in Africa has been hollowed out. This has occurred through the plurality of actors associated with the HIV/AIDS market and through the introduction of new institutions and models for governing health concerns by international donors that are created outside of the health sector. The establishment of these institutions gives rise to the assumption that African health ministries cannot manage health emergencies such as HIV/AIDS and that for a health issue to be afforded high-level political status, it has to be linked to the highest office of government and managed by accountants. Such assumptions are reinforcing: the more health ministries are seen as unable to act, the less they are financed, and the more their mandate is dispersed and thus compromised. Finally, the market for HIV/AIDS has been donor-led and in most countries donor-dependent. The gains made in uptake of antiretroviral treatment, with few exceptions, are principally because of the US government's PEPFAR project. Hence the longevity of progress and the ability of African states to fit the bill of such treatment programmes when international donors inevitably withdraw will yet again make HIV/AIDS a contemporary political hazard for African governments and societies.

The consequence of these factors is that after 15 years of war against the disease, HIV/AIDS has changed how the health sector works in Africa but not necessarily for the good, and those gains that have been achieved could be easily reversed. This will have significant implications for the African state in delivering health and treatment, care and support for people living with HIV/AIDS. A decline in international assistance for HIV/AIDS may present an opportunity for African states to think about how they want to fund and organise their health systems. This would be a welcome opportunity to reflect on and learn the lessons from past vertical financing strategies, to see what worked in HIV/AIDS funding, what the challenges were and how this can be used for health system investment. However, this scenario takes little account of the influence of international donors, non-governmental organisations, accountancy firms, and health policy experts and their accompanied finance that often sways the priorities of African health policy and practice. The challenge of the African state in financing HIV/AIDS care and treatment will be to manage the expectations and interests of international actors, and identify new sources of income to finance both HIV/AIDS interventions and the wider health sector infrastructure. Alternative sources of income could be derived from new types of donor such as the African Development Bank, or would require the state to think about sources of state revenue involving new forms (or reform of old forms) of taxation, particularly of the growing middle class. However, these alternatives come with their own set of problems: new donors follow old forms of conditional-based lending, and new forms of taxation require upfront costs for the state, and a need to show delivery for what the rising middle class is paying for. The legacy of HIV/AIDS financing on the African state and the decline in international commitments present both an internal challenge to the African state in regard to how it delivers health to its citizens and who pays for it, and an external challenge as to how the state manages its relationship with a growing number of public and private international actors interested in health. Given these challenges, the battle to reverse the disease in Africa is beginning all over again for Africans.

Disclosure statement

No potential conflict of interest was reported by the author.

Notes

1. Multiple African government agencies such as national HIV/AIDS councils and presidents have used the rhetoric of a war on or against HIV/AIDS. Kenya has been the most overt with a Total War Against HIV/AIDS project, financed by the World Bank. In addition, the rhetoric of war, battle and fight is often used by the Joint United Nations Programme on HIV/AIDS (UNAIDS).
2. Of the 60 Global Fund projects in Africa (which also includes Palestine, Jordan, Iraq and Syria in the grouping of North Africa and the Middle East), 40 are managed by PriceWaterhouseCoopers. The rest are managed by KPMG, Swiss TPH and UNOPS. For a full list of Local Fund Agents, please see http://www.theglobalfund.org/en/lfa/.

References

AVERT. 2014. "Funding for HIV and AIDS." Accessed October 2014. http://www.avert.org/funding-hiv-and-aids.htm

Barnes, Amy, Garrett Brown, and Sophie Harman. 2015. *The Global Politics of Health Reform in Africa: Participation, Performance and Results.* Basingstoke: Palgrave MacMillan.

Biesma, R. G., R. Brugha, A. Harmer, A. Walsh, N. Spicer, and G. Walt. 2009. "The Effects of Global Health Initiatives on Country Health Systems: A Review of the Evidence from HIV/AIDS Control." *Health Policy and Planning* 24 (4): 239–252.

Eichler, R. 2006. "Can 'Pay for Performance' Increase Utilization by the Poor and Improve the Quality of Health Services?" Discussion Paper, first meeting of the Working Group on Performance-based Incentives, Center for Global Development.

Harman, Sophie. 2009. "Fighting HIV and AIDS: Reconfiguring the State?" *Review of African Political Economy* 36 (121): 353–367.

Harman, Sophie. 2010. *The World Bank and HIV/AIDS: Setting a Global Agenda.* Abingdon: Routledge.

Johnston, Deborah. 2013. *Economics and HIV: The Sickness of Economics.* Abingdon: Routledge.

Kates, Jennifer, Adam Wexler, and Eric Lief. 2013. *Financing the Response to HIV in Low- and Middle-income Countries: International Assistance from Donor Governments in 2012.* Geneva: UNAIDS/Kaiser Family Foundation. Accessed October 2014. http://www.unaids. org/en/media/unaids/contentassets/documents/document/2013/09/20130923_KFF_UNAIDS _Financing.pdf.

Lisk, Franklyn. 2010. *Global Institutions and the HIV/AIDS Epidemic.* Abingdon: Routledge.

McInnes, Colin, and Simon Rushton. 2013. "HIV/AIDS and Securitization Theory." *European Journal of International Relations* 19 (1): 115–138.

Ottersen, Trygve, Aparna Kamath, Suerie Moon, John-Arne Rottingen. 2014. "Development Assistance for Health: Quantitative Allocation Criteria and Contribution Norms." Centre on Global Health Security Working Group Papers. London: Chatham House. Accessed October. http://www.chathamhouse.org/sites/files/chathamhouse/field/field_document/20140901Developme ntAssistanceHealthQuantitativeOttersenKa mathMoonRottingenRevised.pdf.

Pfeiffer, J., P. Montoya, A. J. Baptista, M. Karagiania, M. de Moras Pugas, M. Micek, W. Johnson, et al. 2010. "Integration of HIV/AIDS Services into African Primary Health Care: Lessons Learned from Health System Strengthening in Mozambique – A Case Study." *Journal of the International AIDS Society* 13 (3): 1–9.

Seckinelgin, H. 2008. *International Politics of HIV/AIDS: Global Disease – Local Pain.* Abingdon: Routledge.

Seckinelgin, H. 2012. *International Security, Conflict and Gender: 'HIV/AIDS is Another War'.* Abingdon: Routledge.

Sidibe, Michel and Kent Buse. 2013. "AIDS Governance: Best Practice for a Post-2015 World." *The Lancet* 381 (9884): 2147–2149.

UNAIDS. 2012. "Where Does the Money Go?" Accessed October 2014. http://www.unaids. org/en/resources/infographics/20110607 wheredoesmoneygo/.

UNAIDS. 2013a. "AIDSinfo Online Database." Accessed October 2014. http://www. aidsinfoonline.org/devinfo/libraries/aspx/ Home.aspx.

UNAIDS. 2013b. *Access to Antiretroviral Therapy in Africa.* Geneva: UNAIDS. Accessed October 2014. http://www. unaids.org/en/media/unaids/contentassets/ documents/unaidspublication/2013/201312 19_AccessARTAfricaStatusReportProgres stowards2015Targets_en.pdf.

United Nations. 2000. "The Millennium Development Goals." Accessed October 2014. http://www.un.org/millenniumgoals/.

United Nations Security Council Resolution 1308. 2000. "On the Responsibility of the Security Council on the Maintenance of International Peace and Security: HIV/AIDS and International Peacekeeping Operations." Accessed October 2014. http://www.unaids. org/en/media/unaids/contentassets/dataimp ort/pub/basedocument/2000/20000717_un_ scresolution_1308_en.pdf.

Watt, Nicholas, Sarah Boseley, Lizzy Davies, Kim Willsher, and Philip Oltermann. 2014. "Ebola 'Could Be Scourge Like HIV,' John Kerry Warns World." *The Guardian*, October 18. Accessed October 2014. http:// www.theguardian.com/world/2014/oct/18/ ebola-scourge-hiv-john-kerry.

WHO. 2014. "Global Health Observatory: HIV/ AIDS." Accessed October 2014. http:// www.who.int/gho/hiv/en/.

World Bank. 2007. *The Africa Multi-Country AIDS Program 2000–2006.* Washington: World Bank.

Youde, Jeremy. 2007. *AIDS, South Africa, and the Politics of Knowledge.* Aldershot: Ashgate.

DEBATE

Breaking out of silos – the need for critical paradigm reflection in HIV prevention

Justin O. Parkhurst and
Moritz Hunsmann

Introduction

Since its very beginning, HIV/AIDS has been subject to uniquely intense scientific controversy and political struggles over the origin of the disease and the causes of its epidemic spread in sub-Saharan Africa (Epstein 1996). HIV has also been unique amongst many health problems in its rapid growth, high level of politicisation and unprecedented level of financing, with global resources dedicated to AIDS control rising to over US$19 billion in 2013 (Kaiser Family Foundation and UNAIDS 2014). HIV quickly became enmeshed in ideologically derived debates of human rights, morality, race and development (cf. Wachter 1992; Tarantola and Mann 1995).

In this landscape of HIV, the multiple values of concern and the enormous diversity of agencies involved in HIV-prevention work, as well as the complexity of a health issue often linked to stigmatised behaviours, have challenged consensus building and left ample room for competing narratives about the appropriate design of HIV-prevention policies. The different modes of transmission and the variety and

heterogeneity of contributing factors (or 'drivers') of HIV transmission further make allocative decisions in the field of AIDS control particularly complex.

And yet, despite this complexity, there have been dominant trends in the HIV-prevention response – many of which have through the years been critiqued for being too simplistic or too narrow in their approach. One of the most well-known examples of such thinking has been the dominance of, and continued reliance on, programmes based on information provision (or IEC – Information, Education and Communication) within African epidemics, despite early recognition that knowledge levels are not correlated with lower HIV prevalence (Cleland and Ferry 1995) and that the classic 'Health Belief Model' is limited in addressing HIV/AIDS (Montgomery et al. 1989). 'Information' may be a potentially necessary, but not a sufficient, factor in bringing about shifts in population practices that reduce HIV risk. Moreover, and as discussed below, IEC programmes are often based on a narrowly behaviour-centred causal narrative that overestimates the importance of sexual practices as a driver of HIV in Africa. Despite these well-established limitations to information provision, IEC efforts have continued to dominate HIV-prevention efforts, with a veritable cottage industry of evaluation research that measures programme outcomes in terms of 'awareness' raised, rather than infections averted.

Other examples exist of common responses to HIV that became dominant, or attracted high levels of attention and resources, despite established limitations or problems. The enormous spending on general population prevention even in areas of highly concentrated epidemic spread (leading to vastly different ranges of dollars spent per HIV infection between countries) (Berkley 1994; Pisani 2008), the efforts made to develop multi-sectoral programmes with little concern for how they would address known challenges (Putzel 2004) or the often narrow focus on condom promotion when evidence was mounting that this was having little effect alone (Shelton 2006), represent other cases where the HIV-prevention response has been critiqued for failing to take up existing knowledge to optimise use of resources. We term these criticised approaches 'silos of thinking'. These structured but (often unconsciously) limited ways of considering an issue lead to the exclusion of relevant alternative or, more often, complementary approaches.

We argue that the formation of silos is an inherently political-economic phenomenon that concerns both the dynamics of scientific research and the selective uptake of its results in prevention policies. Silos originate from ideological, disciplinary and institutional roots. These are normal parts of human thinking and human organised functioning. Yet silos can lead to bias – bias in understanding, barriers to new knowledge creation and bias in the priorities set for intervention – all of which continue to hamper HIV prevention.

For an issue as clinically and socially complex as HIV, any tendency to simplify HIV-prevention thinking should be approached with great caution. We see the current discussions and critical thinking about structural approaches to HIV prevention as providing an opportunity to challenge and overcome silo thinking, particularly because of the complex and holistic approach that much structural thinking requires.

Silo thinking in HIV prevention: three examples

This section presents three cases of silo thinking where exclusive reasoning appears to hinder the open discussion and engagement that would, otherwise, be expected as a norm of good scientific practice. Our examples point to seemingly opposed or debated approaches, but our use of the term 'silos' does not necessarily imply that *both* sides of the debate adopt a silo perspective. Nor does it suggest that all players have equal power to deny the validity of the others' claims. So, for example, the disciplinary silo thinking discussed below is arguably reciprocal: we describe two parallel silos – biomedical and social sciences – which coexist, even though the biomedical approach clearly remains dominant in the field. The other silos described, however, are in many ways single silos: one centred around a dominant sexual transmission paradigm that appears to exclude medical transmission, the other focusing nearly exclusively on sexual behaviour, without attention to biological variables that influence the efficiency of sexual transmission.

It is worth noting upfront that our discussion of silos of thinking does not intend to argue for or against a given position. In most cases, the alternatives presented to dominant silos are seeking to expand – not replace – the dominant paradigm of HIV transmission in Africa. We do not set out to *solve* any of these individual questions in the science of HIV (important efforts, but beyond the scope of a single paper). Rather our goal is to reflect on the marginalisation of potentially helpful ideas, and the persistence of problematic approaches to the realities of AIDS in Africa that can arise from adherence to overly narrow institutional, disciplinary or ideologically inspired ways of thinking. Our choice of examples are ones where the removal of silos might realistically lead to progress in HIV prevention as there is already a contrasting set of thinking which could be brought together to improve the rigour and breadth of operational knowledge.

Missing synergies: opposing sexual and iatrogenic HIV transmission

From early in the AIDS response, it was recognised that HIV infections can occur through sexual contact or through the exposure to infected blood, essentially via blood transfusions, the reuse of syringes or the exposure to non-sterilised medical equipment (Vachon, Coulaud, and Katlama 1985; Mann et al. 1986). While the importance of sexual transmission has become the mainstream focus of the vast majority of HIV-prevention work, various researchers have voiced concern about a possible underestimation of transmission via unsafe medical practices (what is termed 'iatrogenic' HIV transmission) (e.g. Gisselquist 2008; Peters et al. 2009; Reid 2009b). These scholars point to identified cases of HIV infection unexplained by sex, such as HIV-positive children whose mothers are uninfected, or they underline statistical correlations between HIV infection and certain medical interventions (such as surgery or vaccination) while excluding reverse causation. The WHO estimated that, in 2000, 2.5% of HIV infections in sub-Saharan Africa were due to the reuse of contaminated syringes for medical care, although a re-evaluation of the model with more realistic variable inputs estimated this was more likely to be 12–17% (Reid 2009a).

Although sexual and iatrogenic transmission obviously coexist, many international agencies and African governments appear to dismiss or ignore iatrogenic HIV transmission. For example, the epidemiological estimates that inform Tanzanian prevention policies (Sando et al. 2014) attribute 2.1% to recreational injection drug use, and 0.0% to iatrogenic transmission (with all remaining infections attributed to sexual transmission). Admittedly, donors such as PEPFAR have invested heavily in blood safety in several African countries over the last decade, and the situation does appear to have improved recently (Pépin et al. 2014). Nevertheless, in a country with well-documented routine failures in infection control and in which 30% of health facilities (and 15% of hospitals) still have no capacity to diagnose HIV (MOHSW 2013, 13), claims of zero iatrogenic transmissions should require strong justification. The fact that these claims continue to go unquestioned illustrates the self-confinement of the leading international AIDS institutions within a silo of sexual explanations of HIV spread.

Epidemiologic reasoning suggests that iatrogenic transmission could be important, even if only representing a small percentage of infections as it could serve as a link between otherwise separate sexual networks. Although this potential trans-network or 'turbo effect' (Vachon, Coulaud, and Katlama 1985) of iatrogenic HIV transmission has been pointed to since the first years of the epidemic, the possible impact of the *interaction* between modes of transmission on the dynamics of sexual HIV transmission remains to be rigorously analysed. Efforts to model one mode of transmission 'against' the other (e.g. French, Riley, and Garnett 2006) risk reinforcing silo thinking that makes little sense in the formulation of prevention strategies.

Social vs medical silos

A second example of silos in the HIV-prevention response can be seen in the repeated claims of an over-medicalisation of the AIDS response, and the continuing struggle of social science to stake its claim around the importance of a social and political perspective on HIV epidemics. The calls and efforts to address structural drivers of HIV are, themselves, a manifestation of this dynamic. In carving out their own corpus of knowledge for HIV prevention, social scientists have also critiqued the implications of exclusively medicalised approaches to social issues. For example, the overreliance on clinical-epidemiological thinking has at times led to assumptions that experimental trials provide evidence of 'what works' for HIV prevention, potentially to the exclusion of all other knowledge sources. Yet an experimental trial is designed to show if what was done had an effect, not whether it will work in the same way elsewhere (Cartwright and Hardie 2012). Human biological similarities that allow generalisation from clinical trials are not necessarily repeated for the social and political factors shaping behavioural intervention effectiveness or the willingness to take up biomedical interventions.

The biomedical response to HIV has also been criticised for a 'political myopia' that fails to engage with the social and political meanings embedded within HIV interventions (such as male circumcision) (Parkhurst, Chilongozi, and Hutchinson 2015) and that abstracts from the structural inequalities that condition access to treatment and prevention. As Nguyen et al. (2011) explain:

> in the rush to paradigm shift, game-change, rollout and scale-up [...] local epidemiological, political, and socio-historical context is once again being ignored, surely only to resurface later as 'culture' once much-heralded interventions fail to deliver. Holding out for a magic bullet – unlikely to ever come – diminishes interest in the hard, messy work required to enable social change and address the social inequalities and structural violence that drive this epidemic. (292)

Or, as Le Marcis (2013) underlines, although biomedical interventions bear great hopes, 'critical analysis is more than ever necessary when a medical response appears set to provide a simple solution to a complex social problem' (our translation).

A critical perspective, however, need not be an oppositional one. The authors making such critiques are not necessarily dismissive of the medical enterprise itself, nor of its importance in the response to HIV prevention. Instead the goal is to delineate the appropriateness of different methods, tools and knowledge to questions surrounding a disease whose spread is deeply embedded in both social, as well as medical, realities. That being said, as the next section shows, the disciplinary barriers to comprehensive learning work both ways.

Not quite 'structural' yet: biological vs behavioural drivers

Our final example brings us back to the structural focus of this special issue. In theory, the recent (re-)emergence of consideration of the structural drivers of HIV transmission provides a window of opportunity to help establish practices that avoid silo-based thinking. Structural approaches are particularly suited to doing this because they are complex and multifaceted in their causal functions, with 'structural approaches' addressing the broader legal, socio-economic and cultural contexts in which HIV risk develops (Parker, Easton, and Klein 2000; Gupta et al. 2008). Nevertheless, structural approaches risk establishing their own form of silo if the only downstream outcome of interest is seen to be a reduction in unprotected sexual contacts. As for any infectious disease, the dynamic of sexual HIV transmission depends on two variables: (1) the number of times uninfected people are exposed to the virus, and (2) the risk of infection per exposure. While the first variable depends to a great extent on individual behaviour, equating the prevention of sexual HIV transmission with behaviour change deprives it of its second key pillar – transmission efficiency.

The reduction of *infectivity* via a reduction of viral load is the underlying rationale of 'treatment-as-prevention'

(TasP) strategies, while the reduction in *susceptibility* drives current efforts to scale up male circumcision. Despite the acknowledgement of the relevance of transmission efficiency in these biomedical interventions, there has been decidedly less attention paid to the control of several parasitic or infectious diseases common in Africa (for which the prevalence has clear structural origins). Malaria, tuberculosis, lymphatic filariasis, soil-transmitted helminths, leishmaniasis, genital schistosomiasis, as well as certain micronutrient deficiencies, have all been shown to potentially increase infectiousness of an HIV-positive individual and/or susceptibility of an HIV-negative individual (cf. Stillwaggon 2006; Kaul et al. 2011). Many of these conditions are highly co-endemic in sub-Saharan Africa, and their geographic distribution is correlated with HIV prevalence (Sawers and Stillwaggon 2010) – potentially explaining why HIV viral loads in treatment-naïve individuals have been measured to be three to five times higher in Africa than in high-income countries (Dyer et al. 1998; Modjarrad and Vermund 2010), or why the per-act transmission risk within sero-discordant heterosexual couples has been estimated to be between 3.75 (male-to-female) and 9.5 (female-to-male) times higher in low-income countries than in high-income countries (Boily et al. 2009).

Yet, most national HIV-prevention programmes in Africa fail to incorporate the effect of various infectious and parasitic diseases (so-called 'cofactors') on HIV transmission efficiency and continue to draw on a nearly exclusive sexual behaviour-centred causal narrative (Hunsmann 2013). Too often, the debates over the importance of any one or another element leads to opposition, with advocates for co-infection control being erroneously accused of denying the role of sexual behaviour – as if addressing the cofactors that increase the efficiency of sexual HIV transmission somehow excludes efforts to reduce sexual exposures overall as well

Transmission efficiency is at the very heart of the increasingly dominant biomedical approach (TasP and male circumcision). Thus, the continuing resistance of AIDS organisations to acknowledge cofactors such as malaria, STIs and urogenital schistosomiasis is all the more paradoxical.

Political-economic origins of silo thinking

The above section provides three examples of cases where silo-based reasoning appears to prevent the unification of thinking and joint planning that can bring together multiple potentially useful efforts and ideas to slow the spread of HIV. We argue that political-economic factors drive the formation and perpetuation of silos – particularly in terms of dominant disciplines, ideologies, and institutional incentives and arrangements.

Political-ideational origins

Disciplines

Disciplines serve to train individuals in methods, theories and concepts to a high level of expertise. Many social scientists are trained as part of their discipline to be self-critical and reflective, challenging if their methods or ideas are appropriate to understand best the question at hand. Public health officials trained in clinical medicine or epidemiology may struggle to recognise the limitations of individualistic and medical interventions to address an epidemic so deeply shaped by social factors, as they have been trained primarily to search for universal solutions rather than to take into account the contextual complexity of the social world (where the fundamental mechanisms by which cause and effect occur can vary over place and time [cf. Pawson and Tilley 1997]). More fundamentally, and beyond the sole issue of contextual validity of public health knowledge, the formulation of HIV prevention policies necessarily involves trade-offs between social values and policy objectives – among which the pursuit of population health is but one (Parkhurst 2012). As Brecht (1959) noted over half a century ago, such policy decisions represent choices of what a 'good society' looks like, questions that science alone cannot answer. Such decisions concerning HIV-prevention policy cannot be exclusively based on a technocratic process that relies on public health specialists' suggestions or epidemiological data. They are irreducibly *political* decisions in the sense that they lie outside the realm of optimisation (Hunsmann 2012).

Yet while social scientists continue to challenge the neglect of the social world in HIV programming (induced by the predominance of the biomedical paradigm), the disciplinary barriers to comprehensive learning manifestly work both ways. Biomedical literacy among social scientists is often disconcertingly low and, being trained to analyse human behaviour, social scientists risk reductionism of HIV prevention to behavioural determinants – paying inadequate attention to the non-behavioural factors that shape susceptibility, infectiousness and thus risk of transmission.

Values

Academics and scientists like to believe they are free of ideology. Yet for those working in HIV/AIDS, they most likely do so *specifically because of* their values. Research from the field of cognitive psychology has shown repeatedly that our existing morals and value positions will lead to simplification heuristics and biases in processing and understanding complex information (Gilovich, Griffin, and Kahneman 2002; Kahan 2013), an insight recently embraced by the World Bank to reflect critically on its own work in poverty reduction (World Bank 2015). Such biases affect the HIV-prevention community as well. Critical views or alternative hypotheses place those on the receiving end of the critique in a state of cognitive dissonance (Festinger 1957). In such states, humans naturally develop responses to oppose, ignore or dismiss the dissonant ideas – supporting the building and maintenance of silo thinking. In this sense, the reaction against (or *non*-reaction to) scholars warning about iatrogenic HIV transmission could in part be explained by dissonance with the 'doctors-are-beneficent' belief system. Similarly, hostile feelings against those who note the failures of condom promotion could arise from dissonant values. No doubt some opposition to condoms has come from a moral agenda (e.g. religious leaders who see them as part of a 'social problem'). But some have critiqued condom promotion based on epidemiological data of its limited impact (cf. Halperin et al. 2004; Shelton 2006). The embrace of condom promotion has been argued to be consonant with belief systems valuing control over reproduction and sexual freedom (Parkhurst 2011), yet these moral positions common to many in HIV prevention should not prohibit exploring valid scientific queries based on epidemiological data.

Humans also utilise representativeness and affective heuristics that can bias our judgements to assume things must go together because they are similar, or because they align with other things we value (Finucane et al. 2000). Several authors have argued that the uncontrolled transfer of the behavioural explanation of HIV epidemics from Western countries to Africa was facilitated by widespread, pre-existing, culturalist assumptions about sexual promiscuity in Africa (cf. Packard and Epstein 1991; Stillwaggon 2003, 2006). Similarly, Parkhurst (2013) has explored cases where ideological values seem to have perpetuated incorrect or oversimplified conclusions in the HIV field – such as poverty or gender inequality 'driving' HIV spread (oversimplifications), or Senegal's early political response being labelled as a 'success story' (a spurious conclusion as it has historically had similar HIV prevalence to its non-proactive neighbours).

The initial reaction to critical insights challenging consensus ideas is often one of disbelief, denial or anger. None of these *should* be the initial reaction of a scientific mind, but all are typical of a human mind – a mind designed to build protective silos around ideological positions, draw affective conclusions and avoid cognitive dissonance.

Institutional-economic origins

As noted in the introduction, the HIV response has grown to over US$19 billion in recent years. While the resulting institutional pressure to spend funds has led to various inefficiencies and perverse outcomes in HIV-prevention programmes during the mid-2000s (Pisani 2008; Hunsmann 2013), the vertical structure of the international AIDS response – which was in part chosen to ensure accountability – has further entrenched silos of thinking and preventive action. In several African countries, over 90% of AIDS-related expenses are funded by PEPFAR and the Global Fund, both disease-specific programmes. However, vertical programmes are externality-prone: the restrictive definition of their targets, the fragmented funding structures and the narrowly HIV-centred reporting processes impel HIV-prevention players to consider only those effects that concern their project's closely circumscribed objectives (Stillwaggon 2006, 173–176; Hunsmann 2012).

Another source of silo-based practice lies in forms of institutional rigidity that derive from organisations' relative specialisation. Organisations that specialise in behaviour-centred prevention measures, for instance, are unlikely to be suitable implementing agencies for prevention measures unrelated to sexual behaviour (Stillwaggon 2006, chap. 9, esp. 190–194). In Tanzania, Hunsmann (2012) found that incomplete

convertibility from one activity to another of AIDS NGOs and government departments, combined with their desire to ensure their institutional survival, led them to act as a political constituency against policy change, hampering the adoption of cofactor-based measures. Finally, the perceived complexity of multi-factor interventions appears to be another important source of bias towards 'simple' single-intervention approaches (*Ibid.*), and that irrespective of the degree to which the desired outcome is actually amenable to policy intervention.

Discussion

Too many studies have taken an authoritative tone which is not warranted by the data available and in doing so have encouraged a premature closure of African AIDS research. (Packard and Epstein 1991, 782)

As the date on the quote above attests, we are not new in our concern over how silos of thinking may adversely affect the HIV/ AIDS response in Africa. This paper has attempted to illustrate the continued presence of such silos, but also to explore the potential origins of silo thinking in an effort to consider ways to avoid it in the future. Overly reductionist thinking is always problematic in scientific exercises, and perhaps the greatest risk to silo thinking is when it gives rise to scientific exclusion or blacklisting. We can see instances of this in some of the examples described above. Those who warn against the risks of blood-borne HIV transmission and ask for better evidence to replace speculation have, for example, been accused of causing thousands of deaths by scaring Africans away from vaccination campaigns and health care (for illustrative examples, see Hunsmann 2013, 78–81). Similarly, social science researchers who develop critical perspectives on biomedical approaches continue to be accused of putting 'lives at stake' (Nguyen et al.

2011) or of having 'blood on their hands' (Le Marcis 2013) by hampering the rapid roll-out of interventions. Finally, researchers interested in non-behavioural drivers of sexual HIV transmission have at times been labelled HIV 'denialists' – grouping them with those who argue that HIV is not the cause of AIDS. Although this claim is not true, since variations in HIV-transmission risk are at the very heart of their argument, it continues to fuel researchers' fear to be 'pushed in the wrong corner' by exploring unpopular or non-mainstream research questions about the spread of HIV (Hunsmann 2013, 80–81).

Nearly a quarter century after Packard and Epstein's words of caution noted above, our point is not to call eternally for more research. Potentially more useful is to enable collaborations across disciplines that can break down silos by exploring synergies between different factors and modes of transmission – and thus between different prevention interventions. Breaking out of institutional, disciplinary or ideologically based silos is easy to call for, but will require deliberate effort and strategies on the part of the public health and HIV-prevention community. A first step may be efforts making us more aware of our ideologies and perspectives, and how these bias or frame our thinking. The critical reflection that many social sciences include in their training derives from an identified need for such perspectives when studying social settings and problems. As the public health field turns to study such issues, it would be prudent to consider what skills and insights are needed for this new area of investigation. Public health training would be wise to consider the 'public' element as much as the 'health' component of its name, reflecting on how dealing with the social world (in terms of behaviours, politics and choices) may differ from dealing with natural (clinical or biochemical) phenomena. A self-reflective approach further provides a starting point to identify our values and positions,

considering if these bias our views of evidence or conclusions. When conflicting or dissenting views are presented, it is essential that HIV scientists reflect on the origins, source and merit of such critical perspectives, being willing to embrace those which expand and complement the goals of HIV prevention.

A second strategy that can be taken up within the contemporary efforts to define structural approaches to HIV prevention is to reconsider the dominant hierarchies and thinking about evidence. Some researchers have begun to undertake randomised controlled trials of single interventions purportedly addressing 'structural determinants'. This is a natural response that emerges from disciplinary traditions which have embraced experimental trials as the best, and often the only, form of evidence to guide practice. Experimental trials can be incredibly useful at times, but any such efforts addressing social, political and economic factors need to be well justified in addressing questions about their generalisability. There should also be reflection as to how much can be learned from single trials of social change phenomenon, as opposed to, for example, historical or ethnographic learning from real-life examples of successful population HIV-prevention efforts.

A final approach to HIV prevention that can help to avoid silo thinking, but is particularly suited to the structural approaches being proposed, is to start from a position that assumes HIV prevention is a complex endeavour. Many social scientists already have a healthy scepticism of simplistic solutions in HIV prevention, but the current efforts to define what a structural approach looks like can do more to establish explicitly that the starting point for HIV prevention should be one of complexity, holding that any attempt to intervene in a simple (single-focused, short-term etc.) way needs clear justification. To date, the reverse has often been true – that simple solutions have been the norm and that more complex, multi-faceted approaches required defending to HIV funding bodies and international donors. Treating HIV prevention as complex would further encourage, rather than discourage, attempts to synthesise and integrate knowledge on the *interactions* between modes of transmission, and between biological and social factors that condition infection risk and access to HIV services. Because of the broad and non-linear reasoning it adopts, a complexity focus also would lend itself more naturally to take account of synergistic effects between multiple prevention interventions (some of which are very inexpensive, but still have been marginalised), as well as of some interventions' positive 'externalities' (i.e. not immediately HIV-related effects) on population health (Stillwaggon 2009).

The above discussion and examples have meant to be illustrative of some of the challenges facing HIV prevention, and some of the possible means to think towards solutions. We believe that breaking away from silo thinking would help to ensure we answer questions in the most rigorous, scientific and efficient ways, and to ensure that our institutional responses align institutional incentives with good practice. The renewed emphasis on structural approaches to HIV prevention may provide a window of opportunity in this respect. However, while the language of 'combination' HIV prevention by UNAIDS (2010) is potentially useful, there is a risk that combination prevention becomes reduced to a narrow set of interventions that are believed to 'work' (e.g. circumcision + antiretroviral therapy + condoms = combination approach). Such an approach does not fit with the idea that HIV prevention requires comprehensive and locally informed approaches. A 'paradigm shift' requires disciplinary change and institutional change. Neither is easy, but the existing discussions about structural approaches to HIV provide an opportunity to press for such change. Windows of opportunity do not stay open long, however. There may be indications that the structural and combination approaches are already being co-opted into modalities that risk burying their useful insights within new silos of thinking. We hope that discussions such as this one can prevent this from happening.

Disclosure statement

No potential conflict of interest was reported by the authors.

References

Berkley, S. F. 1994. "Public Health Measures to Prevent HIV Spread in Africa." In *AIDS in Africa*, edited by M. Essex, S. Mboup, P. Kanki and M. Kalengayi, 473–495. New York: Raven Press.

Boily, M-C., R. F. Baggaley, L. Wang, B. Masse, R. G. White, R. J. Hayes and M. Alary. 2009. "Heterosexual Risk of HIV-1 Infection per Sexual Act: Systematic Review and Meta-analysis of Observational Studies." *The Lancet Infectious Diseases* 9 (2): 118–129.

Brecht, A. 1959. *Political Theory: The Foundations of Twentieth-century Political Thought*. Princeton, NJ: Princeton University Press.

Cartwright, N., and J. Hardie. 2012. *Evidence-based Policy: A Practical Guide to Doing it Better*. Oxford: Oxford University Press.

Cleland, J., and B. Ferry, eds. 1995. *Sexual Behaviour and AIDS in the Developing World*. London: Taylor & Francis.

Dyer, J. R., P. Kazembe, P. L. Vernazza, B. L. Gilliam, M. Maida, D. Zimba, I. F. Hoffman, et al. 1998. "High Levels of Human Immunodeficiency Virus Type 1 in Blood and Semen of Seropositive Men in Sub-Saharan Africa." *The Journal of Infectious Diseases* 177 (6): 1742–46.

Epstein, S. 1996. *Impure Science – AIDS, Activism and the Politics of Knowledge*. Berkeley: University of California Press.

Festinger, L. 1957. *A Theory of Cognitive Dissonance*. Stanford: Stanford University Press.

Finucane, M. L., A. Alhakami, P. Slovic, and S. M. Johnson. 2000. "The Affect Heuristic in Judgments of Risks and Benefits." *Journal of Behavioral Decision Making* 13 (1): 1–17.

French, K., S. Riley, and G. Garnett. 2006. "Simulations of the HIV Epidemic in Sub-Saharan Africa: Sexual Transmission Versus Transmission Through Unsafe Medical Injections." *Sexually Transmitted Diseases* 33 (3): 127–134.

Gilovich, T., D. W. Griffin, and D. Kahneman, eds. 2002. *Heuristics and Biases: The Psychology of Intuitive Judgement*. Cambridge: Cambridge University Press.

Gisselquist, D. 2008. *Points to Consider: Responses to HIV/AIDS in Africa, Asia, and the Caribbean*. London: Adonis & Abbey Publishers.

Gupta, G. R., J. O. Parkhurst, J. A. Ogden, P. Aggleton, and A. Mahal. 2008. "Structural Approaches to HIV Prevention." *The Lancet* 372 (9640): 764–75.

Halperin, D. T., M. J. Steiner, M. M. Cassell, E. C. Green, N. Hearst, D. Kirby, H. D. Gayle, and W. Cates. 2004. "The Time has Come for Common Ground on Preventing Sexual Transmission of HIV." *The Lancet* 364 (9449): 1913–1915.

Hunsmann, M. 2012. "Limits to Evidence-based Health Policymaking: Policy Hurdles to Structural HIV Prevention in Tanzania." *Social Science & Medicine* 74 (10): 1477–1485.

Hunsmann, M. 2013. *Depoliticising an Epidemic. International AIDS Control and the Politics of Health in Tanzania*, PhD thesis, Paris: École des Hautes Études en Sciences Sociales and Albert-Ludwigs-Universität Freiburg. https://tel.archives-ouvertes.fr/tel-01055458

Kahan, D. 2013. "Ideology, Motivated Reasoning, and Cognitive Reflection." *Judgment & Decision Making* 8 (4): 407–424.

Kaiser Family Foundation and UNAIDS. 2014. *Financing the Response to HIV in Low and Middle Income Countries: International Assistance From Donor Governments in 2013*. Menlo Park, CA: Kaiser Family Foundation.

Kaul, R., C. R. Cohen, D. Chege, T. J. Yi, W. Tharao, L. R. McKinnon, R. Remis, O. Anzala, and J. Kimani. 2011. "Biological Factors That May Contribute to Regional and Racial Disparities in HIV Prevalence." *American Journal of Reproductive Immunology* 65 (3): 317–24.

Le Marcis, F. 2013. "Permanence des impensés de la lutte contre le sida et nécessité d'une pensée critique." [online] *Genre, sexualité & société* 9 (June). https://gss.revues.org/2857?lang=fr.

Mann, J., H. Francis, F. Davachi, P. Baudoux, T. Quinn, N. Nzilambi, N. Bosenge, R. Colebunders, P. Piot, and N. Kabote. 1986. "Risk Factors for Human Immunodeficiency Virus Seropositivity among Children 1–24 Months Old in Kinshasa, Zaire." *The Lancet* 328 (8508): 654–57.

Modjarrad, K., and S. H. Vermund. 2010. "Effect of Treating Co-infections on HIV-1 Viral Load: A Systematic Review." *The Lancet Infectious Diseases* 10 (7): 455–463.

MOHSW. 2013. *Tanzania Service Availability and Readiness Assessment (SARA) 2012*. Dar es Salaam: Ministry of Health and Social Welfare.

Montgomery, S., J. Joseph, M. Becker, D. Ostrow, R. Kessler, and J. Kirscht. 1989. "The Health Belief Model in Understanding Compliance with Preventive Recommendations for AIDS: How Useful?" *AIDS education and prevention* 1 (4): 303–323.

Nguyen, V-K., N. Bajos, F. Dubois-Arber, J. O'Malley, and C. M. Pirkle. 2011. "Remedicalizing an Epidemic: From HIV Treatment as Prevention to HIV Treatment Is Prevention." *AIDS* 25 (3): 291–293.

Packard, R. M., and P. Epstein. 1991. "Epidemiologists, Social Scientists, and the Structure of Medical Research on AIDS in Africa." *Social Science & Medicine* 33 (7): 771–783.

Parker, R. G., D. Easton, and Ch. Klein. 2000. "Structural Barriers and Facilitators in HIV Prevention: A Review of International Research." *AIDS* 14 (1): S22–S32.

Parkhurst, J. 2011. "Evidence, Politics and Uganda's HIV Success: Moving Forward with ABC and HIV Prevention." *Journal of International Development* 23: 240–252.

Parkhurst, J. 2012. "HIV Prevention, Structural Change and Social Values: The Need for an Explicit Normative Approach." *Journal of the International AIDS Society* 15 (Suppl. 1): 1–10.

Parkhurst, J. 2013. "The Subtle Politics of AIDS: Values, Bias, and Persistent Errors in HIV Prevention." In *Global HIV/AIDS Politics, Policy, and Activism*, edited by R. Smith, 113–139. Santa Barbara, CA: Praeger.

Parkhurst, J., D. Chilongozi, and E. Hutchinson. 2015. "Doubt, Defiance, and Identity: Understanding Resistance to Male Circumcision for HIV Prevention in Malawi." *Social Science and Medicine.* doi:10.1016/j.socscimed.2015.04.020.

Pawson, R., and N. Tilley. 1997. *Realistic Evaluation.* London: Sage Publications.

Pépin, J., C. N. Abou Chakra, E. Pépin, V. Nault, and L. Valiquette. 2014. "Evolution of the Global Burden of Viral Infections From Unsafe Medical Injections, 2000–2010." [online] *PloS One* 9 (6): E99677. http://www.ncbi.nlm.nih.gov

Peters, E. J., D. D. Brewer, N. E. Udonwa, G. T. A. Jombo, O. E. Essien, V. A. Umoh, A. A. Otu, D. U. Eduwem, and J. J. Potterat. 2009. "Diverse Blood Exposures Associated with Incident HIV Infection in Calabar, Nigeria." *International Journal of STD & AIDS* 20 (12): 846–851.

Pisani, E. 2008. *The Wisdom of Whores: Bureaucrats, Brothels, and the Business of AIDS.* New York: Norton.

Putzel, J. 2004. *Governance and AIDS in Africa: Assessing the International Community's 'Multisectoral Approach'.* Annual Meeting of the American Political Science Association, Chicago. 2–5 September, 2004.

Reid, S. 2009a. "Increase in Clinical Prevalence of AIDS Implies Increase in Unsafe Medical Injections." *International Journal of STD & AIDS* 20 (5): 295–99.

Reid, S. 2009b. "Non-vertical HIV Transmission to Children in Sub-Saharan Africa." *International Journal of STD & AIDS* 20 (12): 820–827.

Sando, D., S. Sumba, G. Somi, and R. Kalinga. 2014. *Epidemiology of HIV and Access to Prevention Services, Tanzania.* Dar es Salaam: Report submitted to the Joint Biennial HIV National Response Review (November 2014).

Sawers, L., and E. Stillwaggon. 2010. "Understanding the Southern African 'Anomaly': Poverty, Endemic Disease and HIV." *Development and Change* 41 (2): 195–224.

Shelton, J. D. 2006. "Confessions of A Condom Lover." *The Lancet* 368 (9551): 1947–1949.

Stillwaggon, E. 2003. "Racial Metaphors: Interpreting Sex and AIDS in Africa." *Development and Change* 34 (5): 809–832.

Stillwaggon, E. 2006. *AIDS and the Ecology of Poverty.* New York: Oxford University Press.

Stillwaggon, E. 2009. "Complexity, Cofactors, and the Failure of AIDS Policy in Africa." [online] *Journal of the International AIDS Society* 12 (12). http://www.ncbi.nlm.nih.gov/pmc/articles/PMC2717915/

Tarantola, D., and J. Mann. 1995. "AIDS and Human Rights." *AIDS and Society* 6 (4): 1–5.

UNAIDS. 2010. *Combination HIV Prevention: Tailoring and Coordinating Biomedical, Behavioural and Structural Strategies to Reduce new HIV Infections.* Geneva: UNAIDS.

Vachon, F., J-P. Coulaud, and C. Katlama. 1985. "Epidémiologie Actuelle du Syndrome D'immunodéficit Acquis en Dehors des Groupes à Risque." *La Presse Médicale* 14 (38): 1949–50.

Wachter, R. M. 1992. "AIDS, Activism, and the Politics of Health." *The New England Journal of Medicine* 362 (2): 128–133.

World Bank. 2015. *World Development Report 2015: Mind, Society, and Behavior.* Washington, DC: The World Bank.

DEBATE

Microfinance and HIV prevention

Janet Seeley

This article provides a brief overview of both the broader microfinance arena and the current evidence on the impact of microfinance on HIV prevention. The available information suggests that the impact of microfinance, as well as the impact of microfinance linked to HIV-prevention programmes in sub-Saharan Africa, show a mixed picture. This is not surprising given the very different contexts in which interventions have been implemented and the varied and sometimes questionable impact of microfinance for the poorest and the less-poor (women and men, older and younger) recipients. While there is little evidence that microfinance alone prevents HIV infections, there is information on unintended outcomes of microfinance as women face HIV-related risks as they struggle to repay debts. Structural changes remain a necessity if HIV prevention and development programmes are to respond to the broader economic and social issues poor women and men face, in Africa and elsewhere.

Writing a decade ago, Julia Kim and Charlotte Watts (2005) suggested that HIV-prevention initiatives could build on the successes of microfinance initiatives in many developing countries to bring about change. The provision of credit and savings to poor women was widely reported to be leading to improvements in household food security as well as individual benefits for the women involved who, through the microfinance interventions, acquired economic and business skills (see for example, Hulme and Moore 2006; Kabeer 2005; Sanyal 2009; Swain and Wallentin 2009; van Rooyen, Stewart, and de Wet 2012). There were direct benefits for reproductive health: Kim and Watts (2005, 770) noted that women in Bangladesh involved in microfinance programmes were reporting an increase in their control over contraception and wider sexual and reproductive health decisions; control that they suggested might be translated in other settings to HIV-prevention initiatives. Anderson et al. (2002) had also suggested that microfinance could have an impact on HIV transmission. However, they sounded a more cautious note in the light of reported benefits of microfinance for HIV-affected households in Zimbabwe and Kenya. They concluded that 'microfinance represents a potentially powerful tool [for HIV programme planners], but the precise benefits and effects of access to credit are often difficult to determine' (7). Much has happened since the papers by Kim and Watts, and Anderson and colleagues were written – HIV interventions studies, which have included microfinance, have been put in place and impact assessments carried out. So, with a growing body of evidence on the impact of these interventions, where are we now in our understanding of the role of microfinance in HIV prevention?

In this short article, I provide a brief (and inevitably incomplete) overview of both the broader microfinance arena and the current evidence on the impact of microfinance on HIV prevention. I focus on credit and savings and do not include conditional or unconditional cash-transfer interventions (see Pettifor et al. 2012 for a review of cash-payment interventions to prevent HIV). I begin with some background on the growth of the microfinance industry, to provide some context for the discussion of the potential of microfinance for HIV prevention and mitigation.

Microfinance or microcredit is a term used to describe financial services which are available to people who may not have access to formal banking services through which to seek a loan. Microcredit, or micro-debt (as Hulme [2000] reminds us it might more accurately be termed), can provide opportunities for poor people to access '"lumps" of money so that they can improve incomes and reduce vulnerability' (Hulme 2000, 26). Microfinance has a very long history which includes both informal and formal institutions: money lenders, friendly societies and cooperatives, for example. Bateman and Chang (2012, 14) note that these institutions:

> especially those from the 18th and 19th century onwards, arose from a desire to transform the lives of the poor and the new industrial working classes, as they struggled to cope with the growing perils and exploitation associated with the rise of industrial capitalism.

The recent interest in the provision of microfinance services in developing countries grew out of similar aspirations. In Bangladesh in the 1970s, Muhammad Yunus set up projects to provide small loans to village women, to test his idea that access to modest amounts of money could make a significant difference to poor people's lives. This led to the formation of the Grameen Bank and similar microfinance organisations in Bangladesh

and elsewhere. The aim of the Grameen Bank, and other non-governmental institutions such as BRAC and PROSHIKA in Bangladesh, was to provide financial services to poor men, but particularly women, in a targeted, convenient and systematic way. Building on the Bangladesh experience, there has since the 1980s been a proliferation of organisations supporting the provision of small loans to individuals and groups for micro-enterprise development or self-employment initiatives with an ever-growing literature describing these projects (see, for example, Basu and Srivastava 2005; Duvendack et al. 2011; Hulme and Moore 2006; Khandker 1998; Rutherford 2001). By the 1990s, microfinance was being viewed by many international development organisations as a solution to poverty alleviation, a 'golden bullet' (Bateman and Chang 2012; Morduch 1999a). However, as Bateman and Chang (2012, 25) remind us, the growth of microfinance as an international development tool came at a time when neoliberalism was being enthusiastically embraced in countries supporting that development. Microfinance initiatives foster small-scale entrepreneurship and competition in what is often a limited market, while encouraging borrowers to see a route to prosperity (or indeed out of poverty) to be through their own efforts, not through state intervention.

> Microfinance thus offers to neoliberals a highly visible way of being seen to be addressing the issue of poverty, but in a way that offers no challenge whatsoever to the distorted structures of wealth and power that historically are mainly responsible for the creation and perpetuation of poverty. (*Ibid.*, 25)

In addition to Bangladesh and India, other early centres of this new wave of microfinance were Bolivia and Indonesia. In Bolivia from the mid 1980s, microfinance organisations provided credit for micro-enterprises and in Indonesia, also from the mid 1980s, local outlets of Bank Rakyat

Indonesia successfully sought to serve the whole population with access to microfinance (with no particular poverty focus). This difference in the target population for microfinance has led some commentators to make the distinction between Bangladesh, where finance was provided for the '*poorest of the poor*', and Indonesia and Bolivia, where the target was 'the *economically active poor*' (Rutherford 2001), a distinction I return to below.[1]

Given the enthusiasm shown by international development organisations for microfinance as a vehicle for poverty reduction, there has over the last 30 years been a plethora of microfinance activity in Africa (Blavy, Basu, and Yülek 2004). But, as in South Asia, this has met with mixed results (Buckley 1997; van Rooyen, Stewart, and de Wet 2012).

Questions over the beneficial impact of microfinance projects on poverty are not new. Since the early experiences with microfinance in Bangladesh, there have been many who have expressed concerns about assumptions that 'microcredit is the answer to the problems of poverty' (Hulme 2000, 28). There is a large literature where questions have been raised about the targeting, delivery and content of microfinance interventions (Banerjee et al. 2013; Chemin 2008; Hulme and Moore 2007; Morduch 1998, 1999a, 2000). Indeed, there has been a sometimes acrimonious debate on impact assessments of microfinance in Bangladesh and elsewhere (see, for example, Bateman and Chang 2012; Duvendack and Palmer-Jones 2012; Pitt and Khandker 2012; Roodman 2012), which raises questions about the microfinance and assumptions that it benefits poor people and is particularly beneficial to women. Perhaps most important for the purposes of this article, these debates serve as a reminder to look at both the context and the timing of interventions as well as the sustainability of any beneficial change.

As noted above, there had been an assumption in Bangladesh in the 1970s/ 1980s that the microfinance projects of the Grameen Bank, BRAC and PROSHIKA were targeting the 'poorest of the poor'. Increasingly, this assumption was questioned in the 1990s and 2000s both by the organisations themselves and by the international donor community. David Hulme (2000), in his article on 'the dark side of microfinance', reminds us that microcredit organisations seldom work with the poorest because very poor people do not want to, and cannot afford to, get into debt,[2] nor do they have the time and resources to sustain involvement in microfinance group activities. The model for microfinance promoted by the Grameen Bank and similar organisations, for example, was based on women's groups holding regular (often weekly) meetings where members deposited low-value compulsory weekly savings and received loans which were intended for investment in new or existing businesses (but not necessarily for consumption needs [Nourse 2001]) and which had to be repaid in weekly instalments. Loans were secured against the track record of the borrowers and with the support of fellow group members, sometimes with borrowers being liable for each other's loans. Many poorer families could not afford regular savings, or the time to attend group meetings. In addition, existing group members might not welcome members who are not similar to them (by socio-economic or ethnic group, for example) and may pose a risk to the rest of the group (Bosher, Penning-Rowsell, and Tapsell 2007; Thorp, Stewart, and Heyer 2005). The realisation that microfinance organisations tend to benefit the 'not so poor' rather than the poorest has led over the last 15 years to considerable efforts in Bangladesh, India and elsewhere to develop interventions which may include some elements of savings and credit which are sensitive to the needs of the very poor (Hulme and Moore 2007; Matin and Hulme 2003). Even for those who are not the poorest, the necessity of ensuring repayments (with, as the sector has become increasingly commercialised, interest repayments [Stewart et al. 2010]) can place enormous pressure on individuals who may easily slip back into chronic or extreme poverty (Hulme, Moore, and Shepherd 2001). If a microfinance intervention is coupled with a health or education project, people who drop out of, or have never been a part of, the microfinance initiative may also not access related components.

Microfinance is also seen as a tool for women's empowerment. As Rankin (2002, 2) observes:

[the] rhetoric of 'solidarity' implies that women who participate in group lending will identify collectively to resist their common oppression [. . .] Yet in practice, the financial imperatives for sustainability often lead microfinance programs to engage the collective only in the most instrumental manner – reducing administrative costs and motivating repayment – at the expense of the more time-consuming processes of consciousness-raising and empowerment. Mere participation in the group borrowing process is often considered a proxy for empowerment, and assumed to generate ample quantities of social capital (in the liberal sense of the term).

Rankin goes on to show, through case material from Nepal, how women's groups formed to access microfinance fit within existing gender hierarchies, and are not vehicles for social transformation. Others have made similar observations (Ballard 2013; D'Espallier, Guerin, and Mersland 2013; Fouillet et al. 2013), urging caution over claims that poor people's (particularly women's) engagement in micro-credit programmes will necessarily be a catalyst for social change. Indeed, prevailing power structures, influenced by politics, history and societal norms, are not easily transformed by a financial intervention targeting poor people. It is more likely that intervention will be contained within and shaped by those existing structures.

I now want to return to the discussion of the development of HIV-prevention initiatives and microfinance. The Intervention with Microfinance for AIDS and Gender Equity (IMAGE) study in South Africa was a 'poverty focused microfinance initiative that targeted the poorest women in communities with a participatory curriculum of gender and HIV education' (Pronyk et al. 2006, p. 1973). This project was reported to have led to reductions in intimate partner violence among participants, but had less impact on rates of unprotected sexual intercourse or HIV incidence. Secondary analysis of the data did show evidence of an impact of the intervention on the sexual behaviour of young women (Pronyk et al. 2008). A recent systematic review of income-generation activities for HIV prevention by Caitlin Kennedy and colleagues has assessed the impact of the IMAGE study, and other microfinance initiatives on HIV prevention. In their analysis of the 12 studies which met the criteria for their systematic review, they looked at the impact of microfinance alone, rather than in combination with health education or other interventions, on HIV-related behaviours. In the two studies where this was assessed, they found no consistent pattern of association between the microfinance intervention and HIV-related behaviour when compared to the control group (Ashburn, Kerrigan, and Sweat 2008; Kim et al. 2007; Pronyk et al. 2006, 2008). In five studies where the impact of microfinance combined with health education was assessed (Kim et al. 2009; Sherer et al. 2004; Ssewamala et al. 2010), changes in HIV-related behaviours as well as a reduction in intimate partner violence, as already described above for the IMAGE study (Pronyk et al. 2006, 2008), were found. Kennedy et al. (2014, 671) note that even though only a small number of studies were included in the review, they represented very different target populations, 'settings, study designs and outcomes, we cannot know whether differences in efficacy were due to intervention components or other factors'. They conclude that 'the evidence that income generation interventions influence HIV-related behaviours is inconclusive' (659). This assessment is not surprising when we look more broadly at impact assessments of microfinance initiatives in Africa and elsewhere.

A systematic review of the impact of microfinance in sub-Saharan Africa carried out by van Rooyen, Stewart, and de Wet (2012) shows a mixed picture. They conclude that 'specific elements of microfinance seem to work in specific contexts' but, because of the variation in the nature of poverty as well as the types of intervention, 'it is hard to draw generalizable lessons' (2258). Nevertheless, based on information from seven studies which included evidence of the impact of microfinance on health, they concluded that there was a positive impact on the health of poor people because they were sick less often and levels of nutrition had improved. They included the IMAGE study among those assessed and note, as Kennedy et al. (2014) had done, that that intervention 'included far more than just micro-credit, with considerable investment in gender and HIV awareness training' (van Rooyen, Stewart, and de Wet 2012, 2256).

I have thus far focused on HIV-prevention and microfinance projects. There is another way that microfinance may be linked to HIV. MacPherson et al. (2015), writing in this journal, describe the experience with microfinance of women fish traders on the shores of Lake Malawi. The loan procedures followed a pattern in common with the operating procedures of microfinance programmes in many parts of the world: loans were provided to groups and the membership then assumed responsibility for loan repayment together. Larger loans could only be accessed if repayment was completed on time. Men could access loans, but women were preferred by the five organisations providing the loans in the study site because they were seen to be more trustworthy and reliable, and therefore more likely to repay. The microfinance organisations were only providing microcredit services; they were not linked to any health intervention. While most women appreciated the loans and valued being part of a micro-credit group, there was a negative side to the engagement in microfinance. A number of the women worried over loan repayment and the strategies that some had to employ to get money to repay. Women engaged in transactional sex to get the money to repay loans, a strategy which put them at risk of HIV infection in a context of high HIV prevalence.

While some studies have noted a decrease in domestic violence when a woman joins a microfinance group, others suggest an increase in violence perhaps because of a spouse's concern over a woman's increasing independence because of access to money (or their failure to secure a loan for the household) and their involvement with the group (Kabeer 2005). Other examples of adverse outcomes or adverse incorporation (Wood 2003) may include accessing money at a high interest rate from a money lender or another loan source in order to pay off a microfinance debt (Anderson et al. 2002), or being a member of a group which places demands on an individual beyond the microfinance activities which are hard to meet (Howson 2013).

The considerable and varied experience with the implementation of microfinance projects and programmes in general, and the more recent experience with microfinance initiatives linked to HIV prevention, point to the importance of not seeking a 'one-size-fits-all' approach to economic programmes linked to HIV (Dworkin and Blankenship 2009). Recent trials of interventions such as SHAZ! in Zimbabwe (Dunbar et al. 2010), which did include a microfinance component, and the SHARE and SASA! trials in Uganda (Abramsky et al. 2014; Jewkes 2015; Wagman et al. 2015), which did not include microfinance but which built on the learning from the IMAGE study, point to the value of interventions that have a range of components, and which do not just target one particular group in a community. However, even these initiatives demand time which may be difficult for the poorest people or marginalised ethnic/social groups to commit to. Women and men who are unable (or prefer not) to take part in group activities also need HIV-prevention support tailored to their circumstances. The quest for a new approach, a new magic bullet, reminds me of Patricia Bonnard's (2002) short paper in which she suggested that the impact of HIV could be mitigated if we used what we know already to encourage general development, rather than looking for something new. Organisations engaged in microfinance need to continue to take an approach which is 'based on an empirically-based understanding of the relationship between context, approach and impact' (Kabeer 2005, 4709) with HIV-prevention interventions also building from this understanding. That is not to say that women such as the fish traders on the shores of Lake Malawi should not have access to microcredit if that is what they want; there are many benefits from having access to loans. But, perhaps with the growing body of information on the unintended outcomes from such projects, microfinance models might be adjusted or additional support put in place, to try to limit negative unintended consequences.

The intimate link between the enthusiasm for microfinance as a poverty-alleviation strategy and neoliberalism should not be forgotten. Encouraging people, particularly women, to take loans may provide short-term benefits, including benefits to health, but does not transform the power structures in society if poor women and their families are locked into loan repayments (often at high rates of interest). The reality is that small adjustments will not

be enough. Structural change is a necessity if HIV prevention and development programmes which include microfinance are to respond to the broader economic and social issues poor women and men face, in Africa and elsewhere (Seeley et al. 2012); that may be an aspiration but it is one worth aiming for.

Disclosure statement

No potential conflict of interest was reported by the author.

Notes

1. Donor funding in Bangladesh enabled microfinance institutions to offer poor people rates of interest on loans that are significantly lower than those charged by microfinance institutions in some other countries (Morduch 1998, 1999b).
2. The consequences for people with problems repaying loans have been played out with tragic consequences in India, Bangladesh and elsewhere with a spate of suicides of people unable to repay their loans (Bateman 2012; Karim 2011; Taylor 2012).

References

Abramsky, Tanya, Karen Devries, Ligia Kiss, Janet Nakuti, Nambusi Kyegombe, Elizabeth Starmann, Bonnie Cundill, et al. 2014. "Findings from the SASA! Study: A Cluster Randomized Controlled Trial to Assess the Impact of a Community Mobilization Intervention to Prevent Violence against Women and Reduce HIV Risk in Kampala, Uganda." *BMC Medicine* 12 (1): 122. doi:10.1186/s12916-014-0122-5.

Anderson, L., Mary Kay Gugerty, O. R. Levine, and Marcia Weaver. 2002. *Microfinance and HIV/AIDS: Five Key Questions on Programme Impact.* Seattle, Washington: Center for Health Education and Research, University of Washington.

Ashburn, Kim, Deanna Kerrigan, and Michael Sweat. 2008. "Micro-credit, Women's Groups, Control of Own Money: HIV-related Negotiation among Partnered Dominican Women." *AIDS and Behavior* 12 (3): 396–403.

Ballard, Richard. 2013. "Geographies of Development II Cash Transfers and the Reinvention of Development for the Poor." *Progress in Human Geography* 37 (6): 811–821.

Banerjee, Abhijit V., Esther Duflo, Rachel Glennerster, and Cynthia Kinnan. 2013. "The Miracle of Microfinance? Evidence from a Randomized Evaluation." MIT Department of Economics Working Paper 13–09.

Basu, Priya, and Pradeep Srivastava. 2005. "Exploring Possibilities: Microfinance and Rural Credit Access for the Poor in India." *Economic and Political Weekly* 40 (17): 1747–1756.

Bateman, Milford. 2012. "How Lending to the Poor Began, Grew, and Almost Destroyed a Generation in India." *Development and Change* 43 (6): 1385–1402.

Bateman, Milford, and Ha-Joon Chang. 2012. "Microfinance and the Illusion of Development: From Hubris to Nemesis in Thirty Years." *World Economic Review* 1 (1): 13–36.

Blavy, Rodolphe, Anupam Basu, and Murat Â. Yülek. 2004. *Microfinance in Africa: Experience and Lessons from Selected African Countries*. Washington, DC: International Monetary Fund.

Bonnard, Patricia. 2002. "HIV/AIDS Mitigation: Using What We Already Know." *Technical Note No. 5*. Washington, DC: USAID.

Bosher, Lee, Edmund Penning-Rowsell, and Sue Tapsell. 2007. "Resource Accessibility and Vulnerability in Andhra Pradesh: Caste and Non-caste Influences." *Development and Change* 38 (4): 615–640.

Buckley, Graeme. 1997. "Microfinance in Africa: Is it either the Problem or the Solution?" *World Development* 25 (7): 1081–1093.

Chemin, Matthieu. 2008. "The Benefits and Costs of Microfinance: Evidence from Bangladesh." *The Journal of Development Studies* 44 (4): 463–484.

D'Espallier, Bert, Isabelle Guerin, and Roy Mersland. 2013. "Focus on Women in Microfinance Institutions." *The Journal of Development Studies* 49 (5): 589–608.

Dunbar, Megan S., M. Catherine Maternowska, Mi-Suk J. Kang, Susan M. Laver, Imelda Mudekunye-Mahaka, and Nancy S. Padian. 2010. "Findings from SHAZ!: A Feasibility Study of a Microcredit and Life-skills HIV Prevention Intervention to Reduce Risk among Adolescent Female Orphans in Zimbabwe." *Journal of Prevention and Intervention in the Community* 38 (2): 147–161.

Duvendack, Maren, and Richard Palmer-Jones. 2012. "High Noon for Microfinance Impact Evaluations: Re-investigating the Evidence from Bangladesh." *The Journal of Development Studies* 48 (12): 1864–1880.

Duvendack, Maren, Richard Palmer-Jones, James G. Copestake, Lee Hooper, Yoon Loke, and Nitya Rao. 2011. *What is the Evidence of the Impact of Microfinance on the Well-being of Poor People?* London: EPPI-Centre, Social Science Research Unit, Institute of Education, University of London.

Dworkin, Shari L., and Kim Blankenship. 2009. "Microfinance and HIV/AIDS Prevention: Assessing its Promise and Limitations." *AIDS and Behavior* 13 (3): 462–469.

Fouillet, Cyril, Marek Hudon, Barbara Harriss-White, and James Copestake. 2013. "Microfinance Studies: Introduction and Overview." *Oxford Development Studies* 41 (sup1): S1–S16.

Howson, Cynthia. 2013. "Adverse Incorporation and Microfinance among Cross-border Traders in Senegal." *World Development* 42: 199–208.

Hulme, David. 2000. "Is Microdebt Good for Poor People? A Note on the Dark Side of Microfinance." *Small Enterprise Development* 11 (1): 26–28.

Hulme, David, and Karen Moore. 2006. *Why has Microfinance been a Policy Success in Bangladesh (and Beyond)?* Manchester: Global Poverty Research Group (GPRG).

Hulme, David, and Karen Moore. 2007. "Assisting the Poorest in Bangladesh: Learning from BRAC's 'Targeting the Ultra Poor' Programme." Brooks World Poverty Institute Working Paper (01).

Hulme, David, Karen Moore, and Andrew Shepherd. 2001. *Chronic Poverty: Meanings and Analytical Frameworks*. Manchester: Chronic Poverty Research Centre Manchester, United Kingdom.

Jewkes, Rachel K. 2015. "SHARE: A Milestone in Joint Programming for HIV and Intimate

Partner Violence." *The Lancet Global Health* 3 (1): e2–e3.

Kabeer, Naila. 2005. "Is Microfinance a 'Magic Bullet' for Women's Empowerment? Analysis of Findings from South Asia." *Economic and Political Weekly* 40 (44/45): 4709–4718.

Karim, Lamia. 2011. *Microfinance and its Discontents: Women in Debt in Bangladesh*. Minnesota: University of Minnesota Press.

Kennedy, Caitlin E., Virginia A. Fonner, Kevin R. O'Reilly, and Michael D. Sweat. 2014. "A Systematic Review of Income Generation Interventions, Including Microfinance and Vocational Skills Training, for HIV Prevention." *AIDS Care* 26 (6): 659–673.

Khandker, Shahidur R. 1998. *Fighting Poverty with Microcredit: Experience in Bangladesh*. Oxford: Oxford University Press.

Kim, Julia, Giulia Ferrari, Tanya Abramsky, Charlotte Watts, James Hargreaves, Linda Morison, Godfrey Phetla, John Porter, and Paul Pronyk. 2009. "Assessing the Incremental Effects of Combining Economic and Health Interventions: The IMAGE Study in South Africa." *Bulletin of the World Health Organization* 87 (11): 824–832.

Kim, Julia C., and Charlotte H. Watts. 2005. "Gaining a Foothold: Tackling Poverty, Gender Inequality, and HIV in Africa." *British Medical Journal* 331 (7519): 769–772.

Kim, Julia C., Charlotte H. Watts, James R. Hargreaves, Luceth X. Ndhlovu, Godfrey Phetla, Linda A. Morison, Joanna Busza, John D. H. Porter, and Paul Pronyk. 2007. "Understanding the Impact of a Microfinance-based Intervention on Women's Empowerment and the Reduction of Intimate Partner Violence in South Africa." *American Journal of Public Health* 97 (10): 1794–1802.

MacPherson, Eleanor, John Sadalaki, Victoria Nyongopa, Lawrence Nkhwazi, Macwellings Phiri, Alinafe Chimponda, Nicola Desmond, et al. 2015. Exploring the Complexity of Microfinance and HIV in Fishing Communities on the Shores of Lake Malawi." *Review of African Political Economy* 40 (145): 414–436. doi:10.1080/03056244.2015.1064369.

Matin, Imran, and David Hulme. 2003. "Programs for the Poorest: Learning from the IGVGD Program in Bangladesh." *World Development* 31 (3): 647–665.

Morduch, Jonathan. 1998. *Does Microfinance Really Help the Poor? New Evidence from Flagship Programs in Bangladesh*. Research Program in Development Studies, Woodrow School of Public and International Affairs.

Morduch, Jonathan. 1999a. "The Microfinance Promise." *Journal of Economic Literature* 37: 1569–1614.

Morduch, Jonathan. 1999b. "The Role of Subsidies in Microfinance: Evidence from the Grameen Bank." *Journal of Development Economics* 60 (1): 229–248.

Morduch, Jonathan. 2000. "The Microfinance Schism." *World Development* 28 (4): 617–629.

Nourse, Timothy H. 2001. "The Missing Parts of Microfinance: Services for Consumption and Insurance." *SAIS Review* 21 (1): 61–69.

Pettifor, Audrey, Catherine MacPhail, Nadia Nguyen, and Molly Rosenberg. 2012. "Can Money Prevent the Spread of HIV? A Review of Cash Payments for HIV Prevention." *AIDS and Behavior* 16 (7): 1729–1738.

Pitt, Mark M., and Shahidur R. Khandker. 2012. *Replicating Replication: Due Diligence in Roodman and Morduch's Replication of Pitt and Khandker (1998)*. Washington, DC: World Bank.

Pronyk, Paul M., James R. Hargreaves, Julia C. Kim, Linda A. Morison, Godfrey Phetla, Charlotte Watts, Joanna Busza, et al. 2006. "Effect of a Structural Intervention for the Prevention of Intimate-partner Violence and HIV in Rural South Africa: A Cluster Randomised Trial." *The Lancet*. 368 (9551): 1973–1983.

Pronyk, Paul M., Julia C. Kim, Tanya Abramsky, Godfrey Phetla, James R. Hargreaves, Linda A. Morison, Charlotte Watts, et al. 2008. "A Combined Microfinance and Training Intervention can Reduce HIV Risk Behaviour in Young Female Participants." *AIDS* 22 (13): 1659–1665.

Rankin, Katherine N. 2002. "Social Capital, Microfinance, and the Politics of Development." *Feminist Economics* 8 (1): 1–24.

Roodman, David. 2012. *Due Diligence: An Impertinent Inquiry into Microfinance*. Washington, DC: Center for Global Development Books.

van Rooyen, Carina, Ruth Stewart, and Thea de Wet. 2012. "The Impact of Microfinance in Sub-Saharan Africa: A Systematic Review of the Evidence." *World Development* 40 (11): 2249–2262.

Rutherford, Stuart. 2001. *The Poor and Their Money*. New Delhi: Oxford India Paperbacks.

Sanyal, Paromita. 2009. "From Credit to Collective Action: The Role of Microfinance in Promoting Women's Social Capital and Normative Influence." *American Sociological Review* 74 (4): 529–550.

Seeley, Janet, Charlotte H. Watts, Susan Kippax, Steven Russell, Lori Heise, and Alan Whiteside. 2012. "Addressing the Structural Drivers of HIV: A Luxury or Necessity for Programmes?" *Journal of the International AIDS Society* 15 (Suppl. 1): 17397. doi:10.7448/IAS.15.3.17397.

Sherer, Renslow D., John D. Bronson, Caroline J. Teter, and Randolph F. Wykoff. 2004. "Microeconomic Loans and Health Education to Families in Impoverished Communities: Implications for the HIV Pandemic." *Journal of the International Association of Physicians in AIDS Care (JIAPAC)* 3 (4): 110–114.

Ssewamala, Fred M., Leyla Ismayilova, Mary McKay, Elizabeth Sperber, William Bannon Jr, and Stacey Alicea. 2010. "Gender and the Effects of an Economic Empowerment Program on Attitudes toward Sexual Risk-taking among AIDS-orphaned Adolescent Youth in Uganda." *Journal of Adolescent Health* 46 (4): 372–378.

Stewart, Ruth, Carina van Rooyen, Kelly Dickson, Mabolaeng Majoro, and Thea de Wet. 2010. "What is the Impact of Microfinance on Poor People? A Systematic Review of Evidence from Sub-Saharan Africa." *Technical Report*. London: Social Science Research Unit, Institute of Education, University of London.

Swain, Ranjula Bali, and Fan Yang Wallentin. 2009. "Does Microfinance Empower Women? Evidence from Self-help Groups in India." *International Review of Applied Economics* 23 (5): 541–556.

Taylor, Marcus. 2012. "The Antinomies of 'Financial Inclusion': Debt, Distress and the Workings of Indian Microfinance." *Journal of Agrarian Change* 12 (4): 601–610.

Thorp, Rosemary, Frances Stewart, and Amrik Heyer. 2005. "When and How Far is Group Formation a Route Out of Chronic Poverty?" *World Development* 33 (6): 907–920.

Wagman, Jennifer A., Ronald H. Gray, Jacquelyn C. Campbell, Marie Thoma, Anthony Ndyanabo, Joseph Ssekasanvu, Fred Nalugoda, et al. 2015. "Effectiveness of an Integrated Intimate Partner Violence and HIV Prevention Intervention in Rakai, Uganda: Analysis of an Intervention in an Existing Cluster Randomised Cohort." *The Lancet Global Health* 3 (1): e23–e33.

Wood, Geof. 2003. "Staying Secure, Staying Poor: The 'Faustian Bargain'." *World Development* 31 (3): 455–471.

Index

Note:
Page numbers in *italic* type refer to tables
Page numbers followed by 'n' refer to notes

Abuja+12 Special Summit (2013) 130
Abuja Declaration (2001) 130
Action on Social Drivers to End AIDS (2014)
    129
Adams, V. 15–16
affliction 72
African Development Bank (AfDB) 141
African state 138–40
agency 106–7, 111, 113
AIDS Dependency Crisis (UNAIDS, 2012) 124
AIDS industry 53
AIDS Transition 127
AIDS2031 Consortium (2011) 9, 11
Akeroyd, A. 53
Alma Ata Declaration (1978) 122
alternative approaches 2–4
Anderson, L., *et al.* 154
Andhra Pradesh (India) 82, 93
Angola 128
Annan, K. 123
Annual Review of Public Health 13
antiretroviral therapy (ART) 9, 20–1, 46, 123,
    126, 129, 137, 140; adherence 21–2
antiretrovirals (ARVs) 1, 4, 44–5, 54, 62, 73–5,
    116, 126, 137, 140
apartheid (South Africa) 18, 31, 33, 129
Asia 125
asset index 46
Association of Entrepreneurs Against HIV and
    AIDS, Tuberculosis and Malaria (ECOSIDA)
    20
at-risk populations 125
Auerbach, J., Parkhurst, J. and Cáceres, C.
    10–11
awareness 143

Bachmann, M., and Booysen, F. 44
Bailey, B. 32
Baird, S.J., *et al.* 71
Banda, J. 86

Bangladesh 82, 90, 97, 154–6, 159n1
Bank Rakyat 155–6
Bärnighausen, T., *et al.* 77n5
Basu, S., McKee, M. and Stuckler, D. 74
Bateman, M., and Chang, H.-J. 82, 155
Bauchet, J., *et al.* 90
Baylies, C. 5, 53
behaviour: promiscuous 90; rational 44, 54–5;
    risk 44, 55; sub-optimal 64
behavioural drivers, *vs.* biological drivers
    146–7
behavioural intervention 2, 8–9, 11, 17, 62, 104,
    107, 146
best-evidence intervention 13
big man leadership 139
bio-political process, structural prevention
    19–22
bio-social political economy 8–9, 17–19
biological drivers, *vs.* behavioural drivers
    146–7
biomedical innovation 60 2
biomedical intervention 1–2, 4, 8–9, 11, 17, 62,
    104, 107, 126, 144, 146–7, 149–50
Björkman-Nyqvist, M., *et al.* 64
Bogle, K. 32–3
Bolivia 155–6
Bonnard, P. 159
booty call 32
Booysen, F., and Bachmann, M. 44
Bourgois, P. 33
boyfriend/girlfriend relations 30, 34–8
BRAC (NGO) 155–6
Braga, C.M.T. 22
Brecht, A. 148
Bujra, J. 5, 45, 47, 51–2, 55, 73
Bush, G.W. 123, 133

Cáceres, C., Auerbach, J. and Parkhurst, J.
    10–11
Caldwell, J., Caldwell, P. and Quiggin, P. 31

Campbell, C. 18, 20, 74
capacity, agent 52
Cape Town (South Africa) 34
capital 20–1
capitalism 3–4, 18, 23, 31, 108, 112–13, 117
CAPRISA 007 RHIVA project 75
cash transfers 2–5, 45, 115; conditional 12–13, 16, 53, 105, 107–8, 115, 155; unconditional 13, 155
casual lovers 37
casual sex 32
casualisation 73–4
CD4 126, 128
Center for Global Development (CGD) 127
Centers for Disease Control (CDC) 126
challenges to response 124–30
Chang, H.-J., and Bateman, M. 82, 155
charity girls 32
child anthropometry 75
choice 61, 65–6, 107; agent 52
choice architecture 64
choice-disabled women 65
chronic unemployment 35, 37
circumcision, male medical 1, 5, 31, 61, 73, 126, 146–7
civil society 133, 135, 139–40
class 45, 47, 49, 51–2, 54–5
Clement, E. 32
Clift, C. 129
Clinton Health Access Initiative (CHAI) 128
coercion 65, 107–8, 110–11, 113–14
cofactors 147
Cold War (1947–91) 121
collective action 12, 16, 24, 116
combination prevention 11, 13, 151
commercial sex 65, 73
commercial sex workers (CSW) 14–15, 46, 104, 106, 122, 125
Commission on Global Governance and Health (University of Oslo, 2014) 129
Commission on HIV/AIDS and Governance in Africa (CHGA, 2003) 123
Commission on Macroeconomics and Health (CMH, 2001) 123
concurrent partners 3, 65, 73
conditional cash transfers 12–13, 16, 53, 105, 107–8, 115, 155
condoms 8–9, 11, 14, 20–1, 23, 28, 31, 33, 36–8, 44, 52–3, 65–6, 70–1, 104–6, 116, 126; promotion 38, 144, 148
confluent love 32
Congress of South African Trade Unions (COSATU) 21
consensus indicators 29
consumerism 108, 112, 114, 117
contemporary relations 36–7
contextualisation 14, 17
Cornwall, A., and Edwards, J. 82, 98

corrective rape 125
COSATU (Congress of South African Trade Unions) 21
Côte d'Ivoire 125
Country Coordinating Mechanisms (Global Fund) 137, 139
credit performance 82
critical political economy assessment 72–5

dates 32
De Walque, D.: Dow, W. and Gong, E. 105–7; et al. 62, 64; and Medlin, C. 64–5
de Wet, T., van Rooyen, C. and Stewart, R. 158
Deane, K.: and Long, D. 3–4, 42–59; Parkhurst, J. and Johnston, D. 10; and Wamoyi, J. 3, 103–20
debt 82, 93, 97, 111, 114, 154, 156, 158
Deci, E., Koestner, R. and Ryan, R. 63
denialists 150
Development Assistance for Health (DAH) 136
Disability Adjusted Life Years 122
disciplines 147–8
distal determinants 10–11, 17, 23
doctors-are-beneficent belief system 148
Dodoma (Tanzania) 46
Domba project 14–15
donors 115–16, 124, 127–8, 130, 138–41, 159n1
Dow, W., Gong, E. and De Walque, D. 105–7
Dunbar, M.S., et al. 16

East Africa 98
Eastern Europe 122
Easton, D., Parker, R. and Klein, C. 9
Ebola 126, 134–5
Economic Commission for Africa (ECA, UN) 123
economic intervention 45, 107–8
economic power 53, 73, 108, 111–12, 114
Economic Reference Group (ERG, World Bank) 128
economic vulnerability 86, 90–1, 99
economically active poor 156
economics, mainstream 3, 45, 51, 54, 103–5, 112–14, 116
ECOSIDA (Association of Entrepreneurs Against HIV and AIDS, Tuberculosis and Malaria) 20
educational attainment 77n5
Edwards, J., and Cornwall, A. 82, 98
empowerment, women's 5, 53, 63, 103, 105, 107, 115–16, 157
Engels, F. 31
epidemic (2015), history 121–4
epidemiology 5, 11, 17–19, 21, 29, 145–8
Epstein, P., and Packard, R. 149–50

Ethiopia 128
evidence based medicine (EBM) 11, 15–17
exchange, sexual 104–15, 117

Fassin, D. 15
female empowerment *see* empowerment
feminism 32
Fenton, L. 44
fiancé 37
Findings from the SASA! Study (Abramsky *et al.*) 158–9
Findings from SHAZ! (Dunbar *et al.*) 16, 84, 158–9
fish-for-sex exchanges 84, 98, 113
fling 37
flu, pandemic 1134
Food and Agriculture Organisation (FAO, UN) 85
force 107
Fraser, N., and Wilson, D. 128
freedom 65, 90, 116, 148

game-changers 1, 5, 61
Gates Foundation 17–18
Gauteng (South Africa) 13–14
Geertz, C. 17
gender consciousness, sex workers 13–14
gender inequality 11, 23, 31, 35, 62, 71, 76, 115, 148–9
gender relations 3, 11, 14–15, 29, 97, 107, 109, 111, 115–16, 125
gender training 83–4; and microfinance 12
gendered power relations 3, 80, 82, 84, 86, 98, 104–5, 112, 114
geographical shifts 35–6
Giddens, A. 32
gifts, Valentine's 31–3, 38, *see also* sex–love–gifts
girlfriend/boyfriend relations 30, 34–8
Global Burden of Disease (GBD) (2014) 125
Global Fund to Fight AIDS, Tuberculosis and Malaria (Global Fund) 9, 20, 22, 123, 127, 133, 135–9, 149; Country Coordinating Mechanisms 137, 139
Global HIV/AIDS Program (World Bank) 62
Global North 52
Global Programme on AIDS (WHO) 122
Global Report (UNAIDS, 2013) 62
Global South 80, 84, 93
Goetz, A.M., and Gupta, R.S. 82
going Dutch 32, 36
gold standard (EBM) 9, 11, 16, 126
Gong, E., De Walque, D. and Dow, W. 105–7
government expenditure *124*
grace period 81, 91, 96
Grameen Bank 97, 155–6
grassroots movements 115–16
group lending 81, 93, 97

Guinea 126
Gupta, G.R., *et al.* 10
Gupta, R.S., and Goetz, A.M. 82
gwaza (bribe) 34

Hallfors, D., *et al.* 63, 71
Handa, S., *et al.* 63, 70
Harare (Zimbabwe) 84
Hargreaves, J.R. 11; *et al.* 71, 77n5
Harman, S. 1, 63, 76, 133–42
health: expenditure 4, *124*; sector 122, 125, 129–30, 134, 136–41
Health Belief Model (HBM) 143
Heise, L., *et al.* 62, 70
herpes simplex virus (HSV) 66, 70–1
Hickel, J. 73–4
HIV Prevention Trials Network (HPTN) 052 trial 126
HIV1 13
HIV2 13
hooking up 32–3, 36–7
Hooking Up (Bogle) 32
HPTN052 trial 126
Hulme, D. 156; and Matin, I. 82, 98
Hunsmann, M. 15, 53, 149; and Parkhurst, J. 2, 143–53
Hunter, M. 3, 28–41, 52, 72–3

iatrogenic transmission 145, 148
Iliffe, J. 128
ilobolo (bridewealth) 33–5, 37
IMAGE (Intervention with Microfinance for Aids and Gender Equity) Study 12, 14, 16, 83–4, 157–9
India 82, 93, 155–6
Indonesia 155–6
inequality: gender 11, 23, 31, 35, 62, 71, 76, 115, 148–9; social 11, 34–5
infectivity 146–7
informal sexual relationships 105–6, 110, 113
Information, Education and Communication (IEC) 143
interaction (modes of transmission) 145, 151
International AIDS Conference; XI (Vancouver, 1996) 122; XIII (Durban, 2000) 123; XVIII (Vienna, 2010) 62; XX (Melbourne, 2014) 127
International AIDS Society (IAS) 62
International Conference on Primary Health Care (1978) 122
International Monetary Fund (IMF) 34, 124
intersectionality 15
Intervention with Microfinance for Aids and Gender Equity (IMAGE) Study 12, 14, 16, 83–4, 157–9
intimacy 72–3, 76
intimate partner violence (IPV) 14–15, 104, 125, 157

intravenous drug users (IDU) 122, 125
intrinsic motivation 63
Investing in Health (World Bank, 1993) 122
Iringa (Tanzania) 46
Is Microdebt Good for Poor People? (Hulme)
    156
ishende (secret lover) 37
isiZulu 31
istraight/iqonda (straight) relationships
    36–7

Johnston, D. 3–4, 10, 43, 55, 60–79; Deane, K.
    and Parkhurst, J. 10
joint liability 81, 94
Joint United Nations Programme on HIV/AIDS
    (UNAIDS) *see* UNAIDS

Kabeer, N. 82–3, 98
Kagera Region (Tanzania) 46
Kaiser Family Foundation 123
Kalofonos, I.A. 21
Karim, L. 90, 97
Kark, S. 129
Katz, A. 123
kauni fishing 85
Kennedy, C., *et al.* 157–8
Kenya 44, 63, 66, 70–1, 105–6, 124, 141n1,
    154
Kim, J., and Watts, C. 154
Kippax, S., and Stephenson, N. 17
Klein, C., Easton, D. and Parker, R. 9
Koestner, R., Ryan, R. and Deci, E. 63
Kohler, H.-P., and Thornton, R. 66
kuunika (to give light) 99n2
KwaZulu-Natal (South Africa) 31, 33–4, 36–7,
    73, 126

labour 20–1
Lake Malawi 5, 84, 158–9
Lambdin, B.H., *et al.* 22
Lancet Commission 62
Lancet, The 30, 84, 129
Langa (Cape Town) 34
Latin America 125
Le Marcis, F. 146
Leclerc-Madlala, S. 52
Lesotho 128; lottery 60, 64, 66, 71
Levin, R. 34
Liberia 126
life expectancy 4, 44, 51, 121, 127, 129
Limpopo (South Africa) 12, 14, 16
loan repayments 5, 16, 80–2, 87–98, 156,
    158–9, 159n1&2; experiences 90–2;
    procedures 89–90; stress and anxiety 92–5,
    see also microfinance
local value chains 103, 114; and sex 110–12
Loewenson, R., and Whiteside, A. 15
London cholera epidemic (1854) 23

London School of Hygiene and Tropical
    Medicine (LSHTM) 12
Long, D., and Deane, K. 3–4, 42–59
long-term plans 130
love: confluent love 32; romantic 32, 36,
    see also sex–love–gifts
Love, R. 5
lovers: hidden 37; secondary 37
lubambo (customary institution) 113, 118n4
Lugalla, J.L., *et al.* 113
Luke, N. 105–7, 114
Lurie, M., and Rosenthal, S. 30

McKee, M., Stuckler, D. and Basu, S. 74
McMichael, A. 11, 23
MacPherson, E., *et al.* 5, 80–102, 107, 158
main lovers 36–7
mainstream economics 3, 45, 51, 54, 103–5,
    112–14, 116
Malawi 12, 14, 16, 62–3, 66, 70–2, 80, 84–6,
    99, 107, 124
mali kauli (credit practice) 111
Mangochi (Malawi) 84–5
Marais, H. 65
market, sex 105–7, 112–14
Marks, S. 8, 65
Marr, A. 93–4
marriage rates 3, 33–5, 38, 70
Marxism 18
Matin, I., and Hulme, D. 82, 98
Mayoux, L. 83, 97
Mbeki, T. 133
Médecins Sans Frontières (MSF) 127
medical silos, *vs.* social silos 145–6
Medium Term Programmes (MTPs) 122
Medlin, C., and De Walque, D. 64–5
men who have sex with men (MSM) 122, 125
microbicides 126
microcredit 12, 16, 23, 155–9
microdebt 155
microfinance 2–5, 16, 45, 53, 103, 105, 108,
    115, 117, 154–9; and gender training 12,
    see also loan repayments
Middle East 125
Millennium Development Goals (MDGs) 115,
    123, 125, 133, 137–8
Millennium Summit (UN, 2000) 123
Ministry of Finance 136–7, 140
Ministry of Health 22, 137, 139–40
Mishra, V., *et al.* 43–4, 50
mobility 108–9
monogamy, serial 29
morbidity 44
Mozambique 20–2, 124, 129
Multi-Country AIDS Program (MAP, World
    Bank) 133, 138
Mutharika, B. 86
Mwanza Region (Tanzania) 108

National AIDS Control Programme (NACP, Tanzania) 46
National Institute on Drug Abuse (NIDA) 13
neoclassical principles 51–2, 122
neoliberalism 18, 60–1, 74, 122, 124, 155, 159
Nepal 157
Nguyen, V.-K., *et al.* 146
Nigeria 34, 128
non-governmental organisations (NGOs) 2, 11–12, 14, 16–17, 21–2, 133, 135, 139–41, 149
norms: sexual 3–4, 72–4, 76, 103, 109, 113, 115–16; social 30, 65, 82–3, 85, 113, 115–17
North Africa 125
North America 125
nudging (choices) 60
nutrition 4, 18, 21–2, 31, 73, 75, 158

objective measures 64
Office of the President/Prime Minister 140
O'Laughlin, B. 3–4, 8–27, 63, 72, 74–5
one-night stand 37
one-size-fits-all approach 5, 158
options 60, 65–6
Origin of the Family, Private Property and the State (Engels) 31
orphans and vulnerable children (OVCs) 63, 66, 70–1
Oster, E. 51
otherness 2
outsider groups 53
Over, M. 127
Oya, C. 98

packages, prevention/intervention 9, 11, 14, 17, 19–20, 23
Packard, R., and Epstein, P. 149–50
pandemic flu 134
paradigm shift 146, 151
Parker, R., Klein, C. and Easton, D. 9
Parkhurst, J. 10–11, 14, 16–18, 23, 42–3, 46, 49, 72, 148; Cáceres, C. and Auerbach, J. 10–11; and Hunsmann, M. 2, 143–53; Johnston, D. and Deane, K. 10
passive victims 52, 106, 110, 113
Pathfinder International 11
patriarchal bargain 34
PEPFAR (President's Emergency Plan for AIDS Relief) 9, 20–2, 123, 128, 133, 136, 138, 140, 145, 149
Pettifor, A., *et al.* 62
Philipson, T., and Posner, R. 51
Pink Ribbon Red Ribbon (PRRR) 137
Piot, P. 135
playboy status 73
polio 121
political class 51
political decisions 148

Political Declaration on HIV/AIDS (UN, 2011) 127
political myopia 146
politics 130
poorest of the poor 156
positive externalities 151
positive-progress narrative 134–6
Posner, R., and Philipson, T. 51
poverty 3–5, 9–10, 16, 22, 35, 62–4, 71–2, 103, 106, 108, 112–13, 115, 117, 129, 156–9; alleviation 44, 46, 62–3, 76, 80–2, 97, 148, 155, 156, 159; compared with wealth 42–7, 49–54
power over 53
President's Emergency Plan for AIDS Relief (PEPFAR) 9, 20–2, 123, 128, 133, 136, 138, 140, 145, 149
Pretoria (South Africa) 13
prevention 81–4, 115–16
price, sexual transaction 106, 114
PriceWaterhouseCoopers (PwC) 138, 141n2
prison of the proximate 11, 17, 23
processes 29–31
promiscuous behaviour 90
property confiscation 80, 87, 89, 91, 93–8
PROSHIKA (NGO) 155–6
prostitution 30, 32–3, 35–6, 38, 52
provider love 36
proximate determinants 10–11, 17, 23
public health 20–1, 115–16; local care 21–2

Quiggin, P., Caldwell, J. and Caldwell, P. 31

Rahman, A. 82
randomised control trial (RCT) 2, 9, 11, 13, 16–17, 66, 70, 75–6, 126, 150
Rankin, K.N. 157
rape, corrective 125
rational behaviour 44, 54–5
rational choice 103, 105, 108, 113–14
reductionism 2–3, 65, 76, 105, 148–9
relative wealth 8, 42–4, 46, 48–50, 52, 54–5
representative individual 65
Resolution 1308 (UNSC, 2000) 123
RESPECT Project 64, 66, 70–1
response, challenges to 124–30
Results for Development Institute (R4D) 128
Rigsby, M.O., *et al.* 62
risk 95–6; behaviours 44, 55; factor 43, 49–50; groups 55; premium 106; situations 42, 55
risky sex 12–14, 16, 52, 60, 64–5, 74, 84, 104, 106
Robinson, J., and Yeh, E. 105–7
rolling contract 32
romantic love 32, 36
Rose, G. 18–19, 22–3
Rosenthal, S., and Lurie, M. 30
Rowden, R. 124–5

Russia 122
Ryan, R., Deci, E. and Koestner, R. 63

Sawers, L., and Stillwaggon, E. 30–1
scaling up 11, 14, 16, 23
Schoepf, B. 29–30
school girls 12–13
School of Public Health (Witwatersrand University) 12
Schooling, Income and HIV Risk (SIHR) 66, 70–2
Seckinelgin, H. 139
secondary lovers 37
secular changes 16–17
Seeley, J. 5, 154–62
Sen, A. 22
Senegal 122, 125, 148–9
serial monogamy 29
seroconversion (HIV) 77n5
sex 29, 33, 115, 117; casual 32; commercial 65, 73; and local value chains 110–12; risky 12–14, 16, 52, 60, 64–5, 74, 84, 104, 106; survival 106; transactional 3, 5, 10, 13, 15, 51–2, 63, 70–1, 73, 84, 92, 95–6, 98, 158; unprotected 12–13, 51, 63, 106, 146, 157; unsafe 47, 62, 64–5, 105–6
Sex and the City (1998–2004) 32
sex workers: commercial (CSW) 14–15, 46, 104, 106, 122, 125; gender conscious 13–14
sex-for-fish exchanges 84, 98, 113
sexual barter 32
sexual debut 63, 70–1, 126
sexual exchange 104–15, 117
sexual interaction 5, 104–10, 112–13, 116
sexual networking 28–9, 35, 51, 73, 145
sexual norms 3–4, 72–4, 76, 103, 109, 113, 115–16
sexual revolution 32
sexual transmission 9, 23, 144–5
sexually transmitted infections (STIs) 14, 31, 60, 64–6, 70–1, 73–5, 106
sex–love–gifts 30–3, 36–7; South Africa 33–6; US 31–3
shadow price 51
SHARE (Jewkes) 158–9
Sherr, K.H., *et al.* 22
Short Term Programmes (STPs) 122
Sidibé, M. 1
Sierra Leone 126
silo thinking 150–1; institutional-economic origins 149; political-economic origins 147–9; political-ideational origins 147–9; prevention examples 144–7
smallpox 121
Smart Investments (UNAIDS, 2013) 127
Snow, J. 23
social drivers 8–11, 19, 23, 46, 104, 129; limits 14–17

Social Drivers Working Group 9, 11
social inequalities 11, 34–5
social issues 2, 146, 154, 159
social norms 30, 65, 82–3, 85, 113, 115–17
social problem 146, 148
social protection cash transfers 63–5, 70–1, 76
social sciences 2, 4–5, 144–5, 149–50
social silos, *vs.* medical silos 145–6
social vaccine 12–13
social work cash transfers 63–5, 70–1, 76
society, good 148
socioeconomic status (SES) 43, 52
solidarity 157
South Africa 43–4, 52, 73–5, 83–4, 123–4, 128–9, 133, 135–6, 157
South Asia 81–3, 97, 156
Stephenson, N., and Kippax, S. 17
Stewart, R., de Wet, T. and van Rooyen, C. 158
Stillwaggon, E. 2, 4, 9, 45; and Sawers, L. 30–1
Stoebenau, K., *et al.* 107
Strathdee, S.A., *et al.* 15
stratigraphic conception of human life 17
structural adjustment 9, 34
structural causes 8–11, 20–1, 23–4
structural determinants 20, 150
structural drivers 2–3, 10, 14, 16, 42, 45, 53–4, 145–7
Structural Drivers meeting (Cape Town, 2013) 129
structural intervention/prevention 2–3, 5, 8–10, 22–3, 53–4, 83, 98, 105, 144, 146, 150–1; bio-political process 19–22; constitution 23–4; experimental 11–17
structural issues 2
structural tensions, ethical and political 22
Stuckler, D., Basu, S. and McKee, M. 74
sub-optimal behaviour 64
sub-Saharan Africa 3, 28–30, 43–5, 61, 74, 81–3, 104, 111, 115, 125, 133–6, 138, 143, 145, 147, 151, 154, 158
substance use 13–14, 64
sugar daddies 13, 15
sugar production 20–1
Sukuma 109
Summertown (South Africa) 18, 20
survival sex 106
susceptibility 147–8
Sustainable Development Goals (SDGs) 125, 134
Swahili 109
Swaziland 73–4, 124, 129

Tanzania 3–4, 62, 64, 66, 70–1, 73, 139, 145, 149
testing 42, 47, 50–1, 53–5
Thornton, R., and Kohler, H.-P. 66
3 x 5 campaign (WHO, 2003) 123
Tongaat-Hulett 20

Total War Against HIV/AIDS Project (World Bank) 141n1
Trade Related Aspects of Intellectual Property Rights Agreement (TRIPS, 1995) 74
transactional sex 3, 5, 10, 13, 15, 51–2, 63, 70–1, 73, 84, 92, 95–6, 98, 158
transmission, modes of 121, 143, 145, 150–1
transmission policies, fashions and fads 4–5
Treatment Action Campaign (TAC) 9, 17, 21, 24, 135
treatment as prevention (TasP) 5, 45, 61, 128, 146–7
treatment tension 1
tuberculosis (TB) 63, 74, 126, 129, 130
turbo effect 145

Uganda 34, 46, 122, 124, 133, 138, 158–9
Ukraine 122
umakhwapheni (hidden lover) 37
umkhwenyana (fiancé) 37
UNAIDS 1, 3, 5, 11, 17–18, 29, 44, 46, 48, 61–2, 122, 124, 127–9, 134–5, 151; *AIDS Dependency Crisis* (2012) 124; *Global Report* (2013) 62; *Smart Investments* (2013) 127
unconditional cash transfers 13, 155
unemployment, chronic 35, 37
unequal gender relations 3, 107, 111, 116
unequal power relations 104–5, 107, 114
United Kingdom (UK), Department for International Development (DfID) 21
United Nations Development Programme (UNDP) 135
United Nations Security Council (UNSC) 123, 133; Resolution 1308 (2000) 123
United Nations (UN) 122, 126; Economic Commission for Africa (ECA) 123; Food and Agriculture Organisation (FAO) 85; Millennium Development Goals (MDGs) 115, 123, 125, 133, 137–8; Millennium Summit (2000) 123; *Political Declaration on HIV/AIDS* (2011) 127; Sustainable Development Goals (SDGs) 125, 134
United States of America (USA), Department of Defense (DOD) 121
unprotected sex 12–13, 51, 63, 106, 146, 157
unsafe sex 47, 62, 64–5, 105–6
usipa fish 85

Valentine's gifts 31–3, 38

value for money 128
values 148–9
van Rooyen, C., Stewart, R. and de Wet, T. 158
variables 29–31
Vilakazi, A. 34
Visvanathan, N., and Yoder, K. 82
vulnerability 84

Wamoyi, J.: and Deane, K. 3, 103–20; *et al.* 109–10
War on HIV/AIDS 133–6, 138–41
Watts, C., and Kim, J. 154
West Africa 97, 126, 135
Western Europe 125
Whiteside, A. 1–2, 121–32; and Loewenson, R. 15
Wilson, D. 62; and Fraser, N. 128
Wojcicki, J.M. 43, 72
women: choice-disabled 65; empowerment 5, 53, 63, 103, 105, 107, 115–16, 157
Women's Health CoOp 13–15
World AIDS Day 1, 134
World Bank 9, 12, 16–18, 21–2, 34, 62, 124, 128–9, 133, 138–9, 148; Economic Reference Group (ERG) 128; Global HIV/AIDS Program 62; Multi-Country AIDS Program (MAP) 133, 138; Total War Against HIV/AIDS Project 141n1; *World Development Report* (1980) 122; *World Development Report* (1993) 122
World Food Programme (WFP) 21–2
World Health Organisation (WHO) 18, 46, 121–3, 125–6, 145; Commission on Macro-Economics and Health (CMH, 2001) 123; Global Programme on AIDS 122; 3 x 5 campaign (2003) 123
World Trade Organisation (WTO), TRIPS (1995) 74
World War, Second (1939–45) 121

Xinavane Sugar Estate (Mozambique) 20

Yeh, E., and Robinson, J. 105–7
Yoder, K., and Visvanathan, N. 82
Yunus, M. 155

Zambia 71, 113
Zanzibar 47
Zimbabwe 16, 63, 71, 83–4, 154, 158–9
Zomba (Malawi) 12

For Product Safety Concerns and Information please contact our EU
representative GPSR@taylorandfrancis.com
Taylor & Francis Verlag GmbH, Kaufingerstraße 24, 80331 München, Germany